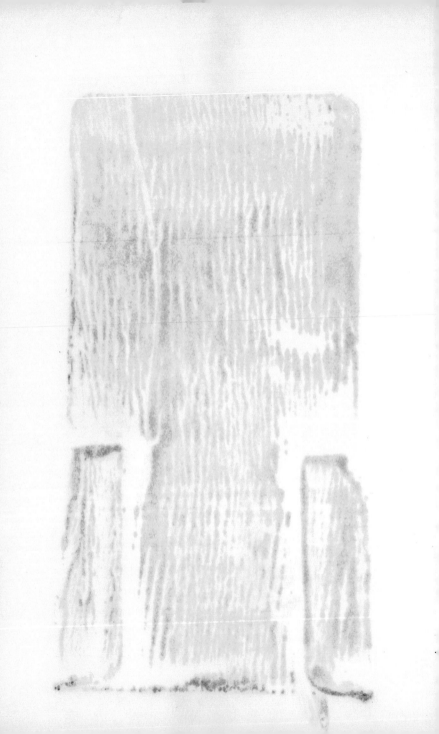

MARXISM
An Autopsy

MARXISM

AN AUTOPSY

Henry Bamford Parkes

PHOENIX BOOKS

THE UNIVERSITY OF CHICAGO PRESS : CHICAGO & LONDON

Parts of Chapters III and V were originally published in *Scrutiny* and in *The Southern Review*. I am indebted to the editors of those magazines for permission to reprint them.

H. B. P.

THE UNIVERSITY OF CHICAGO PRESS, CHICAGO & LONDON
The University of Toronto Press, Toronto 5, Canada

Introduction to the Phoenix Edition

THIS book was written during the autumn and winter of 1938–39, at a time when sympathy for Soviet Communism was still widely prevalent among American and West European intellectuals. While it contains little that I would now wish to change and some suggestions that I can fairly claim to be prophetic, my conclusions were expressed more tentatively than would have been the case if I had written at a later period and addressed myself to a different kind of audience. I was speaking primarily to liberals who accepted the basic values of Western civilization but who were turning toward Communism in the mistaken belief that it would bring about a fuller realization of those values. In 1938 Communist fellow-traveling had passed its peak; the Moscow trials, beginning in 1936, had started the process of disillusionment. But the appeal of Communism to the intellectuals had not yet been shattered by the Nazi-Soviet pact and by the revelation that Soviet foreign policy could be brutally imperialistic.

After nearly twenty years of cold war, during which Americans have become accustomed to regard the Soviet Union as the enemy of everything in which they believe, it is difficult to recapture the mood of the thirties when Soviet Communism was widely regarded as on the side of the forces of light, being criticized only because of some roughness in its methods and a tendency to underrate the importance of individual liberties. In the retrospect of a quarter of a century the vogue of Communism during the thirties seems like an extraordinary demonstration of mass delusion—the more disturbing in that it was strongest among the intellectual groups whom one would expect to be least prone to this kind of irrationality. Yet a considerable proportion of American writers and artists, along with many scholars and scientists, had some kind of record of sympathy for the left-wing movement at some point during the 1930's, and they could be considered fortunate if this record was not subject to public exposure during the McCarthyite hysteria of the early 1950's. Many of them felt impelled to explore for themselves the validity of the Communist view of life by some kind of commitment and participation, however brief; and those whose infection ended relatively early can presumably claim some superiority over more gullible comrades who were less easily disillusioned by the policies of Stalinism.

Primarily, of course, the spread of fellow-traveling was an expression of loss of faith in the traditional institutions of Western civilization. The West seemed incapable of dealing successfully with the economic problems of the great depression—problems which were so clearly due not to natural obstacles but to the mechanisms of a man-made system of distribution. Roosevelt's New Deal was not sufficiently successful to convince the intellectuals that capitalism, even when fused with some elements of a welfare state, could be saved or was worth saving. Meanwhile Hitler was threatening to destroy the whole Western heritage of humanistic liberalism and was apparently being encouraged by the appeasement policies pursued by Britain and France. Naziism, and not Communism, seemed to be our main enemy, and surely with good reason, since it represented a much more fundamental repudiation of the basic values of our civilization.

While the West seemed intent on committing suicide, the Soviet Union had apparently discovered the secret of economic progress, without depressions, and between 1934 and 1939 it supported foreign policies of collective security and seemed to be the only major power that recognized the menace of Hitlerism. Little was known in the West about the great famine of the early thirties, the continuing economic failures, the emergence of a new ruling class, and the severe repression of all opposition elements. Thus the Soviet system seemed to be superior to Western capitalism, and its superiority was attributed to its adoption of a whole new philosophical system first formulated by Marx and afterward developed by Lenin. Marx was supposed (at least by those sympathizers who did not actually attempt to read *Das Kapital*, with its numerous fallacies and inconsistencies and its tedious stretches of abstract argumentation) to have explained the end of capitalism and drafted blueprints for the new Communist society. Marxism was presented as a kind of new religion, giving its adherents a complete and convincing account of all that was wrong with the world as it was, with a promise of rapid salvation through the building of a Kingdom of Freedom. The proletariat was destined to fulfil a messianic role; and, just as in a mystical religion the ordinary convert is asked to take on trust the doctrines which the mystical initiate asserts to be true from his own direct experience, so intellectual sympathizers with Communism were assured that any doubts and misgivings they might feel about its policies were caused by their clinging to bourgeois attitudes and their failure to identify themselves with the proletariat.

In writing this book, I gave Western Communists credit for good intentions and a continuing belief in liberal values. This was undoubtedly true of most of the Communist sympathizers of the thirties. Even those misguided individuals who became so deeply and tragically involved in Communism as to engage in espionage for the benefit of Soviet foreign policy did so with noble purposes, their errors being intellectual rather than moral. This important fact was generally overlooked during the era of McCarthyism. My main objects were to demonstrate that Communism did not actually promise the fulfilment of liberal values and that Marxist doctrine was a liability rather than an asset to any healthy progressive movement.

Starting with a study of the actual record, I argued that the kind of revolution that Marx had predicted was an impossibility; the working class was not actually a revolutionary class, nor would it ever be strong enough to establish any "dictatorship of the proletariat." The only revolutions likely to occur in the modern world were peasant revolutions in relatively backward countries—a proposition that has been abundantly confirmed during the past two decades. Nor were Communist principles likely to bring about freedom, prosperity, and peace. The failures of the Soviet Union were not to be ascribed to economic backwardness or to capitalist antagonism but were the logical results of Marxist theory. No aspects of Soviet policy during the thirties seemed so well established as its opposition to Hitlerism and its rejection of imperialism, and in suggesting that Stalin might make a pact with Hitler and that in the event of a European war the Soviets might easily become imperialistic I was making predictions that—in 1938 and early 1939—ran counter to all general expectation. These discussions of Communist practice were followed by an analysis of the philosophy of Marxism designed to show that insofar as it had any validity it did not support the political conclusions which Marxists attempted to deduce from it.

Since one of the main reasons for the appeal of Communism was the belief that there was no satisfactory alternative, I concluded with a discussion of an American program of economic reform. Rereading it twenty-five years later, I feel that parts of it were too specific and too detailed but that as a statement of general objectives it remains basically sound. My main purpose was to retain the private-enterprise system but to change some of the rules of the game by means of increased government control of the financial structure and new definitions of property rights, in order to reduce economic inequalities and assure wage-earners of greater job security. I argued that such a program was economically sound, politically possible, and in accord with liberal ideals of justice.

H. B. P.

Contents

I. Introduction

I. Introduction

THAT western civilization is today in greater danger of destruction than at any time since the fall of the Roman Empire is a proposition which scarcely needs to be defended. There have been other periods of gloom and disorder — periods, like the fifteenth century, when one social system was decaying and its successor had not yet been fully organized, or, like the age of the Mongol invasions, when Europe was threatened by a barbarian conquest. But never before have powerful nations been dominated by a movement which did not even profess to be based on truth and aiming at justice; never before have civilized men been confronted by so insoluble a dilemma — either of surrendering to Fascist aggression or, by organizing to fight against it, of themselves adopting a dictatorial form of government and a war psychology similar to that of Fascism. Indeed, parts of Europe may now have reached an epoch corresponding to the fifth century, when, as Stanley Casson has pointed out, groups of Roman gentlemen, living in provinces already overrun by the barbarians, continued to practise the arts and to feel confident that the disorders of the time would shortly end and that civilization would continue.

There are, however, significant differences between the problems of today and those of decaying Rome. For whereas the economic system of the Romans was unprogressive and production tended to decrease, society today, for the first time in history, has the technical equipment necessary to guarantee everybody an adequate livelihood and security against famine; the economic problem of today is not to prevent scarcity but to distribute a surplus. And whereas in the Roman Empire a majority of the population, politically illiterate, submitted

3

passively to exploitation and sought consolation in the hope of an after-life, one of the cardinal characteristics of the society of today is an almost universal concern with politics and an extension of political criteria to activities, such as science and the arts, which formerly were left to specialists. Indeed, the difficulties of contemporary society might almost be ascribed to an excess of political energy rather than to a lack of it. If the ignorance and prejudice displayed in Fascism are so triumphant, it is perhaps because backward groups, who in earlier ages were left to their obscurity, have for the first time been aroused from slumber, mobilized into political armies, and encouraged to demand political power

These facts mean that the dilemmas which confront us are not wholly beyond solution, as were perhaps those of the Roman Empire. A remedy is at least theoretically conceivable. And it is notable also that there is a considerable measure of agreement as to the ends toward which our energies should be directed. In the democratic nations a majority of the people, however bitterly they may dispute with each other about methods and policies, profess similar standards of value and are in harmony as to what is ultimately desirable. They desire personal freedom, economic security, a greater degree of economic justice, and civil and international peace. The task of a progressive movement is to find a program by which these ideals may seem likely to be fulfilled and which is capable of winning the support of a sufficient majority of the population.

The most obvious reason for the fact that political factions, which profess to desire analogous ends, fight so bitterly with each other about the means of achieving them, is the desire of privileged groups to retain their privileges. Any change always disturbs vested interests; and the more fundamental the changes which may be necessary, the more furiously will vested interests resist them. To ensure a general liberty and security it is necessary to restrict the liberty and diminish the wealth of a few; to guarantee international peace it is necessary that national governments should accept limitations of their sovereignty and that imperialistic governments should surrender their claims to colonial empires. Privileged groups who are fighting against change win support by arousing the patriotic, racial, and religious prejudices of ignorant persons. These facts are too notorious to require elaboration. One should not, however, be content merely to dismiss the victories of prejudice as an additional proof of the malevolence of ruling classes; the moral to be drawn from them is the necessity of proposing reforms which are at least capable of fulfilment and of recommending them in phraseology which is likely to win assent. To circumvent a hostile combination of forces is often wiser than to meet it in open combat.

Freedom, security, justice, and peace are the aims of the various left-wing parties in modern politics; and those ideals are unquestionably shared by a majority of mankind. Yet during the past half-dozen years the left-wing movement has met with a long series of disasters, and almost every day brings reports of some new defeat. The question presents itself, therefore, as to whether progressivism has not failed as a result more of its own errors than of the strength of its opponents. The ideology which dominates the left-wing movement is that of Marxism. The disciples of Marx are the most energetic, the most self-sacrificing, the most self-confident, and the most disciplined group in modern society. Left-wing tactics are based, to a greater or less degree, on Marxist theory, and disagreements within the left-wing movement are most frequently caused by variant interpretations of Marxist doctrine. Anyone who wishes to find his bearings in modern politics must therefore begin by examining the assumptions and practices of Marxism.

The Marxists promise to create a society characterized by universal freedom, security, justice, and peace. The methods

which they advocate are, however, different from their ultimate ends. They believe that the road to a better society runs
through class warfare, revolution, and dictatorship. The
working class must rise against the capitalist class, seize
power, and — during the transition period between capitalism and communism — create a proletarian dictatorship.
This discrepancy between means and ends is not, in itself, any
argument against Marxism. Unquestionably, however, it
diminishes the capacity of the progressive movement to attract converts. The Marxist emphasis on the necessity of a
proletarian dictatorship alienates the farmers and the middle
classes. Unreflecting persons, who fear revolution and civil
war, are frightened into the Fascist camp. The result is an
irreconcilable conflict about methods between groups who
cherish similar ideals. Marxists claim that a proletarian revolution is possible — that it is, in fact, not merely possible but
inevitable; that by a proletarian revolution freedom, security,
justice, and peace can be achieved; and that they cannot be
achieved by any other method. Anyone who believes that
these claims are justified can only devote himself to fighting
for the revolution. If, on the other hand, these claims are not
justified, then Marxism, owing to the stimulus which it gives
to Fascism, must be regarded as a liability rather than an asset
to the progressive cause.

II. The Evidence of History

II. The Evidence of History

I. SOCIAL-DEMOCRACY

THE Marxist creed of proletarian revolution was first proclaimed in the *Communist Manifesto* of 1848. It began to be an active force in politics with the formation of the German Social-Democratic Party and its partial adoption of Marxist principles in the eighteen-seventies, and with the rising of the Paris Commune in 1871. The history of Marxist politics covers, therefore, a period of some seventy years. This period is long enough to illustrate the consequences of Marxist theory in political practice.

According to Marxist theory the working class is inherently, by virtue of its rôle in the capitalist system of production, a revolutionary class. Its struggles for higher wages and a shorter working day are impossible of fulfilment under capitalism, and must bring it into conflict, not only with the capitalist class, but also with the power of the state. For the state — even the bourgeois-democratic state — is not a neutral power, but is merely an instrument of capitalist domination; to defend bourgeois democracy is to defend capitalism. The economic struggles of the working class must inevitably, therefore, assume a political character and develop into a struggle for a revolutionary transformation of society. Owing, moreover, to the economic laws immanent in capitalism, the working class will grow stronger and more numerous and will at the same time suffer from a steadily increasing exploitation; its ultimate victory is therefore certain.

The victory of the working class will mean that mankind has left the kingdom of necessity and entered the kingdom of freedom. The workers constitute the majority of mankind

9

throughout the world, and they can triumph only by abolishing class distinctions and creating a society characterized by equality. Since the state is an instrument of class dominance, the disappearance of class distinctions will make it unnecessary; coercion will cease, and the state will gradually wither away. The abolition of economic inequalities and the co-operative planning and control of economic life will, moreover, create a universal security and prosperity; while the rationalization of economic and social life will destroy those mystical and unscientific doctrines which are accepted only because society is irrational. It is therefore the historic destiny of the proletariat to achieve justice and truth; justice and truth, in fact, in the present historic epoch, find their only concrete meaning in the will of the proletariat.

These two doctrines — that the proletariat will revolutionize society, and that the proletarian revolution will mean the entrance of mankind into the kingdom of freedom — are the core of Marxism.

The first efforts of the Marxists were devoted to stimulating the political and class consciousness of the workers and to the building of political parties which would represent their interests. This was accomplished in the major European countries before the end of the nineteenth century. The working class had already begun to create trade unions for the protection of their economic interests; and the trade unions now began to accept Marxist theory and to enter the field of politics. Socialist and Social-Democratic Parties were formed in Germany, France, Italy, Austria, and Russia. In England the Labor Party, though repudiating the philosophy of Marxism, represented a similar combination of forces. Only in the United States, among the great powers, did the trade-union movement remain aloof from politics and refuse to adopt a Socialist program.

The attitudes which these working-class parties began to

develop were, however, from the Marxist viewpoint, distinctly disconcerting. In Russia, whose government was not a bourgeois democracy but a despotism, they continued to support revolution. But in western Europe, while still professing revolutionary principles, they began to work for a slow and gradual reform of the social system, to be achieved by legal and parliamentary methods, and for immediate improvements in the condition of the workers under capitalism; and in these efforts they won definite successes. They came to believe that the bourgeois-democratic state was not merely an instrument of capitalist domination, but that under a democratic system it was possible for the workers to win reforms; and being anxious to establish complete independence and liberty of action for the trade unions, they recognized that this independence was possible only under a democratic system and that it would be destroyed by a proletarian dictatorship as much as by a capitalist despotism. The working classes continued to suffer from insecurity and unemployment, and from low wages and long hours of labor; but trade-union pressure, coupled with unemployment and health-insurance schemes and other social legislation enacted by the state, made their condition definitely better than in the nineteenth century. The result was a steady weakening in the impulse toward revolution. In the early years of the twentieth century working-class struggles in Europe were less militant and less violent than in the nineteenth century. A similar tendency was evident also in the United States, where the nation-wide strike movements of the eighteen-seventies and eighties were more widespread and resulted in more bloodshed than any which have occurred since.

On the European Continent Marxism continued, nevertheless, to be the official creed of the working-class parties. In Germany Bernstein elaborated a revision of Marxist doctrine, which reflected the tendencies actually visible in German Social-Democracy, and according to which capitalism would develop into Socialism in a gradual and peaceful manner. Revisionism, however, was never officially accepted. But despite professions of faith in Marxist dogma, revolutionary Marxism almost disappeared among the working classes in western Europe. It was kept alive not by workers but by persons similar to its original creators — in other words, by middle-class intellectuals and men of letters. The only important revolutionary force among the working class was not Marxism but Syndicalism, which won considerable support in Spain, Italy, and France. Syndicalism represented the trade-union mentality of the working class expressing itself in a revolutionary rather than a reformist manner. Rejecting the Marxist doctrine of inevitability, the Syndicalists proclaimed instead a Bergsonian faith in the freedom of the human will. And repudiating the Marxist advocacy of a centralized dictatorship as the instrument for creating a Socialist society, they demanded independence for the workers' organizations in each industry.

The failure of Marxism was vividly dramatized in 1914. Marx had proclaimed union among the workers of all nations and had declared that, since the bourgeois state represented only the interests of the capitalist class, the workers should refuse to give support to capitalist wars. This faith in an international union of the proletariat had been embodied in an international organization, the Second (or Socialist) International. When war came, however, the Socialist and Labor Parties in every country voted support for their own governments. And though in every country there were minorities who opposed the war, these minorities had little support among the working classes and were led, not by the trade-union leaders, but by middle-class intellectuals whose viewpoint was pacifist rather than revolutionary, and who often belonged to the right rather than to the left wing of the Socialist movement and did not even profess Marxist principles.

This was the case with MacDonald and Snowden in England, with Jaurès in France, and with Bernstein in Germany.

II. COMMUNISM

MEANWHILE a new beginning had been made in Russia. Russia, unlike the countries of western Europe, was obviously ripe for revolution. Its government was a corrupt and inefficient despotism, and its system of landownership was still semi-feudal. Almost all Russian intellectuals were agreed as to the necessity of overthrowing czardom, and throughout the nineteenth century a large number of them had been accustomed to engage in revolutionary conspiracies. A class of professional revolutionaries, which had no parallel in any western nation, had appeared. They were compelled to adopt methods of secrecy, had a tendency to engage in terroristic activities, and had no close affiliation with any economic class. They disagreed as to the social system which was to follow the revolution, some favoring a system of peasant communes and others Marxist Socialism. Their mentality was strongly marked by the religious and racial traditions of Russia; they saw life in mystical and messianic terms, and even when they rejected supernatural religion, they employed, in defending materialism, a religious dogmatism and fanaticism and a religious faith in millenarian utopias. In their choice of methods, moreover, they appear to have been influenced by the most peculiar of Russian religious traditions — the belief that good may come from evil, and that the idealist may, with the noblest intentions, employ evil means to achieve a good end. Meanwhile the masses of the Russian people were seething with discontent. The peasants wanted a distribution of the big feudal estates, while the working classes, suffering from a severe governmental repression of trade-union activities such as had disappeared in the more advanced capitalist countries, were more disposed than the workers in western Europe to adopt revolutionary activities.

It was in such a milieu that Lenin appeared. Himself the son of a minor member of the aristocracy, he had adopted from boyhood the revolutionary attitudes of the intelligentsia; and in spite of the realism and sanity, and the ordered personal life and emotional self-control, which made him so markedly superior to most other Russian revolutionaries, he was strongly marked by the peculiar traditions of his country. The strange combination of dogmatic religiosity and hardboiled realism which was to characterize Russian Communism showed itself in the manner in which Lenin adapted Marxism to Russian conditions. Throughout his life Lenin continued to profess a most superstitious reverence for the words of Marx, and he accepted as the basis of all his thinking the fundamental Marxist dogma — its messianic faith in the revolutionary destiny of the proletariat. Yet Lenin's Marxism was often verbal rather than real, and his political practice was marked by significant deviations from the original doctrine. Three of these deviations were to be of decisive importance.

In the first place, Lenin perceived that the inherent tendency of the working class was to adopt not a revolutionary mentality but a trade-union mentality.[1] The most obvious deduction to be drawn from this fact was that Marx had been wrong. Lenin, however, evolved, out of Russian revolutionary traditions, a solution to the dilemma. For the organization of revolution a new kind of political party was required — a small, united, and highly disciplined party of professional revolutionaries. The formation of this party, which took the name of Communist in 1917, was one of the most important political events of the twentieth century. Lenin's Communist Party was not a party of the working class; it was instead to provide the working class with leadership. It was to be the vanguard of the proletariat, embodying and giving expression to its revolutionary will. In a highly mystical sense it was the realization, not of what the proletariat actually was, but of what, according to Marx, the proletariat ideally had to be. Lenin believed that the dictatorship of the Communist Party would result in the creation of a genuine economic democracy. This belief was based on the assumption of an identity between the will of the Party and the will of the proletariat. Such an assumption was, however, unwarranted: for in the first place, the policies of the Party were determined, not by the actual will of the proletariat, but by the Marxist definition of that will; and in the second place, there was the danger that after the Party had established itself as a ruling bureaucracy it might develop a distinct economic interest and political psychology of its own. The ablest revolutionary Marxist in western Europe, Rosa Luxemburg, who still believed that the proletariat would eventually revolt against capitalism by its own volition, denounced Lenin's conception of the rôle of the Communist Party as involving the creation of a bureaucratic tyranny. She found an analogy between Leninism and the advocacy of bureaucracy to be found in the works of Sidney and Beatrice Webb and the English Fabians. The accuracy of this analogy was proved many years later when the Webbs visited Russia and discovered in the rule of Stalin a Fabian paradise.

In the second place, Lenin adopted a new and un-Marxian conception of the rôle to be played by the peasantry in the coming revolution. Marx had regarded the peasants as a backward class, who represented private property in the means of production in its most retrograde form; as in industry, so also in agriculture the disappearance of the small property-owner meant economic progress.[2] Lenin realized, however, that the revolution could not triumph in Russia without the co-operation of the peasants, and he was therefore willing to support their demand for breaking up the big feudal estates. The immediate result of such a policy would be the creation of a strong class of independent property-owners, which might endanger Socialist control of Russia; but Lenin was prepared to take the risk. He would use the discontent of the peasants as an instrument for achieving a proletarian revolution, and afterward force them to abandon their newly won private properties and to adopt collectivism.

In the third place, Lenin attributed a revolutionary significance to the growth of nationalism in colonial areas. Marx had regarded the extension of capitalism to backward countries as a progressive tendency, which was not to be resisted; he had, for example, favored the annexation of Mexico by the United States, and — regarding all Slavs as backward by comparison with his German fellow countrymen — had opposed the growth of Slav nationalism within the Austro-Hungarian Empire.[3] Lenin, on the other hand, believed that all nationalistic revolts against imperialism, even when they were not Socialist or proletarian in character, ought to be encouraged. As in his attitude toward the peasantry, so also in his approach to the colonial question he was willing to seek non-proletarian allies in the struggle against capitalism; and to take the risk that such a policy might eventually result in the growth of new colonial capitalisms and in an intensification of national consciousness which would impede the growth of international unity among the proletariat.

Lenin's genius for political leadership was proved in 1917. Czardom collapsed from its own inner weaknesses, and was at first followed by a bourgeois-democratic régime. But the Russian bourgeoisie were unable to retain power. They were relatively few in number, had never acquired habits of independent political action, had always been accustomed to lean for assistance on the Russian government, and were largely dependent on English and French capitalism. They failed, moreover, to satisfy the demand of the rank and file of the army for immediate peace and the demand of the peasants for an immediate distribution of land. Contrary to the opinion of almost all his associates in the Communist Party, who believed that according to the Marxist timetable feudalism could not pass directly into Socialism, Lenin decided that an immediate seizure of power was possible. The Communist Party won the leadership of the working class; and by advocating an immediate peace and an immediate distribution of land, obtained the support of the army and the peasants. The result was the October Revolution. During the subsequent civil war the reactionary forces consisted chiefly of expropriated landowners and were supported by foreign capitalists, who hoped both to recover their confiscated Russian properties and to carve Russia into spheres of influence under foreign control. The Communist Party was able, therefore, to strengthen its alliance with the peasants and to identify itself with the cause of Russian national independence.

The history of Russia under Communist rule cannot be regarded in its entirety as an illustration of the practical working-out of Marxist doctrine. Any fundamental change in the economic and social structure of a people is always gradual; and the Russian people in 1917 were economically backward, accustomed to a low standard of living, and lacking in any experience of self-government. Under such circumstances it was inevitable that the revolutionary process should be marred by unnecessary cruelties, and that the creation of an efficient economic system should be slow. It is, however, impossible to dismiss all the disturbing features of the Communist dictatorship with such excuses. In its main outlines it is clearly the logical consequence of Marxist and Leninist theory. The purpose of the Communist Parties, moreover, is to erect similar dictatorships in other countries; and though they disclaim the intention of erecting rigid imitations of the

17

Russian model, they accept every feature of the Russian system with an equal approbation.

As was predicted by Rosa Luxemburg, the rule of the Communist Party has meant, not a dictatorship *of* the proletariat, but a dictatorship *over* the proletariat. The nominal purpose of the Revolution was to create a democratic republic, in which power would belong to the workers organized in soviets. This purpose was, however, never realized, even during the lifetime of Lenin. From the beginning of Communist rule the soviets were dominated by the Party; and since the Party was supposed to represent the real will of the proletariat, any opposition to it, even among the working class, was denounced as contrary to that real will and hence as 'counter-revolutionary.' As early as 1921 the workers in Leningrad and Kronstadt, who had been the chief supporters of the October Revolution, began to turn against the Party and to demand freely elected soviets; and this 'counter-revolutionary' movement was crushed without mercy. The subsequent history of the dictatorship, including the rise to power of Stalin, was merely the inevitable realization of tendencies which had been implicit in Leninism from its origins. In order that the Party might continue to dominate the masses of the Russian people, it was necessary that it should remain united, with a single monolithic will; dissensions within the Party might endanger the Party dictatorship, and must therefore be regarded as 'counter-revolutionary.' The dictatorship of the Party over the proletariat was therefore transformed, by gradual but necessary changes, into the dictatorship of a small clique over the Party. Lenin had allowed considerable freedom of discussion within the Party; but after the expulsion of Trotsky in 1926, and the establishment of Stalinite supremacy during the next two or three years, the Party line was determined exclusively by the Party leader, and any criticism of the Party line became treasonable. Henceforth Stalin became the recipient of an adulation equalling, if not excelling, that enjoyed by the *duces* and *fuehrers* of Fascism; and opposition, however honest and legitimate, was forced to adopt conspiratorial methods.

The proletarian revolution would, according to Marx, result in the creation of a society characterized by a universal economic security and prosperity. As to how this desirable consummation was to be achieved, Marx, however, offered no advice. Nothing in the Marxist myth is more remarkable than its refusal to grapple with any of the concrete problems involved in the creation of the promised kingdom of freedom. Marx was concerned only with showing that a proletarian revolution was inevitable and that freedom, equality, and prosperity must be its logical consequences. The construction of the new social order must be left to the proletariat after the revolution; how this order would function could not be predicted. The Communist leaders in 1917 found themselves, therefore, required to create a new society with no guidance from their master as to how to proceed.

The disastrous experiment of 'War Communism,' adopted from necessity rather than from choice, was followed by the New Economic Policy, which combined socialized banking, foreign trade, and large-scale industry with a private property basis for agriculture and internal trade. Subsequently, with the inauguration of the first Five-Year Plan by Stalin in 1928, there began an attempt to create a genuinely communistic society. The peasants were ruthlessly herded into collective farms — a process which necessitated the exiling of hundreds of thousands of recalcitrant 'kulaks' into northern prison camps and which resulted in a large-scale famine — and all the energies of the Russian people were concentrated on the task of creating an industrialized society on the American model. The new social order might best be described as state capitalism. Production and distribution are organized in a manner which resembles private capitalism, the chief difference being that the operations of the whole system are under centralized planning and control, and that profits and losses are assumed by the state instead of by private entrepreneurs. The Russian industrial system, one might say, consists of a single trust, and the managers of this trust constitute the Russian government.

The chief argument in favor of this system, and the chief reason for its growing prestige outside Russia, is that it can avoid the catastrophic depressions and the large-scale unemployment which afflict private capitalism. A centrally controlled economic system can achieve a rapid and consistent growth of the national wealth, can equate consumption with production, and can provide work for the entire labor force of the nation. It can, moreover, dispense with some of the more wasteful forms of activity prevalent under private capitalism (such as commercial advertising and salesmanship) and can provide its working class with insurance against sickness and old age and with other forms of social welfare. The worker under Communism, provided that he remains obedient to the dictatorship and does not offend the local Communist officials, enjoys economic security. It remains arguable, however, that security under Communism is achieved at too high a price, and that similar benefits might have been obtained by less drastic methods.

If Communism can create security, there is, as yet, no evidence for supposing that it can create prosperity. The much-advertised growth of heavy industry under the Five-Year Plan is comparable to that achieved by capitalist nations under analogous conditions, notably by the United States after the Civil War; and it is probable that a bourgeois-democratic Russia would have made progress with a similar rapidity and with considerably less internal friction. The efficiency of the Russian system, moreover, remains questionable. The increase in quantity has often been accompanied by a ruinous sacrifice of quality, and the proportion of damaged goods turned out by the typical Russian factory would never be tolerated under capitalist ownership. The different elements in the Russian economic system make progress at different speeds, so that the rapid growth of industrial production is rendered useless by the backwardness of transportation. Although the achievements of the dictatorship are advertised by the building of elaborate factories and power plants, the supply of consumers' goods — the only ultimate purpose of an industrial system, and the only true test of its efficiency — remains deficient in quantity, poor in quality, and lacking in variety. Twenty years after the Revolution the living standards of the average employed worker in Russia are lower than those of the unemployed worker in the United States. These facts are admitted; what is doubtful is their explanation. Communists attribute them to the economic backwardness of Russia before the Revolution, and to successful acts of sabotage by persistent and ubiquitous kulaks, Fascists, Trotskyites, and agents of the capitalist powers. There are, however, as will be argued in a later chapter, theoretical reasons for expecting inefficiency under a Communist system.[4]

Under the stress of a government-imposed industrialization the other aims of the Revolution — equality and freedom — have been postponed to a distant future. Their fulfilment is promised after the economic basis of a Communist society has been securely established, but hitherto the tendencies of the Russian system have been toward their diminution.

Immediately after the Revolution a considerable degree of democracy was allowed within the factories. Workers' control proved, however, to be incompatible with economic efficiency, and responsibility was gradually concentrated in individual administrators. Power now belongs to the managers of the various industrial units, to the central planning board which governs production and distribution, and to the Communist Party, which supervises the fulfilment of the various plans, enforces general obedience, and suppresses 'counter-revolutionary' malcontents. The right of the workers to criticize the management is tolerated only within narrow limits. Workers may be given freedom to exceed the quotas assigned to them by the national plan, but any tendency to demand shorter hours or less intense methods of labor, or to choose more leisure rather than an increase in the national wealth, may interfere with the successful functioning of the system and is therefore 'counter-revolutionary.' Russia resembles the Fascist nations in that strikes are prohibited and that trade unions are merely the instruments of a party dictatorship. The ultimate basis of the Party control is the monopolistic character of the economic system; insubordinate workers cannot change employers; they can expect only demotion or permanent unemployment and starvation. The practice of employers in capitalistic nations of black-listing agitators is, in fact, considerably less efficient than the Russian method of disposing of them.

The power enjoyed by the ruling bureaucracy is theoretically entrusted to them for the benefit of the proletariat as a whole. All history, however, proves that power corrupts, and that those who exercise power will appropriate wealth and privilege. The fact that Russia has abolished private ownership does not prove that it has destroyed exploitation. Those who control an economic system can assume financial advantages for themselves as effectively as those who own it — a fact of which the recent history of American corporate business offers many illustrations. Disinterestedness may by no means have disappeared among the Russian ruling class, but during recent years there has been a strongly marked tendency toward a greater economic differentiation between the bureaucracy and the workers. The difference in earnings between the average Russian worker and the higher members of the bureaucracy appears now to be almost as large as that between an American worker and the manager of an American corporation. The Russian Revolution has not abolished classes; it has merely created class distinctions in a new form. The limitations upon inheritance and the ability of competent members of the working class to rise into the bureaucracy do not invalidate this conclusion. The fact that class lines are fluid does not prove that classes do not exist. Class lines were almost equally fluid in the United States in the nineteenth century.

The growth of industrialism in Russia has been accompanied by an increase rather than a decrease in the coercive powers exercised by the government. The Communist claim is that this represents a temporary phase, necessitated by the continuance of 'counter-revolutionary' opposition, both internal and external, and that in due course the state will fulfil Marx's prophecy by withering away. Hitherto, however, no evidence has appeared in support of this optimistic belief, nor — under a system where all economic activity is planned by the state — is the disappearance of the state even theoretically conceivable. On the contrary, a planned economic system is impossible unless coercive authority is exercised by the planners. In Russia opposition tendencies are repressed without mercy, and the loyalty of the workers to the requirements of the national plan is maintained by unceasing propaganda, by Communist control over press, radio, and all other agencies for disseminating opinion, and by the inculcation of a perpetual fear of attack by foreign powers without and 'counter-revolutionary' plotters within. Science and the arts have undergone co-ordination — an inevitable consequence of the Communist control over all institutions of learning and over the publishing business; and while scientists receive generous encouragement as long as they devote themselves to the practical tasks imposed by the requirements of production, and writers are rewarded by enormous circulations and large royalties as long as they hymn the triumphs of the Five-Year Plan, both groups are forbidden to arrive at conclusions which contradict the dogmas of the official Marxist creed. The recent adoption of a constitution guaranteeing — at least on paper — a number of civil liberties can scarcely result in a greater freedom, since the Communist Party leadership retains its monopoly of political activity and of all the agencies for forming public opinion, and can continue to apply economic penalties against those who oppose it. As to what extent the dictatorship may represent public opinion one can only speculate; in view of the Communist monopoly of propaganda, such a question is probably meaningless. Scepticism is, however, induced by the prohibition of emigration, by the denial of freedom to opposition political movements, and by the prevalence of 'counter-revolutionary' plots and conspiracies.

That the Communist dictatorship is not fulfilling all the hopes of the October Revolution has been made dramatically apparent by the fantastic series of Moscow trials. Every surviving leader of the Revolution of any prominence (with the exception of Stalin, who remains in power, and of Trotsky, who is in exile), including men who were among Lenin's closest associates and who, in the years immediately following the Revolution, outranked Stalin as leaders and symbols of world Communism, has been convicted of counter-revolutionary' conspiracies, convicted even of having engaged twenty years ago in treasonable activities at the time when they were actually leading the Revolution, and condemned to firing-squads. The full truth about the trials will probably remain one of the unsolved mysteries of history. It is, however, reasonable to suppose that the victims were guilty of conspiring against Stalin, even though the full list of the crimes with which they were charged remains incredible.

And since they were men whose integrity (as judged by their revolutionary past under the czars) can scarcely be questioned — cannot indeed be questioned without impugning that of the whole Communist movement from its origins — and who were likely, from the standpoint of material interest, to gain more by remaining loyal to the dictatorship than by risking their lives to overthrow it, one can only conclude that they regarded Stalinism as a betrayal of the ideals of October and found it morally intolerable to continue to obey it. Two conclusions, at least, can safely be drawn: that when a dictatorship denies free expression to opposition tendencies and drives them underground, they inevitably take the form of sabotage, conspiracy, and murder; and that dictatorship is the end of that Marxist-Leninist-Stalinist chain of logic which began by identifying justice and truth with the will of the proletariat, proceeded by identifying the will of the proletariat with the will of a political party, and has ended by identifying the will of a political party with the will of its leader.

III. THE COMMUNIST INTERNATIONAL [5]

MEANWHILE the rulers of Russia were confidently looking forward to similar revolutions elsewhere. The success of the October Revolution gave enormous prestige to the Russian Communist Party, and enabled Lenin to organize the Third or Communist International, which was intended to uphold, in opposition to the parties of the Second International, the original Marxist faith in revolution. The reformist and patriotic tendencies of the Second International Lenin attributed to corruption and treachery on the part of its leaders, who were supposed to have sold themselves to their class enemies and to have become the hired labor lieutenants of capitalism; to the ability of the capitalists in imperialist countries to give higher wages to the workers at the expense of the exploited populations of the colonies and thereby to 'bribe' them into supporting imperialist policies; and to the fact that the Second International represented, not the working class as a whole, but merely a skilled and relatively well-paid 'labor aristocracy.' It followed that the Second International was the enemy of the proletariat — at least of the proletariat envisaged in the writings of Marx; and Lenin declared an unrelenting war against it. He demanded the adoption of Russian methods, and the formation of Communist Parties, on the Russian model, in western Europe. In 1919 there was general unrest among the working classes in the West, and considerable opposition to the Social-Democratic leaders who had supported the war; and the Communist International won at first the adhesion of several powerful and well-established labor organizations. Lenin insisted, however, that the revolutionary purity of the International must be maintained and that, for this purpose, it must be dominated by the Russians. Russian control was rendered possible, in practice, by the fact that no Communist Party outside Russia was able to make itself financially self-supporting. No large Labor Party in western Europe was able permanently to obey the rules laid down by the Russians, and most of the established organizations which joined the International in 1919 abandoned it within a few years. The ultimate result was that the working-class movement everywhere, in both its political and its trade-union aspects, was split into two mutually hostile groups. The masses of organized labor continued to support the reformist policies of the Second International. The Third International consisted of the Russian Communist Party, of various small and fluctuating groups in western Europe, partly proletarian and partly of middle-class intellectuals, and of representatives of exploited colonial races, particularly in Asia.

For the next twenty years both Internationals continued to look forward confidently to a rapid achievement of Socialism, whether by peaceful or by revolutionary means; and the in-ability of private capitalism to function with any reasonable efficiency made such hopes seem very plausible. Actually, however, the record of Marxism outside Russia was one of unredeemed failure. The only countries which achieved any substantial reforms and where progressive elements could view the future with any optimism — Sweden, Mexico, and, in a considerably smaller degree, the United States after 1933 — were countries where the chief progressive groups did not adhere to Marxist theory or follow Marxist practice.[6] Neither of the two Marxist Internationals won any permanent success, and both of them underwent a number of crushing defeats. The Second International could be militant in defence of po-litical democracy; but its social program was a reformism which grew increasingly milder, more uninspiring, and more difficult to distinguish from the policies of the more enlight-ened members of the capitalist class. The Third International, on the other hand, indulged in a suicidal series of futile revo-lutionary risings, sudden changes of policy, wholesale purges and expulsions, and violent attacks on all working-class lead-ers and organizations outside its own ranks.

The fantastic history of the Communist International can, in part, be attributed to Russian control. None of the Rus-sians had any understanding of western Europe, or of the kind of mentality which had developed under bourgeois demo-cracy; they endeavored to extend to western Europe their own conspiratorial habits, their own belief that any means what-ever were justified in order to achieve the desirable end of revolution. Russian controversies — between Stalin and Trotsky, or Stalin and Zinoviev, or Stalin and Bukharin — spread through the International and resulted in large-scale party purges. And while the Russian Communist Party con-trolled the International, it also governed a nation which had commercial and diplomatic relations with capitalist powers.

The result was doubly unfortunate: for the Communists were accused of spreading revolution in the interests of a foreign government, an accusation which increased the prejudice against them, while at the same time their revolutionary activities, instead of being stimulated, were sometimes restricted, sabotaged, or actually stifled in order to promote friendly relations between Russia and those governments with whom she hoped to establish alliances.

Yet Russian control was not the primary reason for the repeated failures of the International. Under different leadership it would have run a similar course. According to Marxist and Leninist theory the proletariat was a revolutionary class, and the Communist Party was the embodiment of its revolutionary will. Representing not the actual concrete proletariat but the ideal proletariat of Marxism, whose function was to create an ideal kingdom of freedom, the Communist Party was, in fact, in a mystical sense, infallible. Party leaders and Party members might be guilty of errors and betrayals, but the Party itself, in its mystical essence, embodied the historic and predetermined destiny of mankind. And just as in the Catholic Church of the Middle Ages the function of declaring the will of God was gradually lost by the body of the church members and became concentrated in the person of the pope, so in the Communist Party the function of defining the historic duty of the proletariat gradually became centralized in its leadership, Stalin assuming the prerogatives of a Marxist pope or caliph. Actually, however, the proletariat was not revolutionary; at no period, in no part of western Europe, did the masses of organized labor follow Communist leadership. The primary concern of organized labor was to maintain the bargaining strength of the trade unions and thereby to win security, higher wages, and better conditions of labor. Such purposes differed fundamentally from those of the Communists, who wished to use the trade unions, not to achieve security and reform within the capitalist framework, but for their own revolutionary ends. In consequence, there often developed a bitter hostility between the organized proletariat and the Party which claimed to represent it. The refusal of the masses to become revolutionary was attributed to treacherous leadership; the Communists, therefore, attacked the Social-Democratic and trade-union leaders as lackeys of the bourgeoisie, hired labor lieutenants of the capitalist class, Social-Fascists, and allies of Mussolini and Hitler. When they secured admission into a reformist trade union, they indulged in disruptive, splitting, and wrecking tactics, the purpose of which was to discredit reformist policies, but the final result of which was often the ruin of the entire organization. At the same time the Communists were compelled to recognize that even the masses had been corrupted by the same reformist tendencies. They could not, therefore, accept a genuine democracy, even a purely working-class democracy; the Communists must control the working class in accordance, not with its actual will, but with its ideal Marxist will. They sought to dominate every organization which they entered, forming Communist fractions who could work secretly and in concert to secure the adoption of the Party policies, developing a practice of putting forward innocent non-Communist figureheads who could be controlled by the Party from behind the scenes, and — once they had established secure control — reducing democracy to a minimum. The result was that the history of labor organizations under Communist leadership was usually short, tempestuous, and futile, and that those organizations which they did not succeed in capturing frequently found it necessary to expel them and to prohibit all known Communists from membership.

The discrepancy between theory and actuality — between the theoretical revolutionary will of the proletariat and its actual reformist will — caused the International to perform a series of the most extraordinary gyrations. The Party line was constantly veering between two opposite positions. In 1920, 1924, and 1929 the Party leaders denounced all other left-wing and working-class organizations as bourgeois or Social-Fascist, and declared that the Communists must maintain their revolutionary purity by isolation, advocates of a united front being accused of 'opportunism.' In 1922 and 1925 they urged a united-front policy of close association with other organizations, those who believed that the Party should remain isolated being accused of 'sectarianism.' Each time, however, that the International met with defeat — and outside Russia defeat was its invariable experience — it was impossible to attach blame either to Marxist theory or to the Party line, since both were infallible. If the Party line changed, it was not because it had been wrong, but because the situation had changed. Defeat could be explained only as due to corrupt or negligent leaders, who had failed to carry out the Party line — not the high command of the Party in Moscow, who continued to be the only authorized exponents of the Marxist creed, but the local leaders of the Party in the capitalist nations. Each time the high command changed its mind, the leaders who had become associated with its previous policy were liable to be denounced either as 'sectarians' or as 'opportunists,' or occasionally as both at the same time, and were sometimes deprived of their leadership, branded as traitors, and expelled from the Party. The result was an extraordinary lack of continuity both among the leadership and among the rank and file. Discredited leaders either abandoned politics altogether or became members of small, obscure, and futile communistic sects, where they devoted their energies to denouncing Stalin and proclaiming that they themselves were the only true embodiments of the Marxist cause and the revolutionary will of the proletariat. Meanwhile each shift in the Party line brought fresh converts — persons who despaired of reform under capitalism and were attracted by the growing prestige of the Russian experiment and by the discipline and the energy displayed by the Communist Party. Mostly they came from the ranks of the unemployed, or were minor intellectuals and professionals — persons who, for one reason or another, had lost, or had never had, definite class affiliations; though they included also workers in peculiarly depressed and exploited industries, and even a few typical members of the proletariat. Knowing nothing of the Party history, they remained members only as long as their first enthusiasm lasted or until the next turn in the Party line. The annual turnover in the membership of some of the national Communist Parties outside Russia often reached fifty per cent. It is doubtful if more than five per cent could be considered permanent Communists, in the same sense as men were permanent Socialists or Conservatives, Democrats or Republicans.

The conflict between the two Internationals, and the futility which characterized both of them, led to a situation which had not been foreseen in any of the Marxist gospels. Capitalism in western Europe began to disintegrate, but the beneficiaries of the resultant revolutionary situation were not the international proletariat but the Fascists.

Fascism, as developed first in Italy and afterward in Germany, could hardly have come into existence without the aid of the Communists. It borrowed from Russia its system of party dictatorship, and its totalitarian control over every aspect of cultural and political activity; and it won support chiefly by playing on the fear of Communism, promising to protect property-owners, both capitalist and petty bourgeois, against expropriation. Communism was afterward to reciprocate the compliment by aping the Fascist glorification of a leader — building not only Stalin but also its local chieftains, Thaelmann, Thorez, Diaz, Pollitt, and Browder, into miniature *fuehrers* — and by trying to outbid Fascism in appeals to patriotic sentiment. In the thirties the two parties were to feed on each other's growth, since the chief Fascist argument was the menace of Communism and the chief Communist argument was the menace of Fascism. Each party, moreover, was to contribute equally to that growth of fanaticism, and the consequent breakdown of democratic methods of government, which threatened to involve the whole world in the horrors of dictatorship and civil war.

In their social composition the two parties were not wholly dissimilar.[7] The leadership of each party contained a strong element of middle-class intellectuals and professionals — journalists, students, minor poets, ambitious and adventurous characters who had become *déclassés*. The rank and file of each party consisted largely of men rendered desperate by unemployment. In Germany, in 1932, many persons supported each party alternately. Viewed in terms of their objective class character (according to the method which the Marxists have made familiar), both Communism and Fascism might be regarded as instruments by which ambitious members of the lower middle classes hoped to elevate themselves into a ruling bureaucracy. But whereas the subjective element in Communism was a sincere idealism, Fascism was wholly cynical. Both of them were essentially intellectual and aesthetic creations, and not movements genuinely immanent in the course of social development; but while Communism inherited the rationalistic and libertarian ideals of the Hellenic and Christian tradition, Fascism was marked by the pathological sadism and megalomania of a decadent aestheticism. Communism was classicist, but Fascism was a romanticist nightmare.[8] The ends of Communism were good; it achieved evil only because its means were inappropriate to its ends. But Fascism was bad in both means and ends. It came, perhaps, nearer to being the embodiment of positive evil than any other movement in history.

The Fascists achieved power by appealing to all those classes in the social structure, and by playing on all those chords in the gamut of mass sentiment, which the Communists attacked, despised, minimized, or neglected. The Communists threatened the owners of industry with expropriation; but the Fascists promised them protection. The Communists offered to the peasants and the petty bourgeoisie only a collectivized economic system and subordination to a proletarian dictatorship, and at the same time reviled them as belonging to backward, degenerate, and obsolescent social strata; but the Fascists flattered their pride and agreed to fight their battles both against the trade unions and against the bankers and monopolists. Communism was international, egalitarian, anti-religious, anti-mystical, and coldly rationalistic. Fascism played on the consciousness of nation, race, and tradition, appealed to the desire of men for mysticism, their love for emotionalism, and their need for worship, and offered them a debased and barbaric poetry of ritual, ceremony, and myth.

By Marxist theory, Fascism in power had to be regarded as a capitalist dictatorship. All social phenomena were aspects of the class struggle between the capitalists and the workers; and since Fascism did not represent the workers, it must represent the capitalists. Politics, however, is not a mere reflection of economics; governing bureaucracies do not necessarily represent an economic class within the system of production; they are capable of developing independent interests of their own. The Fascists undoubtedly sought power by promising protection to the capitalists; they also collected money from them — a process which the Communists defined as bribery, but which might also be regarded as blackmail. After the triumph of Fascism it was the Fascist bureaucracy and not the capitalist class which had the upper hand; the bureaucracy could, if they found it expedient, expropriate the capitalist

class and still retain power, but the capitalists could not revolt against the bureaucracy without overthrowing themselves at the same time. The ultimate end of Fascism seemed
likely to be a state capitalism which, though reached by a
different road, would in some respects finally resemble the
state capitalism of Russia. Whereas Communism expropriated the previous owners of industry and then created a new
bureaucratic class, Fascism retained the existing ownership,
but confiscated such a large percentage of its profits and subjected it to such an all-embracing state control that ownership
would finally lose all its meaning. But while Communism
was basically pacifistic and its economic system was keyed for
the growth of productive wealth, Fascism, at least in its German and Italian manifestations, sought to build up loyalty at
home by being aggressively imperialistic abroad, and prevented unemployment by an enormous expenditure on armaments.[9]

The chaos and the disillusionment which prevailed throughout Europe at the end of the war might have been expected to
result in Communist revolutions. Actually revolution never
had any chance of success in any highly industrialized country. It may, however, have been possible in some of the peasant nations of eastern Europe, particularly in Bulgaria and
Hungary. Here Communism failed because its leaders would
not ally themselves with the peasants. Lacking the cynical
opportunism of the Russians, who encouraged the growth of
peasant proprietorship in 1917 and forced the peasants into
collective farms in 1929, they regarded the division of the big
estates into individual private properties as a retrograde step.
In Bulgaria they refused to support the Peasant Party of Stambuliski, which attained power in 1919. It was, they declared,
a reactionary movement, representing the opposition of the
country to the towns; both Stambuliski and the feudal aristocracy whom he opposed were merely bourgeois. The result

34

was that three years later both the peasants and the Communists were separately crushed by the forces of reaction. In Hungary, for a short period in 1919, a Communist Party did actually achieve power — or, to speak more accurately, was placed in power by liberals and Social-Democrats who believed that only an alliance with the extreme left could prevent a swing to the extreme right. The alienation of the peasants, the opposition of the British and French governments, and the incompetence and terroristic methods of the Communist chieftain, Bela Kun, led quickly to a triumph of reaction and to a bloody persecution of liberalism as well as of radicalism. The opportunity of revolutionizing these peasant nations, once lost, did not recur. In some of them, such as Rumania, sagacious governments ensured themselves against revolution by themselves distributing land among the peasants. Elsewhere revolutionary parties were crushed too mercilessly for any recovery.

Germany had always been the chief stronghold of Marxism, and from 1919 until 1933 it continued to be the chief hope of the Communists. Blame for the final tragedy should probably be apportioned equally between the two Marxist parties. In 1918 the Social-Democrats, all other political parties having defaulted, assumed the government. It is plain that any thoroughgoing social revolution was impossible; the opponents of Socialism had a majority in numbers, and a still greater superiority in military strength; the German people, already starving, were dependent for their very existence upon the capitalistic governments of Great Britain and France. The Social-Democrats established a democratic constitution and became its most faithful defenders; in 1920 it was the trade unions alone who, by declaring a general strike, prevented the success of a reactionary *coup d'état*. Yet at the same time, faithful to their revisionist attitudes, the Social-Democrats continued to work only for higher standards of living within the capitalist framework, without showing any capacity for solving the grave economic and international problems with which post-war Germany was confronted; and, failing to exhibit even an elementary common sense, they allowed the army, the civil service, and the judiciary to remain strongholds of reaction. Left-wing groups, on the other hand, led at first by such *bona-fide* Marxists as Rosa Luxemburg, afterward by Communists, poured scorn on the constitution, refused to recognize any distinction between a bourgeois democracy and a bourgeois dictatorship, and indulged in a series of futile rebellions and threats of rebellion, which were bloodily suppressed, and the only results of which were to weaken the republic, to drive the Social-Democrats still farther to the right, and to widen the gulf between the reformists and the revolutionaries. The consequent hatred between the leaders of the two left-wing parties continued until they met each other in Hitler's concentration camps. Meanwhile the Russian government, while encouraging the German Communists to rebel, was at the same time selling weapons to the Reichswehr which crushed those rebellions.

It was, however, in Italy that the greatest disaster of the post-war period occurred, though it was long before liberals, and even longer before Communists, began to appreciate its catastrophic nature. For the triumph of Italian Fascism, Moscow, as it happened, was not responsible; the Italian Socialist Party had joined the Third International in 1919, but the opposition of the trade unions to Communist methods had caused a majority of the Party to withdraw two years later. Italian labor, moreover, tended to be Syndicalist rather than Marxist. In 1921 labor troubles in northern Italy led to a lockout, after which the workers took possession of some of the factories and attempted to operate them themselves. They rapidly discovered that successful operation of the factories was impossible, and since they were neither willing nor able to go forward to a revolution, they ended by abandoning them. The result was to frighten the industrialists and to cause them to give support to the bands of Fascist thugs, led by the ex-Socialist Mussolini, who were already engaged in terrorizing militant workers and peasants. The weakness and unpopularity of the democratic politicians, the disappointment of the Italian people with its failure to profit by the World War, the lack of prestige of parliamentary institutions, and the sympathy of reactionary elements enabled Mussolini, in 1922, to achieve the premiership. Two years later, when the murder of the Socialist leader Matteotti threatened to discredit the whole Fascist régime, his rule began to be tightened into a totalitarian dictatorship. For ten years liberals regarded Fascism as a purely Italian phenomenon and of no great importance. Moscow remained faithful to its theory that bourgeois democracy and bourgeois dictatorship were, from a Communist viewpoint, identical, and found it expedient to maintain close diplomatic and commercial relations with the Fascist government.

The period from 1923 to 1929 was to be one of relative tranquillity. European capitalism, with the aid of American loans, appeared to be recovering. The Communist International, therefore, transferred its attention to Asia. Here nationalistic movements were developing, which were plainly antagonistic to British and French imperialism and which — in accordance with Lenin's policy — might appropriately receive Russian support. The International offered encouragement to any movement which might make trouble for the British Empire, even including, at one period, Arabic nationalism in Palestine — a flirtation which was justified on the ground that the Zionists were tools of the British and also bourgeois. Events were to prove, however, that in any alliance between Communism and nationalism it was nationalism which was the gainer. The Bolsheviks were, moreover,

handicapped in their capacity as the organizers of world revolution by the fact that they were also the directors of Russian
foreign policy; and when the two rôles conflicted, it was the
latter which prevailed. Thus the Russian government sought
an alliance with the new Turkey of Kemal Ataturk; Kemal
used Russian help to consolidate himself, and then proceeded
to kill the Turkish Communists. A similar but more spectacu-
lar disaster was suffered by the Communists in China. Moscow supported the Kuomintang, a nationalist party of mixed
bourgeois and proletarian composition. Hoping for an alliance with the Chinese government, it was unwilling to break
with the bourgeois wing of the party; hoping that Chinese
nationalism might eventually develop into Chinese Commun
ism, it encouraged the organization of a Communist Party
among the students and workers. The result was that Chiang
Kai-shek, leader of the right wing of the Kuomintang, was
able to use the Chinese Communists and their Russian advisers
to make himself dictator of central China, after which — in
1926 — he turned against his Communist allies and massacred
them. Moscow, which had dictated every move of the Chinese Communists, could not evade direct responsibility for the
disaster. The result was that Communism, wholly discredited, almost disappeared in the Chinese cities. It was transformed into a peasant movement; and though the insurgent
peasants called themselves Marxists, they had more real affin-
ity with such earlier peasant movements as the Taiping Rebellion than with the Marxists of Russia and the West. Chiang Kai-shek continued to fight the peasant Communists,
with varying success, until 1936; then, with the outbreak of
the Japanese War and the new Popular-Front program of the
International, Moscow suddenly discovered that he was
China's national hero.

The year 1929 marked the end of capitalist stabilization and
the opening of a new era of wars and revolutions. This hap-

pened to coincide with an extreme leftward swing of the International. The Social-Democrats, who at earlier periods had been described merely as traitors to the proletariat and labor lieutenants of the bourgeoisie, were now being denounced as 'Social-Fascists'; they were the supporters of Fascism and the chief enemies of Communism. Any attempt to defend democratic institutions meant, objectively, the defence of capitalism and the frustration of the revolutionary ardor of the working class. Such arguments continued to be the stock-in-trade of the International until 1934 — a period which included the first year of the Roosevelt New Deal. Roosevelt was described as a Fascist, almost identical with Mussolini and Hitler, and — because of his skill in deceiving the working class — even more dangerous, and the New Deal was depicted as being primarily a measure of war preparation, probably directed against the Soviet Union.

The infantile leftism of the theory of Social-Fascism was to be an important cause of the greatest disaster which civilization has suffered in our time — the establishment of the Nazi dictatorship in Germany.

The cessation of American loans in 1929 brought the capitalist house of cards tumbling to the ground, and Germany found herself confronted with all the grave weaknesses in her economic structure which had been caused by the World War and the peace treaties. Bankruptcies and unemployment began to increase catastrophically. Here, if ever there was one, was a revolutionary situation. In Germany, by the year 1932, the objective conditions necessary for the overthrow of capitalism were as fully realized as they are ever likely to be in any highly industrialized country. The result was a steady weakening of those parties which supported the constitution and a rapid growth of the two extremes. A majority of the German people were becoming willing to accept dictatorship, either of the left or of the right, in the hope of ending the intolerable economic insecurity. In the elections of July, 1932, the Communist vote reached five and a quarter million, a large proportion of which came from the unemployed. The Nazis, however, capitalizing on Germany's resentment against the loss of the war and the humiliation of the peace treaties and making enormous gains among the middle classes, had increased even more rapidly, winning a vote of nearly fourteen million. After the July election the Nazis negotiated with the government instead of seizing power, the result being that they began to lose votes and the Communists to gain them — a fact which shows that the two parties were rivals for the support of those groups in the population who had become desperate.[10] Throughout 1932, however, the old German ruling class — industrialists, landlords, generals, and bureaucrats — were able, through their influence with President Hindenburg, to retain control of the situation; and when the Nazis lost strength, they resolved to admit them into the government as a safeguard against the greater evil of Communism. Once possessed of office, Hitler and the Nazi bureaucracy proceeded to appropriate power, and their aristocratic patrons were gradually driven into obscurity. Throughout the *débâcle* of German civilization the two Marxist parties vied with each other in falsifying, by the feebleness of their actions, the predictions of the Marxist faith. The Social-Democrats, who had saved the republic in 1920, but whose organizations were now weakened by the growth of unemployment and by the constant attacks of the Communists, did nothing. The Communists concentrated all their venom on the Social-Democrats, voting side by side with the Nazis against Centrist and Social-Democratic administrations. For more than a year after the triumph of Hitler international Communism continued to proclaim that the Nazi victory was not a defeat but a step toward a Communist victory; it had ended the influence of the Social-Democrats and destroyed the illusions of the masses. When, in the following year, the Austrian Socialists, unlike the German Communist Party, which had capitulated to Hitler without striking a blow, actually took up arms in defence of democracy, the Communists still insisted that the Socialist leaders were betraying their followers, and were merely the tools of the reactionary dictatorship against which they were fighting.

By the summer of 1934, however, it had become obvious, even in Moscow, that the Nazi dictatorship would be more than a temporary interlude, and that its imperialist program was a genuine danger to Russia. The Soviet government had been talking of an attack by foreign imperialisms, usually British and French, since its foundation; but its predictions of war had hitherto been intended primarily for home consumption, as a device for arousing the fervor necessary to a totalitarian state. Now the danger, for the first time, had become genuine. Democracy, moreover, was in danger in other countries besides Germany, notably in France, where the republic had almost succumbed under Fascist attacks in February, 1934. And however much Moscow might insist that bourgeois democracy and bourgeois dictatorship were objectively identical, Communists outside Russia discovered that there were considerable subjective differences between a government which left them free to continue propagandizing and one which tortured and murdered them in concentration camps. The result was a complete reversal in the whole policy of the International and a complete abandonment of all those doctrines which had characterized Communism since its origin. The World Congress of 1935 adopted a program of collaboration with liberals and Social-Democrats in a Popular Front for the defence of democracy and of demanding that Fascist aggression should be checked by a system of collective security. Communists throughout the world suddenly found themselves repudiating every theory which they had professed before 1934 and allying themselves with organizations which, before 1934, they had denounced as instruments of the capitalist class and the Fascists.[11] Bourgeois democracy, instead of being really capitalist dictatorship, had to be defended. Reformist policies, instead of playing into the hands of the capitalists, deserved support. The League of Nations, instead of being the tool of British and French imperialism, was an instrument for checking aggression. Communism now meant democracy, civil liberties, religious freedom, the Americanism of the twentieth century, a strong, free, and happy France, and the united front with Léon Blum, Edouard Daladier, Manuel Azana, Clement Atlee, Chiang Kai-shek, Franklin D. Roosevelt, John L. Lewis, Fiorello H. La Guardia, and all the other Social-Fascists and capitalist 'lackeys' of 1933. Communist leaders even made overtures to the most consistent and inveterate of all the enemies of international Communism, the Roman Catholic Church. From the almost universal distribution of bouquets one left-wing group was, however, rigidly excluded: those who, tainted with the Trotskyite poison, maintained that Stalin had betrayed the Revolution.

The new policy of the International appeared at first to be startlingly successful. In the democratic nations the growth of Fascism was causing a general alarm, and many middle-class liberal and progressive elements were eager for a militant policy in defence of freedom. The Communists still excelled all other parties in their energy, discipline, and capacity for self-sacrifice; and anti-Fascists, taking the democratic professions of the Communists at their face value and knowing nothing of the Party history, began to flock into numerous Communist-controlled organizations. In France and Spain, in the spring of 1936, Popular Front governments, supported both by the working class and by sections of the middle class and the peasants, were elected to office. In France the Communist Party began to become, what no Communist Party outside

Russia had ever been before for more than a year or two, a genuine mass working-class party. In Great Britain and the United States, where the Communists had hitherto been a negligible force, they made few converts among the working class, who had learned in the twenties to regard their disruptive tactics with suspicion; but they made enormous gains among middle-class liberal intellectuals and professionals. While Bloomsbury and Greenwich Village turned Marxist en masse, liberal journalists, university professors, and ministers of religion began to discover that the Soviet Union was a paradise of democracy — a process only partially checked by the execution, in 1936, 1937, and 1938, of hundreds of Trotskyite and Old Bolshevik political leaders, generals, and intellectuals.

It is tempting to regard the new Party line as a sudden reversion to sanity — the first sign of sanity, in fact, which the International had displayed since its foundation. It would, however, be a mistake to regard the new Communist policies with too much optimism. The ultimate aims of the Communists, and the purposes of the Popular Front, remained obscure. The Popular Front, which endeavored to unite the middle classes and the working class on a common platform, was able to win electoral majorities; but its only purpose appeared to be defence against Fascist aggression. No progressive or left-wing movement can, however, be content to remain on the defensive. It can permanently defeat Fascism only by offering an alternative program of social reconstruction. The only positive program of the Popular Front was a Social-Democratic reformism, consisting chiefly of higher wages, shorter hours, and measures of social security for the working class. Whether such reforms were possible within the capitalist framework and without alienating the middle classes was doubtful. Judging from the experiences of the Popular Front in France, their effect was not to transform the

43

economic system but merely to weaken it. The Communists, apparently, regarded a Popular Front government as a preliminary to a social revolution. This was, however, improbable. Either the Popular Front would satisfy its supporters and enact reforms which would stabilize the economic system, in which case there would be no stimulus for any further swing to the left; or else it would disappoint its supporters and increase the economic instability, in which case all the parties of the left would tend to be weakened and discredited and there would be a danger of a swing to the right. In France, in 1939, the latter appeared to be the more probable. What was needed was a positive program of reconstruction upon which the middle classes and the working class could agree. Such a program, however, was impossible without an abandonment of the Marxist creed of proletarian dictatorship and universal socialization. As long as the parties of the left continued to be governed by Marxist dogma, whether it took the Social-Democratic form of reformist legislation or the Communist form of proletarian revolution, the alliance of middle-class liberals and proletarian radicals in a Popular Front could be only a temporary and hazardous expedient.

How seriously the democratic professions of the Communists were to be taken was, moreover, doubtful. Still regarding themselves as the only true interpreters of the will of the working class and the only predestined leaders of the coming revolution, they were still compelled by their own theories to seek to dominate every organization which they entered. They were unable to ally themselves with other organizations on a basis of genuine equality. The Party, moreover, was still controlled from Moscow, and Moscow, in 1937 and 1938, had two cardinal purposes: to build a union of the democratic nations which would check the coming drive of the Nazis against the Soviet Union, and to destroy international Trotskyism. In the pursuit of the first objective the Communists abandoned their earlier policy of opposing war preparations, became militant advocates of collective security, and gave uncritical support to any capitalist government, such as that of President Roosevelt, which seemed willing to check Fascist aggression. The necessity — in Europe — of opposing Fascist aggression may be admitted, but whether the real purposes of progressivism were served by urging the United States to active intervention in Europe and the Far East may be doubted. Meanwhile the Communists continued their vendetta with the Trotskyites, and on this issue, which — at bottom — concerned only the question of who was to govern Russia, were willing to split the left-wing movement throughout the world.

The meaning of the new Communist policy was most vividly exemplified in Spain. Spain, like Russia in 1917, was primarily a peasant country; and like Russia, she had suffered for centuries from all the accumulated evils caused by a feudal landowning caste, a wealthy and reactionary clergy, and a corrupt and despotic bureaucracy. In 1931 there began a revolution — the first genuine revolution which had occurred anywhere since 1917; and the revolutionary movement, originally moderate and liberal, gradually began to assume a peasant and proletarian character. The Spanish Communists, a small and insignificant group, at first remained wholly aloof from the revolution, regarding it as too bourgeois to be worthy of their attention. In 1936, however, the new line of the International made them a part of the coalition for the defence of Spanish democracy; and they were one of the various progressive parties which co-operated in the election of a Popular Front government. The weakness of this government — its inability to carry out reforms with sufficient rapidity and to check either the rioting of the Anarcho-Syndicalist left or the preparations for a *coup d'état* which were being made by the reactionary right — resulted in the summer in the rebellion of General Franco, which was sponsored by the Fascist powers and assisted by the 'non-intervention' policy of the British Foreign Office. Rather than allow Fascism to score another victory, Moscow was compelled to assist the Spanish government, and in the autumn she began, apparently with some reluctance, to ship munitions to Spain. During the two years which followed, international Communism supplied the Spanish Loyalists with allies who displayed a much-needed energy and enthusiasm. Ideologically, they stood nearer to the right than to the left of the Loyalist forces, associating with the Left Republicans rather than with the Socialists and the Anarcho-Syndicalists and insisting that the war was being fought not to achieve a social revolution but to defend democracy. The price which Moscow demanded for her support was high. She never supplied munitions in sufficient quantities to enable the Loyalists to win the war, and for all shipments she required payments in cash. She insisted, moreover, on Communist domination over the Spanish government; and when Largo Caballero showed himself too independent, he was forced out of office in favor of a premier who would be more compliant. Deprived (thanks to the British Foreign Office) of her legal right to buy munitions from the democratic nations, Spanish democracy had no alternative but to obey the wishes of the Kremlin. Meanwhile the democratic pretensions of the Communists in Spain were belied by their antagonism to any left-wing groups who refused to share their reverence for the Soviet government; and the methods of the Russian secret police were introduced into Loyalist Spain to dispose of Trotskyite and Anarcho-Syndicalist leaders.[12]

In 1939 the progressive forces in Europe were everywhere in retreat, and the Popular Front program appeared to have failed almost as fully as the revolutionary program which it had superseded. Its achievements in domestic policy had been insubstantial, while its main purpose — that of creating a union of the democratic powers against Fascist aggression — remained unachieved. The two chief partners in such a union would be the British Foreign Office and the Kremlin, two institutions which rivalled each other in their capacity for cloaking a policy of self-interest with the most idealistic pretensions. They hated and suspected each other as much as either of them feared Hitler; and during the complex diplomatic manoeuvrings of 1938 and 1939 it began to seem probable that each of them was hoping to divert German ambitions against the other. Europe had entered a period of the most cynical power politics. Through 1938 the British Foreign Office continued to encourage the German drive to the east, hoping, apparently, that a war between Germany and Russia would relieve the British Empire from the pressure, at one and the same time, of its two most formidable antagonists; and at Munich Hitler was given a virtual hegemony over all southeastern Europe. In the spring of 1939, however, British policy suddenly reversed itself, and British politicians suddenly adopted the program of collective security. The most plausible explanation of this diplomatic revolution was that they had discovered that Stalin might refuse to save the British Empire by going to war with Germany and that he might, on the contrary, play his trump card and come to an understanding with Hitler. Great Britain then began to woo the Soviet Union; but the Kremlin, which had been urging a program of collective security against Fascism for five years, showed itself remarkably reluctant to accept any terms which Great Britain could offer. It seemed likely that if Moscow could guarantee itself against a German attack and could induce Nazi imperialism to swing westward against Britain and France instead of to the east, self-interest would cause it to choose an understanding with Berlin rather than with London. Such a policy, however, would cause international Communism to be wholly discredited; it would leave left-wing groups with the task of finding a new orientation and a new program. Alternatively, Moscow might decide that it was impossible to head off the German drive to the east and might finally join forces with Great Britain. In this case Communists throughout the world would still be able to represent Russia as the champion of democracy against Fascism; they would, however, be forced more and more to become a war party, and would be compelled to sacrifice all hopes of domestic reform or revolution to the exigencies of war preparation. Either way the extravagant hopes which Marx had first circulated, and which had inspired the left-wing movement for half a century, were perhaps on the verge of liquidation. Progressivism would have to find a new, and non-Marxist, basis.

IV. SOME CONCLUSIONS

THE purpose of this historical survey has not been merely to illustrate the follies of which Marxists have been guilty in practice. Wrong practice is usually a result of wrong theory. The evidence of history would appear to support certain theoretical conclusions, the most important of which are as follows:

(1) Contrary to Marxist theory, revolutions in the modern world occur not in industrialized nations but in peasant nations; they are successful in the degree that they are peasant movements against feudal systems of landownership. The countries where revolutionary movements have either succeeded or come near to success are such peasant countries as Russia, Spain, Hungary, Bulgaria, China, and Mexico. By contrast the highly industrialized nations, such as the United States, England, France, and — to a lesser degree — Germany, have been almost immune from revolutionary disturbances.

(2) Contrary to Marxist theory, the proletariat is not, and

never has been, a revolutionary class. It can be militant in defence of political democracy (as in Germany in 1920, and in Austria in 1934), and where political democracy does not exist (as in czarist Russia) it may support a revolutionary program. But its attitude to social and economic questions is not revolutionary but reformist; it desires a higher standard of living within the capitalist framework. In an industrialized society support for a revolutionary program comes not from the proletariat as a whole but from middle-class students and intellectuals, from workers in peculiarly depressed industries, and from the unemployed.

(3) Contrary to Marxist theory, wherever the lines of conflict are drawn between Fascism and Communism, Fascism is victorious. Fascism has been checked only when the Communists have abandoned their revolutionary policy and allied themselves with reformist middle-class and working-class groups for the defence of democracy. Such an alliance, however, is apt to be unstable and short-lived owing to its failure to find a positive program upon which groups with different class interests can agree. Working-class reformism, when carried too far, is apt to alienate the middle classes.

(4) In the only country where Marxism has been victorious, its ideals — freedom, equality, and prosperity — have not been realized. On the contrary, the attempt to achieve the Marxist ideals by Marxist methods has led to a suppression of freedom and a growth of class differences, and has not hitherto succeeded in creating economic prosperity.

(5) On the other hand, the only countries which would appear to be making any real progress toward those ideals and which are in no immediate danger of falling under a reactionary dictatorship — the United States, Mexico, and Sweden — are countries where Marxist ideas have had little influence and which have not pursued reforms by Marxist methods.

A Note on Trotskyism

The contention of the followers of Trotsky is that Stalin and the bureaucratic group of which he is the leader have betrayed the Revolution, and that its ideals might have been achieved if different policies, advocated by Trotsky, had been adopted by the Russian Communist Party. The argument of this book, on the other hand, is that Stalinism is the logical and necessary consequence of Marxist and Leninist theory, and that the only important difference between Stalin and Trotsky is that Stalin is in power and Trotsky is in exile.

The basis of Stalinism is the Leninist theory of the rôle to be played by the Communist Party; that this theory would result in the creation of a privileged bureaucracy was predicted by Rosa Luxemburg before the Revolution. The organization of such a party was, however, a necessary deduction from the Marxist faith in a proletarian revolution; such a revolution could have been achieved by no other method. The preliminary steps leading to the Stalinite policies, both in Russia and in international affairs, were taken while Lenin was alive and while Trotsky was still a leading figure in the Soviet government. Lenin and Trotsky were in power when the rebellion of the Kronstadt workers was crushed, when friendly relations were established with certain capitalist powers, and when support was given to nationalist movements in Asia. The Communist leadership was, in fact — given the situation in which it found itself — unable to act otherwise.

There are alleged to be fundamental differences in policy between Stalin and Trotsky. Stalin, for example, is supposed to believe in building Socialism in Russia, Trotsky in working for world revolution. This difference is, at most, one of degree. Stalin has always believed in world revolution, Trotsky has always believed in building as much Socialism as possible in Russia. That Stalin has placed most emphasis on building

Socialism in Russia, and has sacrificed the world revolution in order to achieve greater security for the Russian Soviets, was due not to personal choice but to objective conditions. A Communist revolution has never been possible anywhere outside Russia, and for the Soviet government to devote its energies to fomenting revolution outside its own territories would have been suicidal. If Trotsky and not Stalin had become the Soviet dictator, he would have been compelled to adopt a similar attitude. The other theoretical differences between the two men are equally unreal. Before 1928, for example, Trotsky favored a program of rapid collectivization, while Stalin argued that it was necessary to retain the support of the peasants. The initiation of the Five-Year Plan meant that Stalin had adopted the Trotskyite position.

The function of Trotskyism is that of an opposition. It opposes whatever Stalin does, so that when the Stalinite line reverses itself, the Trotskyite line undergoes a reversal also. Before 1935, during the 'Social-Fascist' period, Trotsky argued for a united front. Since the Stalinite adoption of the Popular Front policy in 1935, Trotsky has stepped into the position previously occupied by Stalin and now demands immediate revolutions everywhere. As an opposition the Trotskyites are able to point out all the errors of the Stalinites and to score a number of effective debating points. It does not follow, however, that if Trotsky were in power he would not be guilty of similar errors.

A rejection of Trotskyism does not, of course, involve any belittling of the personality of Trotsky. As politician, military leader, historian, and pamphleteer, he has a combination of talents which are probably unique in the contemporary world and to which there are few parallels in history.

It should be added that Trotsky's most recent study of the Russian situation, *The Revolution Betrayed*, is not a Trotskyite manifesto but a sober sociological analysis. The argument is that Stalinism is a necessary consequence of a revolution occurring in an economically backward country. When the economic system is unable to provide prosperity for everybody, it is inevitable that inequalities should appear and that a bureaucratic class should obtain a privileged position. Such a degeneration is, however, only temporary; and when the productive capacity of the economic system has reached the appropriate level, the bureaucracy will be overthrown. This cannot be called an attack on Stalinism, since it represents Stalinism as historically inevitable. In reality, it is the only plausible *defence* of Stalinism which it is possible to make; it represents the disappearance of freedom and equality in Russia as a temporary phase, and asserts that the ideals of the October Revolution will, in due course, find fulfilment.

III. Revolution and the Proletariat

III. Revolution and the Proletariat

I. THE WORKING CLASS AND
POLITICAL POWER

THE record of the past seventy years gives no support to the Marxist contention that the proletariat will seize power and destroy capitalism; it suggests, on the contrary, that the working class has neither the power nor the will to revolutionize society. It may, however, be illegitimate to draw conclusions from a relatively short period of history. It is possible that the Marxist explanation — that the working class has been temporarily led astray by corrupt leadership and by higher wages paid at the expense of exploited colonial races — may be valid. The theoretical arguments in support of the Marxist position must therefore be examined.

Postponing for later discussion the question whether the proletariat wishes to overthrow capitalism, let us consider first whether it has the power to do so, and under what circumstances a proletarian revolution might be expected to be successful.

Until 1935 the Communist doctrine was that such a revolution, even in the democratic nations, must be achieved by force. The proletariat must seize power, and must then defend itself by establishing a dictatorship and fighting a civil war against its capitalist opponents. Such a seizure of power was — until 1935, when the Communists suddenly discovered the merits of democracy — the avowed purpose of all Communist parties. Marx himself had admitted the possibility that in certain countries, such as Great Britain, Holland, and the United States, the proletariat might achieve power through the ballot; but this possibility was denied by Lenin, who declared that conditions in those countries had changed since Marx's death and that capitalism everywhere could be destroyed only by violence. Such a doctrine appears, when one examines it, to be so preposterous that one would be tempted to suppose that it must have been invented by some red-baiting congressman or newspaper-owner but for the fact that it is included in the official program of the Communist International.[1]

The refusal of Marxists to discuss the concrete steps by which a revolution might be accomplished is almost as remarkable as their unwillingness, prior to 1917, to describe the kind of social organization which would follow the revolution. Communist writers have described in detail the horrors of capitalism and the beauties of Communism, but the vital stage in the argument — the process by which one can be changed into the other — is invariably slurred over in a few vague phrases.[2] The workers, we are told, will in some mysterious fashion proceed to seize power. What is meant, in this context, by the word 'workers,' and by what methods they will seize power, is left in mystery.

Much Marxist argument consists in the manipulation of certain verbal counters, or stereotypes, which are arranged in logical patterns in such a way as to produce certain conclusions, without any reference, at any stage in the argument, to concrete facts. The Marxist faith in revolution is based on the manipulation of the stereotypes 'bourgeoisie,' 'proletariat,' and 'state.' There is, they tell us, a class struggle between the 'bourgeoisie' and the 'proletariat,' and the 'state' is an instrument of class dominance. The 'state' is at present controlled by the 'bourgeoisie,' who use it in order to oppress the 'proletariat.' The 'proletariat' must seize control of it, and transform it into an instrument for crushing the 'bourgeoisie.'

It is obvious, in the first place, that a revolutionary seizure of power would be accomplished not by the 'proletariat' but by some political organization which claimed to represent it. Seizing power means, presumably, taking possession of the machinery of administration and of such vital nerve-centres of the modern social organization as the radio stations, telephone exchanges, electrical plants, and so forth, and establishing a government. This could be accomplished by some relatively small but bold and highly disciplined group of men. After they had seized power, however, they could not hold it permanently unless they had the support either of the armed forces, the bureaucracy, and the owners and managers of industry — in other words, of those small but powerful groups in the community whose viewpoint is apt to be reactionary — or of the large majority of the population. In other words, a right-wing *coup d'état* might conceivably succeed without majority support; a left-wing *coup d'état* is impossible without such support.

Even assuming majority support, moreover, the success of a left-wing *coup d'état* is exceedingly dubious. Unless it had the support of the rank and file of the armed forces — something very improbable except at the end of an unsuccessful war — its enemies would be able to fight a long, destructive, and probably successful war against it. They would, moreover, be able to interrupt the processes of transportation and distribution, without which a modern society cannot survive for more than a few days. The results of a revolutionary upheaval in any highly industrialized community would, in fact, be catastrophic.

What reason is there, however, for supposing that in a democratic nation a left-wing *coup d'état* ever would have majority support? In none of the great powers has any Socialist or Communist Party ever secured majority support by legal and democratic methods. But if the left wing cannot win such support on a program of peaceful reform, it is still less likely to do so on a program of violence and revolution. All the reasons alleged to show the impossibility of securing Socialism by democratic methods — the influence of money, the power of a reactionary press, electoral intimidation, the likelihood of a reactionary *coup d'état* — operate even more forcefully against a revolutionary Socialism. The one political advantage of the left-wing movement is that it can claim to represent the interests of the majority of the population; the only tactic by which it can hope for success is to insist on maintaining the principles of majority rule and of adherence to the law and the constitution. When reliance on constitutional methods is abandoned and political questions are settled by an open trial of strength and by methods of violence, the advantages enjoyed by the forces of reaction are overwhelming.

It is alleged that if the left-wing won an election by democratic methods, it would not be allowed to enjoy the fruits of victory; that reactionary forces would take control of the situation and proceed to overthrow the constitution and set up a dictatorship. This is indeed quite possible, as has been seen in Spain; and any progressive party should be prepared for such an eventuality. It by no means follows, however, that the left wing should themselves anticipate events by seizing power unconstitutionally. On the contrary, it becomes all the more necessary for the parties of the left to advocate a strict obedience to the principles of constitutional government and majority rule, to regard any violation of these principles as criminal, and to allow the opposition no plausible pretext for violating them. Marxists are apt to view society in terms of two opposite forces — a reactionary bourgeoisie and a revolutionary proletariat. Actually, however, large sections of society are swayed by the desire to maintain constitutional order and by the habit of respect for the law.

Parties which respect legality and attain power by constitutional methods, therefore, enjoy an enormous strategic
advantage (as was realized by both Mussolini and Hitler);
and it is the greatest folly for the left wing to sacrifice this
advantage. Communist parties in western Europe and the
United States have never seriously set out to seize power by
force; but their habit — prior to 1935 — of talking as though
this were their intention played into the hands of reaction
and presented Fascist parties with their most effective argument. The rebellion of General Franco against the Spanish
Republic would, no doubt, have occurred even if the left-wing
parties had remained strictly peaceful and law-abiding; but
it would have won considerably less support if it had not been
able to represent itself as a movement for protecting law and
order against the rioting and church-burning of the Anarchists
and against the alleged threat of a *coup d'état* on the part of the
Communists. The Communist Party now professes a strict
loyalty to constitutional methods, but whether it can ever
live down its revolutionary past is doubtful.

If no left-wing party can — in a democratic community —
expect to attain power through a political revolution, even
less can it hope to revolutionize society by methods of economic class warfare. Syndicalists have sometimes expected
the working class to overthrow capitalism by means of a
general strike, the purpose of which, presumably, is to starve
the remainder of the community into submission. The general
strike is sometimes an effective weapon if it is of brief duration, if its objectives are limited and primarily defensive rather
than aggressive, and if those objectives have the sympathy of
other classes in the population. It can, for example, be used
to defend democracy against dictatorship, as happened in
Germany in 1920. Conceivably it might also be used to overthrow a government which, in defiance of popular sentiment,
was about to engage in war. But if its purposes are offensive,

revolutionary, or anti-constitutional, its failure is certain. The effect of a strike of this kind is to antagonize all wavering and non-proletarian groups; and if it is prolonged long enough to cause starvation, the first victims of the starvation are the workers themselves. The failure of the British General Strike of 1926 is a sufficient illustration of these facts. It is true that the leaders of that strike were extraordinarily timid and confused, and that they had no revolutionary intentions; but aggressive and revolutionary leadership would have provoked an even more vigorous reaction on the part of the government and the middle classes.

The Marxist creed of revolution is, in reality, based, not on any concrete study of political strategy, but on certain theoretical propositions about the nature of the state. The state, according to Marx and according to the Communist Party before 1935, is a bourgeois dictatorship, even when it appears to be democratic. The evidence for this proposition must therefore be examined.

It should be noticed, in the first place, that this proposition was first stated in the *Communist Manifesto*, written in the year 1848. At that time none of the European powers had adopted universal suffrage; in Great Britain and France the franchise was restricted by high property qualifications; governments elsewhere were still, for the most part, monarchical. For the proletariat to achieve power by democratic methods was therefore impossible, because the proletariat did not enjoy the right to vote. Obviously the political situation has been radically changed since that time by the adoption of universal suffrage.

The Marxist theory fails, moreover, to distinguish between the two different functions exercised by the state. The state in its legislative capacity is a mechanism by which the will of the electorate is ascertained and translated into law. The state in its executive and administrative capacity is an instrument for enforcing obedience to the existing laws and property relationships. The working class, when it engages in strikes and other forms of class struggle, frequently comes into conflict with the executive and administrative officials of the government. In a capitalist society one of the functions of these officials is to defend the rights of property, in so far as they are guaranteed by law. It frequently happens, moreover, that such officials are themselves biased in favor of the rights of property, or have been bribed by property-owners; and that they violate the legal rights of the workers. But because, in a society where the majority of the population favors capitalism, the state protects capitalist property relationships, it does not follow that the state is itself merely the instrument of the capitalist class. It remains possible for the majority of the population to change the existing laws by democratic methods, and to transform the administrative apparatus of the state into an instrument for protecting property relationships of some other kind. It is true that, in order to make such changes effective, it may be necessary to replace the personnel of the bureaucracy, in order to obtain executive officials sympathetic to the new system; and when Lenin spoke of smashing the bourgeois state, this was really all that he meant. But there is nothing in the nature of the state which makes it impossible for the capitalist system to be changed peacefully, gradually, and by constitutional methods. Actually, in view of the numerous reforms which have been enacted as a result of working-class pressure in Great Britain, France, and the United States — reforms which have been bitterly opposed by the capitalist class, but which have nevertheless been enforced (even though sometimes inadequately) by the official bureaucracy — it is absurd to speak of the democratic state as an instrument of bourgeois dictatorship.

The argument hitherto has denied the possibility of a left-wing revolution in a democratic state. If a democratic form of government is destroyed, it will be by the right and not by the left. The only result of revolutionary talk by the parties of the left is to increase the dangers of a right-wing dictatorship.

Once such a dictatorship has been established, it can, of course, be overthrown only by revolution; and the destruction of a dictatorship of the right might conceivably be followed by a dictatorship of the left. This, indeed, is probably the only method by which a Communist Party could achieve power. It will be recalled that the Communist International welcomed Hitler's accession to power on the ground that, by destroying the democratic illusions of the masses, it had made possible the eventual triumph of the Communists.

It must be realized, however, that a dictatorship of the right may hold power for a much longer period than Marxists have been in the habit of supposing. All history proves that dictatorial régimes can never be overthrown by the efforts of others; they overthrow themselves.[3] As long as a dictatorship retains its energy, its vigilance against internal enemies, and its capacity to gauge the state of public opinion, it can retain power. Marxists believe that Fascism must be short-lived because they identify it with capitalism, and they suppose that capitalism must shortly destroy itself. But Fascism is by no means identical with capitalism. It is closely associated with the capitalist class, who retain their privileged position; but it can modify or transform the system itself in any manner which may serve to prevent an economic collapse. The longer it endures, moreover, the more completely can it wipe out opposition elements and mould the entire population to its own way of thinking. Barring a defeat in war — and in view of the policies of the British Foreign Office, such an event appears to be unlikely for a long time to come — Fascism may be expected to endure as long as its ruling bureaucracy continues to be vigorous, realistic, and free from destructive internal dissensions. As a result of the corrupting effects of excessive power and privilege, the collapse of Fascism may conceivably occur in the near future. There is, however, no good reason for any such optimistic predictions.

Whether the destruction of a Fascist dictatorship will actually be followed by the creation of a proletarian dictatorship is, moreover, dubious. After the fall of Fascism, government will be exercised by whatever group has a sufficient political capacity and a sufficient support from public opinion. There is no reason for supposing that Communism will be favored by a larger proportion of the German people after the fall of Hitler than was the case before Hitler came into power. The chief effect of Fascism, one presumes, will have been to stimulate a desire for individual freedom and for security of person and property. Such a desire could scarcely find satisfaction under a proletarian dictatorship. All historical experience shows that the fall of an autocracy is followed immediately by the establishment of political freedom and representative government. What kind of régime ultimately wins acceptance depends on the state of public opinion and the balance of class forces. Communism would not, therefore, achieve power unless it could convert, by democratic methods, a majority of the population.

It would seem, therefore, that no Socialist or Communist Party can be expected to win power by revolution. The only hope of the parties of the left is to win the support of a sufficient majority of the population by methods of peaceful persuasion. What are their chances of success?

Marx believed that, as a result of the economic processes immanent in the capitalist system, the proletariat would eventually include the vast majority of the population, that it would acquire unity of political interest and sentiment, and that its increasing misery would compel it to adopt a revolutionary program. None of these prophecies, however, has been fulfilled.

Modern society is not divided merely into two classes — the bourgeoisie and the proletariat. On the contrary, a number of intermediate classes still exist, and recent experience shows that these intermediate classes play the decisive rôle in determining the balance of political power. A union of the middle classes and the proletariat (as in the United States and France in the elections of 1936) means the victory of progressivism; a union of the middle classes and the capitalists (as in Germany) may mean Fascism.

The most important of the middle-class groups are the old petty bourgeoisie of storekeepers, small-scale manufacturers and independent artisans, and the farmers. According to Marx the tendency of capitalism toward monopoly would transform both the petty bourgeoisie and the farmers into wage-earning proletarians. Actually large-scale production has by no means wiped out the small producers in the towns, and is of negligible importance in agriculture.

The middle classes have their own grievances against the workings of the capitalist system and against those who control it, but these grievances do not make them willing to accept collectivism or to support a political movement which — like Socialism or Communism — is based primarily on the supposed interests of the proletariat. They are hostile to the bankers and large-scale manufacturers, but they are almost equally hostile to the trade unions, whose policy tends to increase the prices of what they buy and the wages of those whom they employ. Economic depressions transform them not into a proletarian class but into a debtor class. They do not want their property to be collectivized — either by the private collectivism of the big corporations or by the state collectivism of the Communists; they want, on the contrary, to retain their property and to be released from the burden of their debts.

Marxists have — until 1935 — been in the habit of repudiating any alliance with the middle classes as dangerous to the integrity of the revolution, and of ridiculing and abusing them. They have reviled them as backward, conservative, narrow-minded, prejudiced, and destined to be swept away by the march of economic progress. It is therefore understandable, and not without a kind of historic justice, that in certain European countries these middle classes should have responded to Fascist demagogy — a tendency increased by the fact that in eastern Europe money-lending is often a Jewish profession. Actually, however — whatever one may think of the urban petty bourgeoisie — the farmers are very far from being backward or conservative, and show no likelihood of being swept away by the march of progress. On the contrary, some of the most successful progressive movements in the modern world — in Sweden and Denmark, in Wisconsin and other western states, and, before the Nazi Revolution, in northern Germany — have been movements of farmers. A progressive party in which the farmers are included on their own terms is, therefore, theoretically conceivable. Without the support of the farmers, moreover, no progressive movement is likely to be able either to win power or to hold it after it has been won. The program of such a movement cannot, however, be a proletarian collectivism. In this context Russian experience presents both a promise and a warning. The Russian Revolution was made possible by an alliance of the workers and the peasants; the former obtained the collectivization of industry, the latter the division of the big estates. This alliance was broken in 1929, when collectivization was imposed upon the peasants. The result was the intensification of the dictatorship, a large-scale famine, and the growth of an opposition which, in any country where the agrarian population had acquired democratic habits, would have caused the destruction of the whole Communist régime.

Nor is the proletariat that politically united force which Marx imagined it to be. The word 'proletariat' is an abstraction which covers a number of different groups with different and often conflicting interests. If the word is used in its broadest sense, as including all persons who live by wages or salaries, then a majority of the population in the more highly industrialized nations belong to the proletariat. For political purposes, however, it is necessary to make considerable deductions: one must deduct the salaried technicians and administrators (the most vitally important of all classes in an industrial society), the employees in white-collar and distribution occupations (whose psychology is usually petty bourgeois), workers in luxury industries (whose jobs depend on the existence of a wealthy leisure class), workers whose political opinions are determined by racial and religious attitudes or by bourgeois indoctrination, and — at the other end of the scale — those groups of casual laborers and of workers in backward communities who can be classified — in Marxist phraseology — as the *lumpen*-proletariat. Even Marxists do not, in practice, expect the proletariat as a whole to become revolutionary; they place their confidence in the industrial workers. The industrial workers, however, compose only a minority — in the United States about one-third — of the total employed population. These facts explain why — at the end of seventy years of incessant propaganda — no Socialist or Communist Party, even of the mildest and most reformist variety, has been able to win an electoral majority in any important country.[4]

Marxists hope, however, that they may eventually, by dint of more propaganda, win a majority. This hope is unlikely to be fulfilled unless economic changes alter the viewpoint of large sections of the community and make them more responsive to Socialist doctrine than they have been in the past. Unfortunately the tendencies of the economic system do not encourage such a supposition. One of the most important characteristics of the capitalist system of production is the steady increase of mechanization; but mechanization, in its modern form, tends to weaken both the political and the economic power of the proletariat. For the past twenty years the industrial workers have been decreasing both in absolute number and in relative importance; this decrease has been especially rapid during the depression, and is obviously destined to continue.[5] The skilled laborers, moreover, who have traditionally been the backbone of the trade-union movement, are being replaced, at one extreme, by salaried technicians and engineers, and, at the other, by unskilled labor which does not easily acquire the sense of unity and the tradition necessary to a vigorous trade-unionism. Meanwhile surplus labor is flowing into new clerical and distribution occupations which are not normally associated with a proletarian psychology. Twentieth-century capitalism, instead of creating a united and integrated working class, as Marx predicted, is, on the contrary, splitting the working class into a number of different groups with different interests and viewpoints.

Nor will the onset of new economic crises and depressions necessarily improve the prospects of the left. The Marxist belief that, as the proletariat becomes more miserable, it must become more revolutionary, overlooks two important considerations.

In the first place, it is illegitimate to regard political problems in terms of the mechanics of an economic system; one cannot graph the future simply by prolonging the lines indicated by contemporary tendencies. A pure capitalism might eventually become intolerable for the majority of the population; but such a pure capitalism does not exist and never has existed. Pressure from below and intelligent self-interest from above constantly modify its workings in such a way as to forestall revolutionary upheavals. Roughly speaking, the natural tendency of capitalism is for money to flow to the top of society; and capitalism can continue functioning as long as governments continue to skim it off at the top and pour it back into circulation. Such palliatives as unemployment relief serve both to prevent economic crises and to blunt the edges of mass indignation, and are consciously regarded by intelligent ruling classes (as in Great Britain) as an insurance against revolution.

In the second place, an economic crisis may increase the discontent of the working class, but it also weakens it. Labor is never militant during a period of crisis; it becomes militant only during a period of returning prosperity. The effect of a crisis is not so much a lower standard of living shared equally by all members of the proletariat as a growth of unemployment.[6] Unemployed workers, however, are unable to use any of the regular weapons of class struggle, while they constitute a perpetual menace to those workers who still have jobs. Their position in the social structure is anomalous, and if they continue to be without employment for a long time, they tend to become *déclassés*; desperation may make them willing to support extremist policies, but such policies may be Fascist rather than Socialist or Communist. During a depression, moreover, Fascistic movements attract other classes, and flourish on the hysteria, the fear, and the desire to rely on a leader and to find scapegoats which are characteristic of a crisis psychology. All the evidence goes to show that when men turn to desperate remedies, Fascism increases much more rapidly than Communism. If this view seems unduly defeatist, one need only remark that what happened in Germany can happen elsewhere.

II. THE ECONOMIC INTEREST OF THE
WORKING CLASS [7]

THE Marxist faith in a coming proletarian revolution is, however, not in reality deduced from the economics and politics
of capitalism; evidence of this nature is adduced merely to
corroborate it. The basis of Marxism is its interpretation of
history. As the bourgeoisie destroyed the feudal aristocracy,
so it must itself be destroyed by the proletariat. The proletariat is destined by history to be a revolutionary class; and even
if it appears at present to be reluctant or unable to perform its
revolutionary function, its ultimate triumph is certain. Reason may make us sceptical or hesitant; but with the eye of
faith, as illuminated by the Marxist gospels, we can view the
future with confidence.

The Marxist theory of history may be described as follows:
The basic needs of the human race are food, clothing, and
shelter. In the process of satisfying those needs human beings
create different economic and social systems and become divided into different classes. The different classes perform different functions in the task of production, and share unequally
in what is produced. In every society since mankind abandoned primitive communism, a ruling or owning class has
appropriated for itself the major share of the products of the
economic system, while the working class — whether it consists of chattel slaves, feudal serfs, or wage slaves — has been
allowed to consume only as much as is needed to maintain its
physical efficiency. Inequalities of distribution cause struggles between the different classes, and these class struggles
have been the chief motive-power in history.

The economic system forms the base of society, and all
political and ideological constructions belong to the superstructure. The state is an instrument by which the ruling or
owning class enforces its supremacy. Philosophical and re-

ligious beliefs tend to be disguised expressions of economic drives, reflecting the economic system and having the effect either of justifying a privileged class in maintaining its privileges or of encouraging an oppressed class in fighting to destroy those privileges.

Human society is necessarily progressive. Methods of production grow steadily more efficient, and the human race acquires a greater power over nature. Improvements in production result in changes in the social system, these changes being brought about by revolutions which overthrow a degenerate ruling class and create a new and progressive ruling class. Since a ruling class never resigns power peacefully, such changes can be effected only by force. Thus the Roman system of chattel slavery was followed by feudalism, which was based on serfdom; and that, in turn, by capitalism. The increase of productive efficiency under capitalism must lead to a further and final revolution, when the proletariat will overthrow the bourgeoisie and create a society without classes.

This mode of interpreting history is, no doubt, largely true. The economic interpretation is, as will be argued in a later chapter, not all-embracing; but it may be granted that the economic factor is of more importance than any other in determining the course of human development, and that history has consisted, to a large degree, of struggles between different classes for economic advantages. These doctrines, in fact, were not invented by Marx, but were well known to political thinkers in the eighteenth century. What Marx added to the economic interpretation of history was the prophecy that, as the bourgeoisie had overthrown the feudal aristocracy, so it must in turn be overthrown by the proletariat. This prophecy is, however, based on a false analogy.

The classic example of the revolutionary process is the French Revolution. The purpose of this revolution was to destroy the privileges of the feudal nobility and clergy and the powers of the royal bureaucracy. It was accomplished by a combination of the bourgeoisie, both rich and poor, and the peasants. The urban proletariat were an important factor in ensuring the triumph of the revolution, but they did not adopt an independent rôle; their political ideals were indistinguishable from those of the poorer bourgeoisie.

From its origins in the early middle ages bourgeois society had been outside the feudal system. The bourgeoisie did not work for the feudal landowners; they were not even indirectly exploited by them. Bourgeois industry, commerce, and finance grew up as an independent organization. The conflict between the nobility and the bourgeoisie was caused not by any economic connection between the two classes but by the fact that the bourgeoisie, in their rise to wealth and power, eventually became strong enough to claim control over the government and to demand that the whole social system should be reconstructed in order to conform to bourgeois interests and the bourgeois way of life. They resented the social privileges claimed by the nobility; they wanted an extension of the bourgeois ideal of a free market to the feudal and clerical estates; and they finally began to demand control over the economic and financial regulations of the government. The immediate cause of the French Revolution was the financial collapse of the monarchy; the nobility and clergy were exempt from taxation, and the bourgeoisie, without whose financial support the monarchy could not continue to function, finally refused to continue saving it from bankruptcy. The burden of taxation must be more equitably distributed, and the policies of the government must be subjected to bourgeois control.

The two other chief bourgeois revolutions — the English Civil War in the seventeenth century, and the American Revolution in the eighteenth — had similar causes. In England King Charles I attempted for eleven years to govern as an absolute monarch; by the year 1640 his financial resources were exhausted, and the bourgeoisie refused to contribute higher taxes as long as the government remained absolutist. The American Revolution was primarily a nationalist rather than a revolutionary movement, but it was also a bourgeois movement; and the cause of this movement also was the refusal of a bourgeois class to pay taxes without enjoying any control over policy.

The bourgeois revolutions, therefore, were caused by a conflict for political power between quite separate and independent groups: on the one hand, a vigorous, expanding, and ambitious bourgeoisie; on the other, a nobility and a bureaucracy, which possessed power and privilege but which were degenerate and unprogressive. The victories of the bourgeoisie were, moreover, caused by their possession of wealth, which finally made it impossible for governments which lacked their support to continue governing.

In addition to the bourgeoisie, the only other class which has occasionally played an independent revolutionary rôle is the peasantry. The peasants were an important factor in the French Revolution, while those revolutionary movements in the twentieth century which have come nearest to success — in Russia, Spain, and Mexico — have been, to a large degree, peasant movements. Unlike the bourgeoisie, the peasants were directly exploited by the feudal nobility, and this exploitation was too intense to enable them to initiate a revolution. Contrary to popular belief, an oppressed class rarely rebels; rebellion requires energy and initiative — qualities which do not develop among a population which has suffered from prolonged undernourishment. When, however, other classes had initiated the French Revolution, the peasants proceeded to take advantage of it. Their primary desire was for something very concrete and tangible, possession of which would immediately increase their own standards of living — namely, pieces of land. Peasant agriculture, it should be remarked, means primarily subsistence agriculture rather than the production of commercial crops for sale in a national or world market. Once the peasants had acquired the land, they could defend it themselves with their own weapons; and if they were successful in keeping it, they were assured of greater prosperity, without being required to consider any more complex economic and political problems. What the nobles lost the peasants gained; and even a civil war would be unlikely to destroy the value of their gains.

The proletariat in modern industrial society cannot be compared either with the bourgeoisie or with the peasants.

In the first place, the proletariat is not, like the bourgeoisie before the French Revolution, a vigorous, expanding, and ambitious class; it is, on the contrary, a class which is declining both in size and in importance. Revolutions are initiated by classes who are able to change the social system to their own advantage because they are gaining in power and because the system cannot function successfully without their support. The capitalist system requires industrial workers; but as mechanization increases, its need for them decreases, as the growth of permanent unemployment testifies; and unemployment weakens the bargaining power of the working class. By contrast, the class which is gaining in power, and which can be regarded as indispensable to the modern industrial system, is the new middle class of managers and technicians. It is not impossible that this group may develop into a new ruling class — a process already perhaps in process of realization, by different methods, both in Russia and in Germany. Such a change, however, is unlikely to realize the Marxist dreams of a classless society, nor will it necessarily be accomplished by revolution.

In the second place, the capitalist class and the working class in modern society belong to the same intricate and delicately balanced economic organism. The proletariat are not, like the bourgeoisie before the French Revolution, the representatives of a wholly independent system which has become ready to claim universality; neither are they, like the peasantry, eager for the ownership of tangible pieces of property. What is lost by the capitalist class is not necessarily gained by the working class; on the contrary, any prolonged or violent conflict may destroy the mechanisms of exchange and distribution and thereby result in the common ruin of both classes. What is at stake in any class conflict between capital and labor is not the ownership of concrete properties but the distribution of the products of a very intricate system; and the working class, even more than the capitalist class, is dependent for its very existence on the successful functioning of the system. Each class, moreover, needs the other; if the capitalist class cannot make profits unless the working class provides them with labor, the working class cannot make a living without the aid of the financial, managerial, purchasing, and selling activities normally performed by members of the capitalist class. The only justification for the destruction of a class is that (like the aristocracy before the French Revolution) it no longer performs any necessary function and has become parasitical. Certain sections of the capitalist class — the *rentiers* who live by the ownership of stocks and bonds, and the bankers and stock-manipulators who juggle into their own pockets the wealth created by other people — can plausibly be regarded as parasitical; and there are good grounds for viewing the capitalist system of today in terms of a conflict between industry and finance. Such a conflict inside the capitalist class is, however, radically different from the Marxist conflict between capital and labor. That group within the capitalist class which actually operates the industrial system exercises an essential function; and if it is destroyed, it must (as in Russia) be replaced by some other group which will perform similar duties and may, in course of time, claim for itself similar powers and privileges. For these reasons it is useless for the workers to seize control of the factories — an operation which Marxists apparently envisage as a vital part of the revolutionary process. When this was attempted in Italy in 1921, the workers rapidly discovered that they could not operate the factories by themselves, and that the ownership of factories was useless when the processes of exchange had been interrupted. Such considerations do not mean that there will not be conflicts between capital and labor; on the contrary, class conflicts may often be prolonged and bitter. They will, however, be reformist rather than revolutionary in character. The tendency of the working class will be to fight, not for a new kind of system, but for a different distribution of advantages under the existing system. When they have wise leadership they will not make demands which may cause any sudden interruption of the mechanisms of production and exchange; and when they profess Socialist ideals, they will hope for their realization through a gradual and peaceful extension of state ownership and regulation.

Industrial workers who associate with each other in a common task develop a sense of comradeship, a consciousness of belonging to the same class and of having the same interests; and when they associate with each other also in a common struggle with their employers, they acquire a discipline and a loyalty to their trade union and to each other which makes them capable of a self-sacrificing heroism. To betray the union or the common interests of the working class becomes criminal and despicable. For this reason even an unsuccessful strike may, nevertheless, prove to be worth the cost and the sufferings which it causes. It creates a tradition of working-class unity which often endures for generations; and it has an immense moral value in educating and invigorating those who engage in it, in transforming them from mere cogs in an industrial machine into human beings. The moral value of class consciousness caused Georges Sorel, the theoretician of the Syndicalist movement, to consider the class struggle as good in itself, and to contrast the heroism displayed by militant workers with the love for bargaining and for intrigue characteristic of a trade-union bureaucracy and of a parliamentary Socialism. Marx regarded this class consciousness as the embryo of the new co-operative society which would be created after the Revolution, and regarded militant class struggles as necessary in order that the working class might acquire the education and the discipline necessary for the performance of its predestined revolutionary function.

In spite, however, of the value of working-class militancy, it by no means follows that the working class is revolutionary. Historically, the real purposes of a militant working class have been, first, to extend and preserve political democracy; and secondly, to secure a greater measure of economic justice within the capitalist framework.

When, in the English, American, and French Revolutions, the bourgeoisie became the dominant class, they endeavored to restrict political rights to themselves. The franchise was limited to owners of property; education remained a privilege rather than a right; and trade unions were treated as illegal organizations. The working class made its first appearance as an active political force when it began to insist on the full realization of the political equality and freedom implicit in the ideals of bourgeois society. Until the old régime had been destroyed, they functioned as the left wing of the bourgeoisie; afterward they continued to support the bourgeois ideals, but demanded — in opposition to the wealthy property-owners — that those ideals should be genuinely fulfilled. This was the rôle adopted by the proletarian supporters of the Jacobins in France, by the Chartists in Great Britain, and by the working-class parties in the United States in the era of Andrew Jackson.[8] Once these movements had achieved success, the working classes ceased to play an independent part in politics; until the growth of reformist Socialism at the end of the nineteenth century, they confined themselves to trade-union activities. The working class continued, however, to attach a greater value than any other class to political democracy — not only because of the value of the franchise, but also because dictatorship (of the left as well as of the right) destroys the rights of the trade unions. Since 1917 no working-class movement in any country has been militant in the cause of Socialism; the working class has, however — in Germany, in Austria, in Spain, and in France — acted vigorously, and occasionally taken up arms, to defend constitutional government. Today the working classes remain the chief enemies of dictatorship, and a vigorous trade-union movement is indispensable to the preservation of democracy.

Marxists, however, assert that the working class is, by its position in the economic system, forced to adopt a revolutionary attitude. Communism, they believe, is not an intellectual invention, but a real movement objectively present in the course of social development; it is the end implicit in the day-by-day struggle of the working class for a higher standard of living.

This belief has little foundation. The true mentality of the working class is (as Lenin realized) not a revolutionary mentality but a trade-union mentality. Historically, the Socialist and Communist ideals have been created not by the working class but by intellectuals. It is true that in modern society the working class has least to lose by the overthrow of capitalism and therefore, it would seem, most to gain by Socialism; and that for this reason it has been more responsive than other classes to Socialist ideals. But the combination of Socialism with the working-class movement has always been an alliance and not an identity. The working-class movement has interpreted these ideals in a reformist rather than a revolutionary manner, has rarely been willing to take any vigorous action toward their realization, and has, in general, belonged to the right rather than to the left wing of the Socialist movement. Support for a revolutionary program has always come not from the working class as a whole but only from those sections of it who happen to be peculiarly miserable and exploited. For there is nothing in the status of the employed worker in a capitalist industry which is inherently or peculiarly revolutionary. That status would, indeed, if the Russian experience proves anything, undergo little improvement if the ownership of capitalists were replaced by the control of commissars. Industry under Communism, in spite of phrases about the dictatorship of the proletariat, is owned not by the workers but by the state. The difference is important: for while workers' ownership would mean self-government by the workers in each industry, state ownership means centralized control by a bureaucracy. Marxists may declare that under Communism the proletariat will become the ruling class, but such a prophecy is not corroborated either by historical precedent or by Russian actuality. Marx's Judaeo-Hegelian faith in a complete reversal of classes — the last becoming first, and the first last — is the merest mysticism.

It is a well-attested fact that few institutions are more conservative than a successful trade union. Workers who are denied the right to join unions, whose struggles are repressed by the authority of the state, who suffer from long hours and low wages, and who are treated by their employers as members of an inferior species, may adopt extra-legal methods of fighting for their rights, and are sometimes responsive to revolutionary ideals. But let them once become successfully organized; give them the right to bargain freely with their employers; assure them of adequate wages and of treatment as human beings; and they become bulwarks of the capitalist system. The transformation of trade-unionism from a militant into a conservative movement is a process exhibited by the history of each of the great industrialist nations: by that of Great Britain, in the change from the class struggles of both the earlier and the later decades of the nineteenth century to the class collaboration of the modern Trades Union Congress; by that of Germany, in the change from the revolutionary Marxism of the seventies and eighties to the reformism of post-war Social-Democracy; by that of the United States, in the change from the bitter class conflicts of the eighties and nineties to the conservatism of the American Federation of Labor. A trade union is militant only when, as in certain contemporary C.I.O. unions, it is of recent formation and has not yet won recognition from the employers. If the trade-union movement in Russia was still revolutionary in 1917, it was because it had never acquired legal recognition and still suffered from severe governmental repression. The explanation of these facts is that questions of ownership and of the basic elements of the economic structure are not at stake in industrial struggles. Workers who go on strike do not aim at acquiring ownership of the means of production; what they fight for is a larger share in the profits of the employers, for shorter hours and better conditions of labor, for a greater degree of job security, and for the right to make complaints freely against unfair treatment.

The conservatism of successful trade unions has frequently been denounced by the Marxists. From the Marxist viewpoint it is indeed very puzzling that the trade unions should become bulwarks of capitalism. The workers have somehow failed to recognize their historic destiny. Marxists ascribe this dereliction from duty to treacherous leadership, and to the fact that the most successful trade unions have usually represented a skilled-labor aristocracy. This explanation is unconvincing. Corruption and racketeering have undoubtedly been prevalent among the leadership of certain branches

of the American trade-union movement; but no such phenomena can be adduced to explain the reformism of British,
French, and German unionism. And though industrial unions
representing unskilled labor are usually more honest and more
militant than the craft unions of the labor aristocracy, their
purposes are almost equally reformist. In reality, any union
which has won the right to bargain peacefully with the employers ceases to be militant, and must occasionally be willing
to accept wage-cuts. The workers must live, and they usually
have families to support; and while it might be more heroic
for them to refuse to compromise with their class enemies, it
is to their interest, wherever possible, to secure moderate concessions by bargaining rather than, by striking for more ambitious demands, to lose wages and risk a total defeat. When,
moreover, an industry is in a state of depression, it is frequently necessary that its workers should agree to lower
wages; if they refuse, they may handicap their employer in
competition with his rivals, domestic and foreign; and the
end may be a complete shutdown, which means no wages at
all for the workers as well as no profits for the capitalists.
The longest and most intransigent strike in post-war working-
class history — the struggle of the British coal-miners through
1926 — ended in the complete defeat of the workers, and its
only permanent results were the permanent loss of foreign
markets, the permanent unemployment of more than two
hundred thousand of the miners, and the partial ruin of the
entire industry. Those peaceful and friendly conferences between capitalists and trade-union leaders which are so repro-
bated by Marxist critics are not proofs of treachery and betrayal. What they prove instead is that the workers have a
stake in the successful functioning of the economic system and
that the whole trade-union movement is, by its nature, not a
revolutionary or an anti-capitalist movement. For this reason
there is a fundamental incompatibility between the purposes

of trade-unionism and those of Communism. A militant trade union may temporarily accept Communist leadership; but once it has won recognition from its employees, its interests and those of Communism part company. When the Communists endeavor to use a trade union for their own revolutionary ends, their policies run counter to the economic interests of the workers; and when, in the hope of overthrowing a reformist leadership, they adopt disruptive and splitting tactics, they necessarily weaken the union and are thereby guilty of what — from the working-class viewpoint — is the most unpardonable of crimes.

It is, nevertheless, true that successful trade-unionism leads to modifications in the capitalist system of property relationships. Implicit in the union movement is the feeling that an industry should belong to those who work in it no less than to those who invest money in it, that the possession of a job should constitute a property right, and that the responsibility for determining industrial policies should not be left to ownership or management alone, but should be shared by the workers. The desire of the workers to obtain control over policy is probably the chief reason for the bitter hostility to unionism displayed by so many American industrialists. Such a control limits the employers' freedom of action, and violates their conviction that an industry in which they have invested money is their private property. The interest of the workers in obtaining control over policy is not, however, revolutionary. On the contrary, it results, when successful, in a policy of class collaboration such as all good Marxists anathematize. It is impossible to assert a new right without accepting a corresponding obligation; and the more successful the workers are in obtaining rights within the capitalist framework, the greater becomes their responsibility for ensuring the successful functioning of the capitalist system. Actually, a strong union, which has wise leadership, will usually collaborate with its employers in promoting efficiency, preventing waste, and enlarging the market of the industry; such policies, which increase capitalist profits, also increase working-class wages. A statesmanlike union leader will, moreover, find himself compelled to begin formulating industrial policies for the nation as a whole — policies which are planned in terms not of revolutionizing capitalism but of improving it. He may dispute with employers as to how profits, after they have been made, should be divided between owners and workers; but he shares with them an interest in obtaining greater employment and larger markets.

The approach toward industrial democracy which is represented by the trade-union movement is valuable and necessary; but its importance should not be overestimated. It can humanize the economic system, but it cannot cure all its weaknesses. The unions must, for their own safety, aim at monopoly; and a working-class monopoly can be as narrowly selfish and as obstructive to the common good as a capitalist monopoly. The struggle between the capitalist and the worker may have, indeed, very little connection with the struggle for a more equitable social order. For the victims of a trade-union victory are sometimes not so much the capitalists themselves as the remainder of the community. It is often difficult to say precisely against whom a strike is directed — whether against the employing class or against the ordinary consumer, who may suffer by it as acutely as does the employer. And when a trade union succeeds in winning a higher wage or a shorter working day, the bill is not always paid by the employer. Those conferences between the capitalists and their labor lieutenants do, indeed, sometimes acquire a sinister tendency, though not precisely of the kind envisaged by the Marxists. They have occasionally resulted in a common agreement to exploit the middle classes through higher prices. The building unions, for example, both in the United States and in Europe, have notoriously succeeded in raising costs at the expense of the consumer; and some years ago we witnessed a more elaborate scheme of a similar kind in the N.R.A. Responsibility for this ill-fated measure, which endeavored to end the depression by assuring both the capitalists of higher profits and the workers of higher wages, but which had the effect of raising prices at the expense of the middle classes and ultimately, therefore, of curtailing the market, appears to have been divided about equally between certain capitalists and certain union leaders. The hostility between the trade unions and the middle classes which results from this aspect of union policy is one of the bases of Fascism. This fact should be a warning against attaching too much value to the industrial struggles of the working class.

III. MARXIST ECONOMICS

MARXISTS claim corroboration for their faith in a coming proletarian revolution through an analysis of the economics of capitalism. The purpose of Marx's writings on economic questions, and particularly of *Das Kapital*, was 'to reveal the economic law of motion of modern society.'[9] A study of this law of motion would, according to Marx, show that capitalism could only be a temporary and transitional phase in human development, and that at some period in the future it must inevitably be transformed into Socialism. Marxist economics consists primarily of three propositions: first, that the capitalist class will become smaller and the working class larger, and that both classes will acquire international unity, thereby making possible the overthrow of one by the other; secondly, that capitalism in its essence means the robbery of the workers by the capitalists, so that any genuine reconciliation between the two classes is impossible; and thirdly, that the economic laws immanent in capitalism will lead to the increasing misery of the working class and hence will force them to become revolutionary. All of these propositions contain elements of truth; none of them, however, is true in the manner in which Marx stated it. *Das Kapital*, upon which Marx labored for the last twenty-five years of his life and which he was never able to finish, is a remarkably incoherent book, and the power which it has exercised is due to its passion rather than to its logic. The descriptive passages, which deal with the history of capitalism and with the misery which it has inflicted upon the workers, have a great emotional force. Those sections, on the other hand, which purport to reveal the inner logic and future development of the system, are a maze of highly abstract deductive reasonings, which are rarely supported by any factual evidence and which sometimes have little more relationship to concrete realities than the more recondite speculations of medieval scholasticism.

The first of the three propositions into which Marxist economics can be divided is a deduction from experience rather than from logic. It is a generalization from the history of capitalism down to the time at which *Das Kapital* was written. Marx formulated his ideas in the eighteen-forties and fifties, when capitalism was associated with the liberal free-market doctrines of the English Manchester School; and he took it for granted that this kind of capitalism would work itself out to what he believed to be its logical conclusion. Marx's sketch of capitalist development is, in general, valid up to the time at which he wrote. Unfortunately, capitalist society began to move in new directions shortly after Marx had published the first volume of *Das Kapital*; and in spite of the capacity for predicting the future with which he is credited by his disciples, Marx did not foresee how completely the political situation would be transformed by these new developments.

At the point where capitalism emerged out of feudalism

Marx found a process of force and fraud which he called 'primitive accumulation.' On the one hand, the bourgeoisie seized possession of feudal and clerical properties, and of the wealth of America and the Indies. On the other hand, the feudal peasantry were both released from serfdom and separated from the land, so that they became a propertyless proletariat. Thus two classes confronted each other, one of whom owned all the means of production, while the other owned nothing. The proletariat had no alternative but to sell their labor to the bourgeoisie; and since there was always a 'reserve army of unemployed,' they were unable to demand more than a subsistence wage. By the exploitation of the workers and the sale of the commodities which those workers produced, the bourgeoisie were able to amass profits; and their eagerness for the accumulation of profits became the motive-power of the economic system. Toward this system Marx's attitude was ambivalent. Evil in its methods, it was a necessary stage in that historic process which would end in the creation of the kingdom of freedom. By revolutionizing human society throughout the world, and by immeasurably increasing the productive forces of the human race, it was creating the objective conditions necessary for the establishment of a just and rational world-society.

Viewing the development of capitalism down to the time at which he wrote and assuming that the future of the system would be like its past, Marx found in it certain dominating tendencies.

In the first place, capitalism was inherently international. The search for profits was destroying feudal and patriarchal relationships in all countries, was overriding all national boundaries and breaking down all national distinctions, and was driving all peoples into the net of a single world-market. 'In place of the old local and national seclusion and self-sufficiency, we have intercourse in every direction, universal interdependence of nations. And as in material, so also in intellectual production. The intellectual creations of individual nations become common property. National one-sidedness and narrow-mindedness become more and more impossible.' [10] Thus nationalism was a retrograde and a dying force, and capitalism was creating a unified world-system, in which an international bourgeoisie would confront an international proletariat.

In the second place, the ownership of the means of production was becoming centralized, concentrated, and consolidated. Capitalist competition, extending to every form of productive activity, was everywhere ruining the small property-owners and driving them down into the ranks of the proletariat. Capitalist methods would become dominant in agriculture as well as in industry, and the small farmer and the peasant, like the petty bourgeois, would find themselves expropriated and transformed into wage-laborers. All those intermediate classes between the capitalist and the worker were thus rapidly disappearing. Meanwhile the capitalist class itself was shrinking, since individual capitalists were constantly dropping out of the race for profits. From time to time there occurred economic crises, during which many of the weaker capitalists were driven into bankruptcy. Thus one capitalist devoured others, and only the richer and stronger were able to survive.

Capitalism was, however, also creating its own gravediggers. As the bourgeoisie grew fewer and richer, so the proletariat were meanwhile becoming poorer and more numerous. Associated with each other in factories, they were acquiring a sense of unity and habits of common action. While property remained individualistic, labor was becoming socialized. 'Along with the constantly diminishing number of the magnates of capital, who usurp and monopolize all advantages of the process of transformation, grows the mass of misery, oppression, slavery, degradation, exploitation; but with this too grows the revolt of the working class, a class always increasing in numbers, and disciplined, united, organized, by the very mechanism of the process of capitalist production itself. The monopoly of capital becomes a fetter upon the mode of production, which has sprung up and flourished along with, and under it. Centralization of the means of production and socialization of labor at last reach a point where they become incompatible with their capitalist integument. This integument is burst asunder. The knell of capitalist private property sounds. The expropriators are expropriated.' [11]

Most Marxists appear to be so awed by the apocalyptic fervor with which Marx prophesies the coming expropriation of the expropriators that they are unable to realize how completely history has failed to conform with Marx's expectations. It is now obvious that capitalism is not creating any world-state. The growth of imperialist rivalries, of trade barriers, of economic nationalism and ultimately of autarchy — tendencies which began as early as the eighteen-seventies — have decisively checked the movement toward an international world-market. Instead of a unified international capitalism confronting a unified international proletariat, there are a series of nationalistic capitalisms which are fiercely antagonistic to each other. For Marx the international organization of the Socialist movement corresponded to objective economic realities; today, on the contrary, it represents, not an economic reality, but a political aspiration and an ideal.

Nor has capitalism continued to decrease the numbers of the bourgeoisie and to increase the numbers of the proletariat. The tendency toward centralization no longer means that ownership is concentrated into fewer hands. The development of finance capitalism, and of the large-scale corporation as its characteristic institution, means that control is concentrated but not ownership. Since the beginning of the twentieth century the number of individuals who have, through stock-ownership, a financial interest in capitalism has tended to grow larger. Meanwhile certain occupations, and particularly agriculture, have never been conquered by capitalistic methods; and the proletariat is achieving neither a greater unity nor a greater strength.

Though, however, the more obvious tendencies of capitalism have all reversed themselves since *Das Kapital* was written, Marxists still claim that Marx understood its inner logic. Historical accidents may temporarily divert the course of human development into directions which could not have been predicted; but such deviations are of superficial importance. Marx grasped the essentials of the system; and the laws of motion which he formulated must eventually be fulfilled.

The essential element in capitalism, according to Marx, is the exploitation of labor by capital; and the basic concept in the Marxist interpretation is its concept of value. According to Marx all value is an expression of human labor — not, however, of any labor, only of that kind and amount of labor which is 'socially necessary.' Every commodity has a certain ideal value which represents the socially necessary labor which must be devoted to its production. This value will usually be larger than the value which has meanwhile been consumed by the laborers, since it is a characteristic of human labor that it constantly increases the wealth owned by society. Under the capitalist system, however, the workers who create wealth do not receive back, in wages, the full equivalent of what they have created. The capitalist, owing to his ownership of the means of production and to the existence of a reserve army of unemployed, is able to pay his workers only what is necessary to maintain their strength and efficiency, while the remainder of the value which they create, the 'surplus value,' he retains for himself. This robbery of the workers, through the extraction of surplus value, is the primary cause of injustice and of economic maladjustments under capitalism. The capitalist constantly struggles, by means of decreasing wages and lengthening the working day, to increase his surplus value; while the workers, correspondingly, struggle to decrease it. The struggle will end when, under Socialism, the workers are allowed to keep the full value which they produce and surplus value disappears. Marx's theory of surplus value thus constitutes a proof of the injustice of capitalism, as — in the bourgeois revolutions of the eighteenth century — the theory of the social contract was a proof of the injustice of monarchy.

The labor theory of value had been invented by eighteenth-century bourgeois economists, who had used it to prove that the landowning aristocracy, who consumed wealth which they did not produce, were a parasitical class. Certain early English Socialists, from whom Marx borrowed his doctrine of surplus value, had then turned this ideological weapon against its original inventors, and had insisted that the profits of the capitalist were based on the exploitation of other men's labor just as much as the rents of the landlord. The labor theory of value is thus a means of expressing the truth that all life is dependent upon labor, and that those who do not labor themselves are living parasitically upon the labor of others. This sociological truth becomes, however, very misleading when it is translated into terms of economics and made the basis of economic science. Both the economics of Marxism and also, to a considerable degree, that of the classical schools confuse two different questions which belong, in reality, to different categories of thought. Of any group of commodities one can ask, first, In what does their economic value consist? and secondly, To whom is it most just or most expedient that that value should belong? The answer to the second of these questions cannot be deduced by analyzing the first of them.

It is easy to demonstrate that economic value is an expression, not of human labor, but of the interaction of supply and demand. An article is valuable when the potential demand for it is greater than the supply. The varying values of different articles reflect the varying degrees by which supply falls short of demand. By means of a price system it becomes possible to compare these values with each other with considerable precision. Unimproved land, for example, does not embody any human labor, but it may have value; when the land lies in the centre of a city, the value may, in fact, be very high. If there were a scarce but useful mineral which, in the places where it occurred, could be gathered from the surface of the ground, the labor required to collect it might be very small; but its value would nevertheless be great. Even in industry it is impossible to calculate value in terms of human labor; monopolistic practices may inflate the value of a commodity, and overproduction may decrease it; yet the amount of labor required to produce it may remain the same. These facts are, in reality, implicit in the Marxist formula 'socially necessary.' According to Marx not all labor produces value, but only that kind and amount of labor which is 'socially necessary.' The addition of this phrase, the implications of which Marx never explored, virtually destroys the labor theory of value. What it implies is that value is not an expression of labor except to the extent that the labor is socially necessary. It is, in fact, the social necessity and not the labor which determines the value. And the problem of determining whether any particular piece of labor is socially necessary or not — a problem which is obviously of the most vital importance, but which Marx never attempted to answer — can be solved only by the use of a pricing system which shows how far the supply of different commodities falls short of the demand.[12]

Marx occasionally argued that prices were not (except within narrow limits) determined by supply and demand because supply and demand were frequently in equilibrium and hence their influence could be ignored. The value of a commodity (i.e. the amount of labor embodied in it) was 'the centre around which supply and demand caused the market prices to fluctuate.'[13] Such an argument is like saying that when the two sides of a balance are in equilibrium, the weight has no connection with what is being weighed. It is, in point of fact, the price which causes the equilibrium. If there were no prices — if, in other words, commodities could be obtained for nothing — the demand for articles of value would always exceed the supply. Articles of which this would not be true are articles which have no economic value. The function of prices is to balance demand and supply by diminishing demand; and the correct price for any article is the price at which demand and supply are equal. In this manner a pricing system serves to ration commodities — not, however, by allotting to each consumer a fixed quota of everything, but by giving freedom of choice to consumers within the limits of their incomes. A pricing system also makes it possible to determine the relative necessity and utility of different kinds of labor. The most socially useful labor is (or under desirable social conditions ought to be) the labor which produces the largest profits — the labor in which, in other words, there is the largest margin between the value which is added to society and the value which has meanwhile been consumed by the laborers. Profit, therefore, is not, as Marx supposed, surplus value unjustly extracted from the workers; it is the difference between the value of a commodity and its cost of production. And it is only by the method of calculating profits in monetary terms that it is possible to determine the relative usefulness and efficiency of different industries.

Marxists have always supposed that such an interpretation of prices and profits was peculiar to competitive capitalism, and had no broader validity. This is an illusion. The basic laws of economics are true of all social systems, and no society can afford to neglect them. Any society, whether capitalist or Communist, which proposes to regulate its economic life efficiently, must adopt a pricing system by which values can be compared, the distribution of commodities can be rationed, and the profits of different industries can be calculated. The history of the Soviet Union since 1917 has been largely the history of the rediscovery of economic concepts which its rulers had supposed to be peculiar to capitalism. The Soviet Union now recognizes that articles must be priced in proportion to their scarcity, that industry must be conducted in such a way as to produce profits, and that an industry which does not show profits is either inefficient or not sufficiently useful.

The question of how value is determined is, however, quite distinct from the question of how value ought to be distributed; and it is of the greatest importance that this distinction should be recognized. Every society must, in the interests of economic efficiency, adopt an accurate pricing system, and it must recognize the need for such concepts as profit, differential rent, and (at least for the immediate future) interest on savings. But any society which wishes to ensure justice and promote the general welfare should regulate its affairs in such a way that these economic values will not accrue to persons who have not earned them, and that large profits can be secured only through genuine economic efficiency and not by the deliberate creation of scarcities. The classical economists failed to distinguish between these two problems, assuming, for example, that because profit was a necessary element in the economic system, the private appropriation of it by a capitalist class was therefore justifiable. Marx, who was guilty of the same confusion, attempted to evade the consequences of it by abandoning the categories of classical economics and adopting a different, and erroneous, interpretation of value. The correct line of attack on bourgeois economics is to make the proper distinctions. All industry must be conducted in order to produce profits. This does not mean, however, that it is necessarily expedient and equitable that the profit should go to private entrepreneurs and *rentiers*; it might also be taken by the state, or it might be divided among the workers. Scarce minerals and urban real estate are inherently valuable. But there is no good reason why these values should accrue to private owners, who will thereby be enabled to live without working.

All that can fairly be considered valid in the labor theory of value, therefore, is the proposition that the profits of industry should not go to the capitalist class because it has done nothing to earn them, and that when, under capitalism, labor is employed on the production of articles which have economic value, the total value which is produced ought, as a matter of justice, to become the property of labor. Even this doctrine, however, is open to dispute. In the first place, the capitalist class is by no means wholly parasitical. Members of the capitalist class exercise the functions of organization and management, they take risks in the initiation of the new industrial enterprises, and — by abstaining from spending all their incomes — they provide savings for industrial expansion. It is arguable that in the exercise of these functions (and particularly of the last of them) they have frequently been overpaid; but it is not true, as Marx habitually implied, that they contribute nothing to society. In the second place, as Marx admitted in his *Critique of the Gotha Program* but not in *Das Kapital*, any economic system must produce wealth beyond what is taken by the workers for their own consumption. Surplus value is required to provide savings for industrial expansion, to remunerate the managers of the economic system, to meet the expenses of government, and to support intellectuals and other non-productive classes. The difference between Socialism and capitalism is that under Socialism the distribution of surplus value is controlled by the state, whereas under capitalism it remains the property of individuals. Arguments as to the relative justice of the two systems depend on one's definition of justice. Discussion becomes possible only when the question is shifted from grounds of abstract right and wrong to grounds of expediency. The most important questions at issue are: first, Which system would produce the greater total wealth? and secondly, Which system would use its surplus value less wastefully and for more desirable purposes? In the lack of adequate experimental evidence, the answers to these questions must remain matters of opinion and are not susceptible to scientific proof.

The private appropriation of surplus value is not, however, according to Marx, the only vice of the capitalist system. After showing in the first volume of *Das Kapital* how surplus value is extracted, Marx devotes himself, in the third volume, to proving that the extraction of it must grow steadily more intense and the misery of the workers steadily greater, and that any reformist solution is impossible. Marx's argument is not based on any analysis of the system of distribution, or on that growth of overproduction and underconsumption which is emphasized by most modern left-wing economists. Throughout *Das Kapital* Marx devotes himself primarily to a study of production, almost ignoring the economic problems of distribution. Any detailed study of distribution would have involved a recognition of the importance of supply and demand in determining value, and would hence have been incompatible with the value theory with which Marx had chosen to work. Marx repeatedly denounced the capitalist system because it involved inequalities of distribution, but he never analyzed in any detail the economic consequences of that inequality, nor did he regard it as the primary cause of that economic collapse and revolutionary crisis which he so confidently expected.

The coming crisis, according to Marx, will be caused by a fall in the rate of profit; and the reason for this fall is to be found in the distinction between 'constant' and 'variable' capital. Constant capital is the capital which is spent on new means of production (both new raw material and new machinery); variable capital is that which is used to pay wages to the workers. As capitalism develops, the proportion of constant to variable capital grows larger; capitalists spend relatively more of their money on raw material and on new and more elaborate machinery and less of it on wages. Capitalists, however, according to Marx, make their profits only out of the variable capital; all profit consists of the surplus value created by, but not given back to, the workers. The result is that, though the rate of surplus value — i.e. the ratio of profits to wages — may remain constant or even increase, the rate of profit — i.e. the ratio of profits to the total capital invested, both constant and variable — must necessarily decrease. We may ask whether an increase in the rate of surplus value may not compensate for the increase in the proportion of constant capital, so that the rate of profit will remain the same; but Marx assures us that this cannot happen. 'The rate of profit will fall,' he tells us, 'in spite of the increased rate of surplus value, (1) because even a larger unpaid portion of the smaller total amount of newly added labor is smaller than a smaller aliquot portion of unpaid labor was in the former large amount of unpaid labor, and (2) because the higher composition of capital is expressed through the individual commodity by the fact that that portion of its value, in which newly added labor is materialized, decreases as compared to that portion of its value which represents raw material, auxiliary material, and wear and tear of fixed capital.' [14] The result of this fall in the rate of profit (in spite of the fact that it does not mean any fall in the total amount of profit) is that capitalists will constantly struggle to intensify the exploitation of labor; they will force their workers to work for longer hours and smaller wages; and will draft women and children into service. But with the inexorability of a law of nature the fall in the rate of profit will continue to outstrip the rise in the rate of surplus value; and the working class, exasperated by the steady increase in their burdens, will finally rise in their wrath and expropriate the capitalists.

This is the Marxist interpretation of the coming revolutionary crisis, an interpretation which is set forth in detail in the third volume of *Das Kapital*. That other, and now more favored, explanation for the failure of capitalism — the inability, as a result of low wages and high prices, of consumption to keep pace with production — is referred to only in vague terms and is never co-ordinated with the main line of the economic analysis.

In the suggestion that capitalist crises have some connection with the relative increase of constant over variable capital, there is perhaps an inkling of the truth. Marx, however, did not understand the nature of the connection. If one studies capitalism in Marxist terms, it is impossible to explain why the system functions as it does or why crises should occur. Marx, in fact, in the third volume of *Das Kapital*, finds himself involved in contradictions and compelled to abandon some of the assumptions which he has laid down in the first volume.

What happens when a capitalist allots a part of his money to constant capital? He buys new buildings and machinery or new raw material from other capitalists who specialize in the making of such goods; these capitalists, in turn, will have bought their material from the owners of mines or plantations. When the whole process is examined, it will be seen that the entire cost in the creation of wealth (as distinct from the devices by which profit, interest, and rent are distributed among the different kinds of ownership) is the cost of the human labor involved. The constant capital which the manufacturer of consumption goods pays to the manufacturer of capital goods is divided by the latter partly into the variable capital which he pays to his own workers, partly into the constant capital which he pays to the mine or plantation-owner; this constant capital is then converted into variable capital paid to those who are employed in the mine or plantation. If capitalist production is viewed as a unit, then constant capital disappears; all capital is variable capital. This will be plain if we consider a hypothetical industry which controls the whole of its processes of production from the farm or the mine to the finished product, without buying any machinery or raw materials from outside. The entire cost of production in such an industry will consist of its wage bill. The increase of constant capital means merely that the division of labor is increasing, that commodities pass through a larger number of hands before they reach the consumer, and that a larger share of the energies of society are being devoted to the making of machinery and a smaller share to the making of finished products. But why should such a process diminish profits? If the output of finished products were decreasing, then profits might also decrease. But obviously this is not what happens. The introduction of new machinery means an enormous increase in the wealth of society as measured by the production of consumers' goods. Who, then — if, as Marx says, the workers are growing poorer, and the rate of profit is shrinking — is acquiring all this wealth?

Why, indeed, one may ask, if an increase in constant capital means a reduction in the rate of profit, do capitalists ever spend money on new machinery at all? Why do they not invest their savings in new variable capital by drafting into service a part of the reserve army of unemployed? Large-scale unemployment, by such a theory, ought to be impossible. Marx's reply to this question, by admitting that profits depend on relationships of supply and demand and not merely on the robbery of the workers, virtually destroys the whole basis of Marxist economics.[15] As a result of competition, Marx tells us, an average rate of profit is created, and profits in all industries and in all branches of the same industry tend to become the same. When, however, a capitalist increases his investment in constant capital by buying new and more efficient machinery, he is able to decrease his cost of production. The result is that as long as prices remain constant, his margin of profit will be larger. In course of time, however, his competitors will also introduce new machinery, and then, by competition, prices will decrease; and the profits of all those engaged in the industry will again tend to become equal. Marx admits, therefore, that the margin of profit — in Marxist phraseology, the surplus value which the capitalist extracts from the workers — depends on the state of the market. He goes on, however, to declare that the growth of constant capital will cause the average rate of profit to decrease. It may be granted that competition will cause profits to fall at the end of a cycle of technical improvement, when no capitalist enjoys any advantage over his competitors; but why is it necessary that they should fall below what they were before the cycle began? Because, Marx tells us, of the larger proportions of constant capital. But if profits depend, in actual practice, on the state of the market, then the larger proportion of constant capital is totally irrelevant to the issue. Profits will be high when the demand for an article is very much larger than the supply; they will be low when the market is glutted.

The cardinal fact to which Marxist economics attaches insufficient importance is that what the capitalist wants is not 'surplus value' but money. Marxists interpret the economy of capitalism as though it were like that of feudalism, under which the landlord extracted the surplus products of the peasants and used them for his own consumption. But money can be obtained only through the processes of distribution. Capitalist profits are not directly the result of the exploitation of the workers. The capitalist does not make his profits out of the workers when a commodity is made; he makes it out of the consumer when it is sold. It is true that profits may often be larger when the workers are exploited and smaller when they are well paid; but this fact is not fundamental to an understanding of capitalism. A few hypothetical examples will illustrate this point. Assume a monopoly industry which has succeeded in strangling or absorbing all its rivals and which can therefore charge whatever the traffic will bear without having to consider any competitors; suppose also that in such an industry there is a privileged trade union which, by restricting its membership, has obtained a strong bargaining position. The workers will then be highly paid; yet the owners may still make extravagant profits. From whom is the surplus value extracted? The example would be even more forceful if we supposed that such an industry were owned co-operatively by the workers themselves. By Marxist theory there would then be no surplus value; but there would still be exploitation: *by* the workers, *of* the remainder of the community. An industry, on the other hand, which was a victim of cut-throat competition might be unable to pay any dividends or profits whatsoever; its owners might receive sums no larger than management wages. The workers would probably be miserably underpaid. Once again there would be no surplus value, but there would still be exploitation: *of* the workers, *by* the remainder of the community.

Marx himself, when he considers the facts of competition, is compelled to admit that there are discrepancies between his theory of surplus value and the actual functioning of capitalist economy. 'Everything,' he complains, 'appears upside down in competition.' The fact which Marxist economics most signally fails to explain, and which compels Marx virtually to abandon his own system, is that the money invested in different industries produces the same average rate of profit in spite of large variations in the proportion between constant and variable capital; an industry in which only twenty per cent of the capital is variable may be as profitable as one in which eighty per cent is variable. When Marx realizes this fact, he is driven to confess that 'it would seem, then, as though the theory of value were irreconcilable at this point with the actual process, irreconcilable with the real phenomena of production, so that we should have to give up the attempt to understand these phenomena.' He can escape from this dilemma only by admitting that though surplus value may be created by the labor of the workers, it must afterward be 'realized' through the sale of the commodities which they have produced. In the third volume of *Das Kapital* the theory that each commodity has a certain ideal value representing the amount of labor put into it is tacitly abandoned. What we are told instead is that a commodity has a 'cost price,' which is the equivalent of the amount of capital invested in it, both constant and variable, and a 'price of production,' which is 'the cost price plus a percentage of profit apportioned according to the average rate of profit.' But why, according to this theory, the average rate of profit should shrink remains inexplicable. The theory of surplus value survives only as an ideal explanation of social phenomena, which has a moral importance in proving the justice of revolution, but which cannot be used to explain the economics of capitalism.[16]

Twentieth-century left-wing writers have usually preferred

to ignore Marx's theory of a decrease in the average rate of profit. They have adopted Marx's moral attitude to capitalism, as a system of robbery and exploitation, and — while attributing capitalist crises to the failure of consumption to keep pace with production — have praised Marx for predicting those crises. But they have omitted to mention that the reasons which Marx gives for them are not the correct ones. Among recent popular exponents of Marxism, John Strachey, in *The Nature of Capitalist Crisis*, is almost alone in setting forth the true Marxist theory.[17] And yet, as Strachey points out, the whole Marxist theory of revolution is dependent on Marxist economics; abandon Marxist economics, and one abandons also the theory that it is the peculiar destiny of the proletariat to create a new society and that it can do so only through revolution. The belief that it is the workers, and the workers alone, who are being exploited is a consequence of the theory of surplus value. Assume that capitalist profits depend on the market, and it follows that all those various classes whose consuming capacity is unduly limited have an equal grievance against capitalism. The belief that capitalism cannot be reformed but can only be destroyed is a consequence of the theory of a falling rate of profit. Adopt some other theory of capitalist crises — the theory of low consuming power, for example — and it remains possible for capitalism to be transformed by gradual methods.

A consideration of how the economic system actually functions shows that there are certain elements of truth in the Marxist analysis, but that Marx misapprehended them and used them to make erroneous deductions. For the two cardinal conclusions of Marxist theory — that the rate of profit will fall, and that the misery of the working class will increase — there is no factual evidence at all.[18] Throughout the history of capitalism the rate of profit has shown no particular tendency to fall; while the working class, instead of suffering from more intense exploitation, have steadily gained higher standards of living and a shorter working day. Low wages, long hours, and child labor have been characteristic of capitalism, not, as Marx predicted, in its old age, but in its infancy. Nor did Marx himself adduce any evidence in support of these two conclusions; he stated them as logical deductions from theory, not as observed phenomena. Throughout *Das Kapital*, in fact, concrete experience is adduced merely as illustrative detail showing, in general, the misery of the workers under capitalism; it is never used to prove the truth of theoretical reasoning.

What does, however, appear to be true is that capitalist depressions have become more intense, more widespread, and more prolonged. During periods of prosperity both profits and wages increase; but during crises they tend to fall more catastrophically than in the past. Does Marxist economics suggest any explanation for this fact?

The most obvious characteristic of a depression is a deficiency of purchasing power. Producers find themselves with goods on hand which they cannot sell; they begin to close down their factories, dismiss their employees, and lower their prices; new construction ceases, so that the workers in capital goods industries are unemployed; and debts cannot be paid, so that firms go into bankruptcy. What must be explained, therefore, is why there should be any deficiency in purchasing power. The value of the total wealth produced by a community within a given period is, it should be remembered, roughly identical with its total income; theoretically, the total purchasing power must be equivalent to the total prices of the commodities produced. It is obvious, therefore, that if there appears to be a deficiency, it is because money is being hoarded and not spent. The point in the economic system where the circulation of money is most likely to be checked is the channel by which savings flow into the capital goods industries; if money is hoarded and not spent, it is most frequently because the owners of savings no longer invest them in industrial expansion. This is what actually happened in the United States during the prosperity period which ended in 1929. Between 1922 and 1929 billions of dollars of savings, which had been extracted from the productive system, circulated among the propertied classes by means of stock exchange speculation instead of being invested in the development of new industries. Various factors may cause money to be hoarded — fear of war, for example, or lack of confidence in the government; but the causes of the excess of savings in 1929 appear to have been primarily economic and not political. They were due to the mechanisms of capitalism itself.[19]

The purpose for which new industries are developed is the production of more consumers' goods. Consequently there will be no expansion of industry unless the market for consumers' goods is also expanding. If this market is not expanding with sufficient rapidity, producers will have no incentive to build new factories or to invite new investments; and savings will tend to be hoarded instead of flowing into the capital goods industries. Any increase in the money available for capital investment must, therefore, be accompanied by a corresponding increase in consumption. If savings for capital investment increase much more rapidly than consumption, those savings are likely to be hoarded, and the result will be a depression.

The cause of the surplus of savings in the United States in 1929 was that consumption had not been increasing with sufficient rapidity. Two factors appear to have caused such a condition. In the first place, as Marx predicted, capitalism tends toward monopoly. Marx, however, did not foresee the economic effects of monopoly; he regarded it as important chiefly because he believed that it would diminish the numbers of the capitalist class. The real importance of monopoly is that it enables industrialists to keep prices high, the result being that the market for consumers' goods is restricted. When, moreover, a depression begins, monopoly industries limit production instead of cutting prices, thereby causing greater unemployment and restricting the consumers' market still further. The primary victims of monopoly prices are not the workers employed by the monopoly, who may enjoy relatively high wages, but the community as a whole. Monopolists are able to extract super-profits not — as Marx believed — from the workers by keeping wages low, but from the consumers by keeping prices high. That such practices have become prevalent in the United States is notorious. It is true that scarcely any industry is under single ownership and that competition continues; but such competition takes the form of improvements in quality and of excessive advertising rather than of price reductions. Uniform price schedules, whether achieved through trade associations or by less tangible devices, have become the rule in a large number of the more important American industries.

A second factor which results both in too slow an increase in consumption and in too rapid an increase in savings is an increase in the inequality of the distribution of wealth. The poorer classes in the community spend almost all that they earn; the richer classes save a large proportion of their incomes. If, therefore, the incomes of the rich are increasing much more rapidly than the incomes of the poor — as was happening in the United States before 1929 — the result is likely to be an excess of savings. It is possible that Marx had some inkling of this fact when he attached importance to the relative growth of constant over variable capital, though it is impossible to find in *Das Kapital* any clear explanation of why this should cause a depression. The importance of the growth of constant capital is not that it diminishes the rate of profit, but that constant capital (that part of it, at least, which is spent on new machinery) is normally financed out of savings or borrowings and not, like variable capital, out of income. The increase of constant capital means an increase in the debt obligations of industry and in the total invested savings of the community; and on these savings interest must be paid. As capitalism develops, the total capital investment and the total interest payments grow larger. This, in itself, does not mean that capitalism must eventually collapse, since the growth of interest payments is accompanied by a corresponding growth of production. Industrialists can continue to make profits as long as they can find markets; and they can find markets as long as the balance between savings for capital expansion and spendings on consumption goods is not disturbed. The importance of the steady growth of capital investments is that it tends to increase the relative share of the national income which goes to the propertied classes and to decrease the relative share which is paid in the form of wages to the working class, and hence to redistribute wealth for the benefit of the rich. In the price of each commodity a larger proportion will represent profits, dividends, interest, and rent, and a smaller proportion will represent wages. The decreasing importance of labor as compared with machinery does not, as Marx declared, decrease the rate of profit; what it does do is to decrease that proportion of the gross income of industry which is paid back to labor, and hence it tends to upset the balance between savings for capital investment and spendings on consumption goods. The crisis of capitalism is caused, not by a decrease in the rate of profit, but by the increase in the total amount of profit. This, it should be emphasized, does not mean any absolute decrease in the income of labor, any growth of misery and exploitation. As production expands, the absolute income of labor, as measured in real wages, will increase. The important factor in the situation is that while wages increase, profits will tend, by comparison, to increase even more rapidly.

In the nineteenth century capitalism was a self-adjusting mechanism. When a crisis occurred, the consumers' market was enlarged by price reductions; excess savings and capital claims were wiped out by a scaling-down of values, liquidation of debts, and bankruptcies. At the present day such automatic adjustments no longer occur. Monopoly control over industry causes production and not prices to be decreased, the full burden of price reductions being passed on to those occupations which are still competitive, and particularly to agriculture. The system of debts and capital claims has become so intricate, and the process of liquidating them so catastrophic, that governments find it politically impossible to tolerate the necessary chain of bankruptcies. All governments — even a government which, like that of Herbert Hoover, professed to be guided by *laissez-faire* principles — have intervened to protect the credit structure from collapse and to assist industry to meet its debt obligations instead of repudiating them. The result is that private capitalism has ceased to function; political interference with the economic mechanism, of one kind or another, has become unavoidable.[20]

It may seem that if Marx was right in predicting that capitalism would reach an impasse, it is unnecessary to quibble about the details of his analysis. The errors in Marxist economics are, nevertheless, important.

In the first place, Marx declared that, as a result of the fall in the rate of profit, labor would suffer from a more intense exploitation. Actually, however, the misery of the working class has not increased. On the contrary, during periods of prosperity it has gained higher wages and shorter hours, even though its gains have not been sufficiently large to provide the industrial system with adequate purchasing power. The relative share of the workers in the total wealth of the community has decreased, but its absolute income has increased. The result is that, contrary to Marx's expectations, economic conditions have not stimulated them to adopt any revolutionary program.

In the second place, Marx viewed capitalism wholly in terms of a conflict between capital and labor, and regarded the extraction of surplus value and the payment of low wages as the fundamental evil of the system. A more accurate analysis shows that the fundamental cause of maladjustment is to be found, not in the relation between the capitalist and the worker in the process of production, but in the relation between the capitalist and the consumer in the system of distribution. Capitalism is unable to function successfully because monopoly restricts the market by keeping prices high and because the bulk of the community, farmers and middle classes as well as workers, have incomes which are disproportionately low. All those classes whose purchasing power is unduly limited have, therefore, an equal grievance against the capitalist system. The fundamental line of conflict in modern society is not the capitalist against the worker, but the monopolist and the *rentier* against the consumer. Recognition of this fact makes possible the formulation of a progressive political program which has some chance of success. Experience has proved that the proletariat has neither the power nor the will to revolutionize society, and that only the alliance of the proletariat and the middle classes on a common platform can ensure the victory of progressivism. No theoretical justification can, however, be found for such an alliance unless Marxist economics is abandoned.

In the third place, Marx believed that, as a result of the falling rate of profit, capitalism could not be reformed but could only be destroyed. Acceptance of this belief can only induce a very pessimistic frame of mind, since the existing balance of class forces does not offer any hope of such a

IV. The Kingdom of Freedom

IV. The Kingdom of Freedom

I. COMMUNISM AND FREEDOM

ARGUMENTS showing that the proletarian revolution which Marx predicted is not inevitable but, on the contrary, very improbable, and that the most likely result of attempts to stimulate such a revolution will be the provocation of a Fascist reaction, are probably insufficient to dissuade enthusiasts from following the Marxist road. As long as idealists believe that Marx pointed the way to a kingdom of freedom, without class divisions, without coercion, and without poverty, they will be willing to risk their lives and to gamble with the preservation of civilization in the hope of achieving it. The real nature of the Marxist kingdom of freedom, and the degree to which its promises are capable of fulfilment, must therefore be examined.

The Soviet Union is the only country which has undertaken to translate Marxist theory into concrete realities; and in spite of the growth of inequality, the powers of the secret police, the liquidation of the kulaks, the Moscow trials, and the continuance of a very low standard of living, many people continue to persuade themselves that the kingdom of freedom is actually being constructed under Stalin's leadership. A growing number of intellectuals, on the other hand, are becoming disillusioned with the Russian experiment, but they still insist that under different conditions the Marxist ideal is capable of fulfilment. The failure of the Soviet Union is ascribed to its economic and cultural backwardness, to czarist traditions, to the need for defence against foreign imperialisms, or to the treachery of Stalin and the Stalinite bureaucracy. We should, they tell us, continue to work for a collectivist society, but it must be a democratic and libertarian collectivism. The question whether the Soviet Union can fairly be regarded as an illustration of Marxism is obviously of the greatest importance; but the burden of proof would appear to belong to those who deny it. They must be prepared to show, in concrete detail, how a democratic and libertarian collectivism, free from the tyrannies of the Russian system, could actually be made to function. In the absence of any such demonstration, one may justifiably continue to judge Marxist theory by Russian practice. Indeed, as will be argued in this chapter, the main features of the Russian experiment appear to be the necessary consequences of that theory, and cannot be dismissed with a reference to Muscovite backwardness or to the duplicity of Stalin.

According to the Marxists capitalism is the kingdom of necessity because the course of events in a capitalist society is not consciously and deliberately planned. Each individual does what he himself chooses, and the result of this individual freedom is collective anarchy. 'Men make their own history themselves, but not as yet with a collective will or according to a collective plan or even in a definitely defined, given society. Their efforts clash, and for that very reason all such societies are governed by *necessity*, which is supplemented by and appears under the forms of accident.' 'There are innumerable interacting forces, an infinite series of parallelograms of forces which give rise to the resultant — the historic event. This again may be viewed as the product of a power which, taken as a whole, works *unconsciously* and without volition. For what each individual wills is obstructed by everyone else, and what emerges is something that no one willed.' Communism, on the other hand, is the kingdom of freedom because mankind, collectively, will consciously plan its own future. 'Anarchy in social production is replaced by conscious organization on a planned basis. The struggle for individual existence comes to an end.... The conditions of existence forming man's environment, which up to now have dominated man, at this point pass under the dominion and control of man, who now for the first time becomes the real conscious master of Nature, because and in so far as he has become master of his own social organization.... The objective, external forces which have hitherto dominated history will then pass under the control of men themselves. It is only from this point that men, with full consciousness, will fashion their own history; it is only from this point that the social causes set in motion by men will have, predominantly and in constantly increasing measure, the effects willed by men. It is humanity's leap from the realm of necessity into the realm of freedom.' [1]

The Marxist kingdom of freedom is not, therefore, a society in which man, individually, will do what he chooses; it is a society in which men, collectively, will plan their own future. The argument of this chapter is that such a society means, and can only mean, a kind of slavery for at least the vast majority of mankind. The only genuine freedom is the freedom of the individual to do what he himself chooses. The assumption that society has a collective will, that this collective will is identical with the wills of the individuals of which society is composed, and that the individual who obeys the collective will is enjoying freedom, can lead only to tyranny. This fallacious identification of the will of the individual with the will of the collectivity is common to both Communism and Fascism.

The word 'freedom' has acquired such favorable connotations that for one hundred and fifty years the advocates of every political system have tried to appropriate it; even the Nazis speak of having given 'freedom' to Germany. Roughly speaking, there are on the market-place two kinds of freedom; there is the genuine article, which means the right of the individual to do what he chooses; and there is also a spurious brand, which was originally manufactured by Hegel in accordance with a formula devised by Rousseau. The metaphysicians who peddle this second variety of freedom usually declare that the individual has a lower self and also a higher, or moral, or real, or collective, or racial self; and this second kind of self is regarded as finding its true fulfilment in whatever form of political organization the metaphysician wishes to recommend. It follows that by obeying the collectivity, and by merging his own individuality into it, the individual is really obeying his own higher self and is therefore achieving 'real' freedom. This kind of verbal legerdemain has often proved surprisingly successful in inducing men to sacrifice their right to do what they choose in order to receive, in return, a different kind of freedom which proves, on examination, to be merely slavery under a eulogistic name. The original inventor of this trick was Rousseau, who declared that the democratic state had a 'general will,' which was identical with the will of each individual; the individual who obeyed the democratic state could not, therefore, lose any of his individual freedom. What this meant, in practice, became apparent when Rousseau's disciple, Robespierre, announced that men must be 'forced to be free' and began sending to the guillotine anybody whose interpretation of the 'general will' differed from his own. Hegel elaborated in more detail the distinction between the lower and the higher or moral self, and discovered that the moral self had found its perfect and final embodiment in the Prussian monarchy. From Hegel are derived all varieties of the totalitarian state, both Communist and Fascist. The freedom promised by the Marxists is freedom in the Hegelian sense, and not the genuine article.

The motive which caused such genuinely well-meaning and idealistic persons as Rousseau and Marx to offer men slavery in the guise of a more perfect freedom was an unwillingness to admit that so desirable a thing as freedom could never be complete or universal. For if freedom means the right of the individual to do what he chooses, it is obvious that it must always be limited. Men must be prevented from injuring each other; and there must therefore be a state, with powers of coercion. Since, moreover, men must co-operate with each other in the satisfaction of their economic appetites, society must inculcate certain common modes of behavior and must guide the activities of individuals into channels where they will be socially useful. The successful performance of these functions limits the freedom of individuals, but it also increases the total amount of freedom; men enjoy more freedom when the state restricts the power of the strong to oppress the weak; they have a wider range of choice when they organize themselves collectively in order to increase their collective wealth. For these reasons it is easy to jump to the conclusion that individual freedom does not mean freedom at all and that real freedom is to be achieved by giving complete power to the state or to the collectivity. This conclusion, however, is illegitimate. The fact that freedom is increased when it is limited does not mean that freedom will become complete when it is abolished.

An examination of how liberal democracy has attempted to reconcile individual freedom with the need for order and for co-operation will show that the problem is not insoluble.

According to the doctrines of eighteenth-century liberalism the functions of the state were negative; it must maintain order by preventing individuals from injuring each other. For the state to issue positive commands, dictating to individuals what they must do, was tyranny. The maintenance of order, moreover, was not left to the arbitrary action either of majorities or of officials; arbitrary action, whether it took the form of lynch law or of bureaucratic tyranny, was likely to violate the rights of individuals. Justice could be ensured only through the rule of law rather than the rule of men. Both the rights of individuals and the powers of the government must be clearly defined and limited by general rules, to which no exceptions must be allowed. Individuals accused of transgressing their rights were immune from arbitrary punishments; they must be impartially tried by law courts which were immune from political pressure, and must be permitted to defend themselves, before they could be convicted and punished. These guaranties of individual rights were first elaborated by the British people during their struggle with the Stuart kings in the seventeenth century, were written into the American Constitution in the eighteenth century, and were adopted by every civilized country in the nineteenth century.

No social system, however, can restrict itself to the negative function of protecting individuals from each other. The production of wealth, especially in an industrialized society, requires positive co-operative activity. An industrial system is not a static but a dynamic and progressive system, and the manner in which human labor must be distributed among the different kinds of production constantly varies. As agriculture grows more efficient, labor must be transferred to industry; as technical knowledge increases, old industries become obsolete, new industries are developed, and an increasing proportion of the labor resources of the community can be shifted to service and professional occupations. The activity of the individual cannot, therefore, be fixed by habit or heredity, nor can it be left wholly to his own free decision; some kind of social control, which will both determine the immediate needs of society and will distribute labor in such a way as to satisfy those needs with a maximum of efficiency, is indispensable.

According to the familiar Socialist antithesis, production is either for use or for profit. Such a distinction confuses the issues; in reality, production is either for use or for exchange. Men either produce for their own personal needs, or else they produce commodities which can be profitably exchanged for other commodities. In the former case, the individual decides for himself what he needs and how to distribute his labor; in the latter, the exchange of commodities must always create profits (which may accrue to individuals, to groups of producers or to the state), and there must always be collective regulation of the labor of individuals.

There are only two possible methods by which this collective regulation of the distribution of labor can be achieved. One is direct compulsion by the state; the other is a system of rewards and penalties, which does not directly coerce individuals, but which offers such inducements as will cause labor in the mass to distribute itself in accordance with social needs. Direct compulsion is the only method available to a consistent Communism. A fully effective system of rewards and penalties, on the other hand, requires the maintenance of private property, of a free market, and of a competitive economic system.

One hesitates to describe a free-market society by the name of capitalism, since capitalism has come to mean a system under which the means of production are monopolized by a small class, and freedom for the majority of mankind means merely freedom to choose between wage-labor under conditions determined by the capitalist class and starvation. Yet capitalism in its modern form is not a fulfilment of the ideas of the eighteenth-century liberals, but a grotesque perversion of them. The free-market system remains the only system under which it is possible to reconcile the freedom of the individual with the needs of society. The most important duty of contemporary politico-economic theory is to reinterpret the doctrines of the fathers of Anglo-American liberalism,

John Locke and Adam Smith and Thomas Jefferson, in order
to adapt them to large-scale industrialism.

According to the theory of the free-market system the consumer is king. What is produced is determined, not by the
state, but by what the consumer is willing to buy. Those who
are successful in satisfying the consumer are rewarded with
wealth; those who fail to anticipate consumer demand are
penalized by financial losses. As economic processes grow
more efficient, and the wishes of the consumers vary, resources
are constantly redistributed among the different kinds of
production through the mechanism of competitive prices.
When the demand for a commodity exceeds the supply, its
price rises, and more labor is attracted into its production;
when the supply exceeds the demand, its price falls and labor
tends to be diverted into other forms of production. Thus
the distribution of the productive forces of the community
always corresponds roughly to its needs, yet the movement
of labor from one occupation to another is effected by pressure
and not by direct coercion. At a certain stage of economic
development, for example, there may be a surplus of farmers;
this surplus will indicate itself through a decrease in farm
prices and farmers' incomes. If the system is functioning
smoothly, it can be assumed that a sufficient number of young
men who might otherwise have become farmers will respond
to this pressure by seeking other occupations. Yet no individual who wishes to adopt farming is prohibited from doing
so; society penalizes him by paying him a relatively low income, but it does not coerce him. This reliance on pressure
rather than on compulsion, which is characteristic of liberalism, is to be seen also with respect to values and beliefs. Any
social system must inculcate mental attitudes which will be
conducive to its smooth functioning. In a liberal society,
as in all societies, there is inevitably a considerable pressure
toward conformity; yet liberalism is unique in that the indi-

vidual may, if he chooses, resist this pressure; his right to dissent from the prevalent code of ideas is guaranteed.

The discredit into which the free-market system has fallen is due to the fact that it is identified with contemporary capitalism. Bankers and monopolists defend their power to exploit the remainder of the community by speaking of freedom and individual enterprise; and economists support them by maintaining that any political modification of the operations of capitalism is a violation of the eternal and immutable laws of economics. This identification has been accepted by the parties of the left, who claim that the practices of capitalism are the logical result of the principles of economic liberalism. Yet in reality the abuses of the contemporary economic system are the result, not of adhering to the principles upon which it is supposedly based, but of violating them; and the only method of reform by which freedom can be preserved is to return to those principles. Reform undoubtedly requires political interference with economic forces; but any economic system operates within a legal structure determined by political forces; a pure *laissez-faire* system does not exist, and cannot exist. The primary evil of capitalism is the extreme inequality with which wealth is distributed; this inequality is due partly to the right of unrestricted inheritance — a feudal survival which has no necessary connection with a free-market system — and partly to the growth of monopoly, of a *rentier* class, and of financial devices which enable individuals to achieve wealth by plundering the community instead of by serving it. As a result of this inequality the effective demand of the consumers does not correspond to their real needs, and industry produces luxuries for the rich while the needs of the poor are still unsatisfied. As long as this inequality continues, moreover, the right of free speech, when exercised by persons who advocate a greater equality, will be regarded by the rich as a menace; and intellectual freedom will be in danger. Meanwhile the poorer classes have no real freedom of choice; freedom means the power to resist economic and social pressure if one chooses to do so, and is therefore impossible unless one owns the means of one's own livelihood. Under capitalism the business classes are free; the working class is not. In order, therefore, to achieve a genuinely liberal society changes of two kinds are needed: economic rewards must be more closely co-ordinated with social services, so that only those persons can achieve personal wealth who have genuinely increased the wealth of the community; and property rights must be extended to comprise working-class jobs. Such changes, though revolutionary in their implications, do not mean the abolition of private ownership of the means of production, or of the free market, or of competition. They represent, in reality, a return to those principles of eighteenth-century liberalism upon which modern society was built.

For the Marxists, however, the fact that the practices of capitalism have not conformed to the principles of liberalism is a proof that the principles are wrong. Capitalist society is half free and half slave; instead of extending freedom to all, the Marxists propose to abolish the freedom of all. No Marxist has ever recognized the importance of the rule of law and of guaranties of civil liberty. The struggles of the British and American peoples in the seventeenth and eighteenth centuries are interpreted as merely a bourgeois movement against feudalism, caused wholly by economic interests, and nothing more.[2] If a Marxist writer mentions the Habeas Corpus Act or the Bill of Rights, it is only to call attention to the fact that these guaranties have occasionally been suspended or violated; from which Marxists deduce that they are worthless, and that no Communistic society need conform to them. No Marxist has ever admitted that individuals need to be protected from the collectivity. Once class differences between the bourgeoisie and the proletariat have been abolished, it is assumed, conflicts of interest will disappear. The will of all will be identical with the will of each, and mankind will have entered the kingdom of freedom.

Concrete descriptions of how this kingdom of freedom will actually function are, as has been noted before, remarkable by their absence. The clearest formulation available in any of the Marxist gospels is to be found in the concluding paragraphs of Lenin's *The State and Revolution*, which was written in the summer of 1917, a few months before the Bolshevik seizure of power. These paragraphs betray such an astonishing and alarming simplicity that, if Lenin had continued to be merely the leader of an obscure revolutionary sect, one would dismiss them as pathetic. Since, however, they were the work of a man who was about to become the ruler of one-sixth of the land surface of the globe, their simplicity becomes tragic.[3]

The 'state machinery' after the revolution, declares Lenin, will be 'in the shape of armed masses of workers.' As a result of the training and education received by the workers under capitalism, 'it is perfectly possible, immediately, within twenty-four hours after the overthrow of the capitalists and the bureaucrats, to replace them, in the control of production and distribution, in the business of *control* of labor and products, by the armed workers.' 'Accounting and control — these are the chief things necessary for the organizing and correct functioning of the *first phase* of Communist society. *All* citizens are here transformed into hired employees of the state, which is made up of the armed workers. *All* citizens become employees and workers of *one* national state "syndicate." All that is required is that they should work equally, should regularly do their share of work, and should receive equal pay. The accounting and control necessary for this have been *simplified* by capitalism to the utmost, till they have become the extraordinarily simple operations of watching, recording, and issuing receipts, within the reach of any-body who can read and write and knows the first four rules of arithmetic.' 'The whole of society will have become one office and one factory, with equal work and equal pay.' This factory discipline is, however, merely a preliminary stage. Eventually the need for a state will disappear. 'For when *all* have learned to manage, and independently are actually managing by themselves social production, keeping accounts, controlling the idlers, the gentlefolk, the swindlers, and similar " guardians of capitalist traditions," then the escape from this national accounting and control will inevitably become so increasingly difficult, such a rare exception, and will probably be accompanied by such swift and severe punish-ment (for the armed workers are men of practical life, not sentimental intellectuals, and they will scarcely allow any-one to trifle with them) that very soon the *necessity* of observ-ing the simple, fundamental rules of everyday social life in common will have become a *habit*.'

These words exhibit such a startling inability to grasp any of the real problems involved in the building of a Communist society that it is difficult to decide where criticism should begin.

In the first place, it is assumed that once economic class differences have been abolished, there is no longer any pos-sibility of conflict or disagreement. The will of each will be identical with the will of all. All need for those individual and minority rights which are guaranteed in the western democracies is denied. The state no longer consists of any elaborate system of organs of administration, including, among other things, electoral machinery for ascertaining the majority will and an independent judiciary. It consists merely — to cite again that extraordinary and alarming phrase — of 'armed masses of workers'; and the workers, we are assured, 'will scarcely allow anyone to trifle with them.' Only 'sentimental intellectuals' would be so deluded as to suggest that 'swift and severe punishment' by lynch law may not always be in accordance with justice. The obdurate individualist, who resents doing his quota of hours on the task assigned to him in the 'national state syndicate,' is apparently to be knocked on the head. Lenin — it is only fair to add — was, in practice, hardly so brutal as these words suggest; he appears to have taken life only with reluctance. But certainly since his death the 'armed masses of workers,' or whoever else constitutes the government of the Soviet Republics, have shown no unwillingness to administer 'swift and severe punishment.'

To assume, however, that in a Communist society there will no longer be conflicts of interest is extraordinarily naïve; and yet it is only by making this assumption that one can deduce that the state will ever 'wither away.' Equal hours and equal pay do not necessarily mean harmony. Conditions of labor in different occupations are necessarily unequal. Is the coal-miner, whose task is laborious and dangerous, to be placed on an equality with the office clerk? And if, as is highly probable in a community where all wages are equal, nobody is willing to choose mining as his occupation, how (except by coercion) is the need for miners to be supplied? Is, moreover, the highly skilled scientist or technician to be placed on an equality with the manual laborer? There is no universally applicable formula of justice which will prevent men from complaining of injustice. As Aristotle said, justice means either giving equality to all, or giving unequal things to unequal persons; and about these two conceptions men will argue eternally. Even, moreover, if we assume that a rough degree of equality can be established, there are still infinite possibilities of argument. Should the 'armed masses of workers' choose a low standard of living and more leisure, or a high standard of living and more labor? Should they

choose to manufacture more capital goods for future prosperity, or more consumption goods for present prosperity?
Should they choose to improve housing at the expense of
transportation, or transportation at the expense of housing?
Should they choose to give cheap electricity to one province,
or better roads to some other province? These are necessary
decisions, and once they have been made, the defeated party
must be induced to conform to them. There is, therefore, a
need for a state, with adequate machinery for ascertaining the
majority will. The state, as the Marxists insist, exists for the
sake of coercion; but some degree of coercion is always necessary. The fact that everybody is a worker, and works for
equal pay and equal hours, does not mean that men will cease
to disagree with each other.

In practice, these problems can be evaded only by dictatorship, which — as was shown during the French Revolution —
is the logical result of any attempt to identify the will of each
with the will of all. For if all men have the same will, then
that will can be correctly defined and interpreted by some
individual or group of individuals. Some body of men will
claim the right of stating and enforcing the will of the collectivity, and any persons who oppose their decisions will
be denounced as acting in violation of that will, and hence
as 'aristocratic,' 'bourgeois,' or 'counter-revolutionary.'
Thus Robespierre regarded himself as embodying the will of
the French people; and thus Stalin interprets the will of the
Russian proletariat. Thus also Hitler identifies himself with
the will of Germany.

Lenin, however, did not suppose that coercion could immediately be abolished; men must first become accustomed
to obeying the rules which would govern a Communist society. Coercion would cease, and the state would wither
away, when 'the *necessity* of observing the simple, fundamental rules of everyday social life in common will have be-

come a *habit*.' This statement is profoundly true, and deserves careful examination. Individuals and minorities will no longer need to be coerced when they will obey the rules governing life in common from force of habit and will feel no impulse to violate them. These rules, according to Lenin, involve only such matters as the right of all to equal pay and the duty of all to equal work. Yet if coercion is to become unnecessary, they must be extended to cover all questions about which men may legitimately disagree with each; they must include all the details of the economic system and the rôle which each individual must play in it. Only when all such matters are determined by habit, and not by discussion, argument, and coercion by the majority party, can the state 'wither away.' Communities of this kind do indeed exist; certain insect societies are governed by habit. Men, however, have usually regarded any attempt to reconstruct human society along the lines of a beehive or an anthill with some distaste. Yet this is the only method by which the Marxist kingdom of freedom can be realized. As long as human beings retain those characteristics which distinguish them from animals, the state cannot 'wither away.'

II. COMMUNISM AND DEMOCRACY [4]

THESE objections may appear to be somewhat captious, in view of the fact that the Soviet Union does not show the slightest likelihood of conforming with Lenin's predictions. The operations of the economic system are controlled, not by 'armed masses of workers,' but by factory managers, bureaucrats, and technicians. The notion that wages ought to be equal has been officially repudiated; and we are now assured that neither Marx nor Lenin ever believed in equality. [5] Though, moreover, the dictatorship continues to impose 'swift and severe punishment' upon those who dispute its will, it has also adopted a constitution under which — at least according to the letter of the law — certain individual liberties are guaranteed, and electoral machinery is set up by which the will of the majority can be ascertained and translated into law. In theory, the Soviet Union now recognizes that the protection of freedom requires a state. There are, however, certain more immediate, and possibly more important, objections to Lenin's conception of a state 'in the shape of armed masses of workers.'

According to Lenin, all that is needed to manage the economic system is 'accounting and control,' and these can be performed by everybody. The question of control, he adds, 'must not be confused with the question of the scientifically educated staffs of engineers, agronomists, and so on. These gentlemen work today, obeying the capitalists; they will work even better tomorrow, obeying the armed workers.' Society will be a single factory, and everybody will work for equal hours and equal wages. The only administrative function needed is to hand out receipts registering the fact that each individual has done his quota of work, and this can be performed by anybody who knows a little arithmetic.

If society is to become a single factory, owned and operated by 'armed masses of workers,' let us consider some of the things involved in the efficient operation of it. Somebody must decide how many hours of labor shall be required from each individual, and how many shall be left for recreation. Somebody must decide what proportion of the energies of society shall be devoted to the building of new means of production and what proportion to the making of goods for immediate consumption. Somebody must allot that proportion of the total labor which is devoted to new means of production among the various possible kinds of capital goods, deciding, for example, whether it is better to build more new power plants or more new tractor factories, and how many of each. Somebody must similarly distribute the labor devoted to consumption goods, choosing between turning out more radios or more automobiles, more clothes or a greater variety of foodstuffs. Somebody must balance the total amount of money paid out in wages with the prices of the articles offered for sale in the consumption goods industries — a process which means either that the wages of all workers must be smaller than the value of their products, or that after wages have been paid, they must be taken back again through taxes or through compulsory saving by means of forced loans. Somebody, moreover — and this is the most vital element in the whole process of social planning — must co-ordinate all the different forms of productive activity in such a way that they will harmonize with each other to produce the goods needed by the consumer. The output of coal and steel, for example, must be co-ordinated with the needs of the factories; and the output of the factories with the facilities of transportation. Goods must be distributed throughout the country in the quantities needed by each particular area, so that there will not be a surplus in one section and a scarcity in another; and all that incredible variety of articles which the consumer in the industrial state has learned to expect must be made available in each locality and at the same time. In a well-regulated free-market system the co-ordination is achieved automatically, through the operations of the profit motive. The ultimate criterion is the effective demand of the consumer; and wherever there is such a demand somebody is certain to supply it because by so doing he will make a profit. No element in the economic structure can fail for long to be co-ordinated with the rest because the mechanism of competitive prices will divert labor to fill the gap. Under Communism, however, all this delicate organic structure must be planned.

Now even if we assume — which is highly improbable —

that there are human minds capable of planning efficiently an entire economic system, it is obvious that the planning function must be entrusted to individuals; it cannot possibly be performed by 'armed masses of workers.' The workers might conceivably be capable of deciding for themselves how many hours a day they wished to work, and how their energies should be divided between making new means of production and making goods for immediate consumption — though it does not appear that even such elementary questions as these have ever been submitted to a popular vote in the Soviet Union; but only individuals — and individuals, moreover, with a high degree of ability and specialized training — can plan all the complicated details of an economic system. Democratic interference with the planning process can be tolerated only within very narrow limits. Popular insistence that, for example, a railroad should be built here rather than a power plant there, new houses in one city rather than a tractor factory in another, may destroy all that delicate coordination which is vital to the economic efficiency of a plan. Such questions cannot possibly be submitted to a popular vote, or determined in open forum by 'armed masses of workers.' They must be worked out by bureaucratic officials. The only concession to democracy which can safely be made is to allow the people to change their bureaucrats at stated intervals. Both Russian experience and inherent probability point, however, to two limitations on this democratic right: an efficient plan is necessarily a long-term plan, so that it can be subject to repudiation or drastic revision only at very rare intervals; and the bureaucracy will enjoy such dictatorial powers between election periods that it is highly probable that they will be able to assure themselves against defeat on those rare occasions when the 'armed masses of workers' are allowed to express their collective opinion.

The Marxist kingdom of freedom, moreover, does not merely

involve the dictatorship of a bureaucracy; it requires also that this bureaucracy should have power to coerce individuals. A national plan is a plan for the disposal of the labor forces of the nation, and those who carry out the plan must have power to move labor to different occupations as may become necessary. In a free-market system this is accomplished by economic pressure. If one occupation is crowded, its earnings diminish; if another occupation is understaffed, its earnings increase. Groups of people are thus induced to change their occupations, yet, according to the principles of the system (which must not be confused with the practices of capitalism), no individual is directly coerced. Communism, however, must either coerce or forsake its principle of economic equality. If the productivity of agriculture increases so that there is a surplus of farmers who may more usefully be employed in industry, if too many people wish to become clerical workers and too few are willing to work in mines and steel mills, if one industry becomes obsolete while another industry in a different section of the country requires additional labor, the bureaucracy must either forcibly shift individuals from one occupation to another and from one part of the country to another, or else it must ensure that the balance is redressed by adopting large-scale wage differentials. Actually a policy of open coercion has proved too drastic even for the Stalinist bureaucracy; and the Soviet Union has adopted a combination of the two methods. Farmers have been attracted into industry by means of considerably higher earnings and industries which need extra labor are allowed to invite it by raising wage schedules. On the other hand, a number of the more dangerous and unattractive enterprises have been worked, under the supervision of the Ogpu, by the forced labor of 'kulaks,' 'Trotskyites,' and other elements who have incurred official disapproval.

III. COMMUNISM AND EFFICIENCY [6]

THE Marxist kingdom of freedom means, therefore, the rule of a dictatorial bureaucracy; it can mean nothing else. It may, however, be argued that the freedom which is abolished by such a system is a freedom which is not worth saving, and that the efficiency of a planned economy is sufficient to compensate for its disadvantages. The question of the relative efficiency of Communism and capitalism must, therefore, be considered.

Even if we assume that the officials in charge of the planning process have the almost superhuman ability needed for the formulation of a successful plan — and this is a very large assumption — there are certain fundamental reasons for expecting Communism to be less efficient than a free-market system in fulfilling the primary purpose of an economic system — the satisfaction of the wants of the consumer.

In a free-market system the determination of what articles are produced, and how many of each kind, depends ultimately upon what consumers are willing to buy. When the demand for an article increases, its price rises and new labor is attracted into the production of it; when the demand decreases, prices and profits fall and labor seeks other occupations. It can safely be assumed that no consumers' demand will remain unsatisfied for long, and that no goods will be produced very much in excess of what consumers need. Capitalist practice is marred by the gross inequality in the effective demand of different classes of consumers, and by the fact that consumers are inadequately educated and are open to harmful advertising pressure. The remedy, however, is to reform the practice, not to abandon the principles.

Under Communism the supremacy of the consumer is replaced by the supremacy of the officials who plan production. What is produced is determined, not by what the consumers actually want, but by what the planners think they ought to want. A planned production means also a planned consumption; the disposition of the available labor supply among the various kinds of consumption goods means that those goods, and no others, will be available to consumers. Such a system might function efficiently if the planners had accurate knowledge of what the consumers wanted, and of how those wants might most efficiently be satisfied; but once the free-market and the competitive-price systems have been abolished, the acquisition of such knowledge becomes very difficult.

In a system where all prices are fixed by the state instead of being regulated by competition, price is not dependent on demand but demand on price. The price-fixing arrangements of the planners will determine what articles will be bought, and how many of each kind. The fixing of prices is necessarily a somewhat arbitrary matter, and to regulate prices by costs of production does not remove the difficulty; costs of production are themselves variable, for by choosing to invest capital in some particular branch of production, the planners can make it more efficient and thereby reduce its costs. By lowering the price of a commodity, the planners can increase the demand for it; by raising the price they decrease the demand. Without the checking provided by competition it is, however, impossible to say whether a large sale of some particular article means that it gives more satisfaction to the consumers than any of the other articles upon which they might have chosen to spend their money, or whether the sale is due mainly to the fact that its price is relatively low. In a free-market system competition between the producers of rival commodities will produce a roughly accurate distribution of the available labor resources between them. Under Communism the planners are at liberty to choose which commodity to develop; and if they concentrate on one at the expense of others, they can, by lowering prices, ensure an effective demand for it. There is, however, no way of telling whether the wishes of the consumers might not have been more adequately met by making a different choice. Since, moreover, the planners can always be assured of a market for any article which they choose to produce, there is nowhere in the system any sufficient incentive for creating, anticipating, or satisfying a consumer demand. The enormous variety of consumption goods produced by competitive capitalism is caused by the incentive of profits, and by the willingness of individual entrepreneurs to take risks in the hope of making a profit. Under a system which has ended risks and abolished the profit motive, consumption goods are likely, as is actually the case in the Soviet Union, to be of poor quality and to lack variety.

The inability of a Communist system to plan production in such a way as to achieve the maximum consumer satisfaction is inherent in monopoly, and is characteristic also of price-fixing regulations in capitalist monopolies. Capitalism has, however, the guidance of a price system which is at least partially free, whereas under Communism all prices are arbitrary. The kind of question which confronts the planning board in a Communist society, it should be realized, is not whether it is desirable to build a tractor factory in a certain locality, but whether the building of such a factory is preferable to all the other possible uses which might have been made of the same labor and material. To choose to build a factory means that one has chosen not to build a power plant or a railroad or a block of workers' houses. In a free-market system the ultimate criterion is consumer demand; and if mistakes are made, those who make them will be penalized by the loss of their investment. Under Communism such decisions are likely to be made by a hit-or-miss method. What might be expected to happen, and what appears to have actually happened in the Soviet Union, is that the decisions of the planning board will be guided by a desire to advertise the régime and to fill its citizens with pride. The planners will resolve to have the biggest power plant, the largest number of tractors, and the most colossal government building in the world, thereby making visible to all doubters the supremacy of Communism over capitalism. Whether such creations are genuinely — in the economic sense — efficient, it is, however, impossible to say. The supply of tractors in the Soviet Union appears to be considerably in excess of the real economic need for them; and it is probable that the welfare of the consuming public might have been better met by devoting less labor to the building of power plants and to the construction of a Palace of the Soviets higher than the Empire State Building and more labor to such less imposing but more immediately useful objects as workers' apartments and clothing and boots and soap and food.[7]

Nor is inability to co-ordinate production with consumer demand the only economic weakness of Communism. It may be replied that consumers under capitalism are badly educated and swayed by the corrupting influence of unscrupulous advertising, that mankind can well dispense with much of the extraordinary variety of consumers' goods produced by a competitive system, and that a society which gives the public what a group of enlightened planners decide that they ought to want is better than one which caters to all their most degraded whims. Communism, however, is likely to be inefficient, not only in its inability to satisfy the consumer, but also in its own productive processes.

Discussion as to the relative merits of capitalism and Communism has often revolved about the question of incentive. While defenders of capitalism maintain that men will never work for the state as conscientiously as they work for themselves, Communists have replied that such an argument is a slander on mankind, that human nature changes, and that how men will behave under Communism cannot be predicted by observing their behavior under capitalism. Stalin appears now to have settled the argument by adopting the viewpoint of capitalism. The Soviet Union has abandoned any notion of equalizing wages, and has adopted a program of encouraging greater productivity among the workers, paying high wages to those who surpass their quotas, and penalizing the slow and the inefficient, not only through low wages, but also by attempting to brand them with the contempt of public opinion. The result is that the workers are exposed to a competitive pressure which would never be tolerated by a healthy trade union in any capitalist country and which has sometimes caused such acute resentment in Russia that 'Stak-hanovites,' who, by exceeding their quotas, have caused piece-rates to be lowered, have occasionally been lynched by their infuriated comrades.[8] To what extent this kind of incentive can promote genuine efficiency is, however, doubtful. The crucial question is not whether Communism can provide economic incentives for productivity, but to what extent efficiency under a non-profit system can be accurately measured; the real need is not so much for incentives to increase productivity among the workers as for incentives to promote efficiency among the bureaucracy and the management. In a free-market system, where profits and losses are assumed by individual entrepreneurs, each unit in the economic system is independent of the rest; and inefficiency, whether in quantity or in quality, is automatically penalized. If an industry is operated inefficiently, it can be assumed that it will be driven into bankruptcy by the competition of more efficient rivals. Under Communism it is difficult to determine whether any particular factory is being operated efficiently or to fix responsibility for inefficiency. Industries in the Soviet Union are expected to show profits; but such profits may be due to favorable price-fixing arrangements, to low piece-rates paid to the workers (who, in a country where the trade unions are merely instruments of state control, are not usually able to defend themselves), or to an increase in quantity at the expense of quality. Without the checking provided by competition, it is difficult accurately to fix the norm in any particular industry either for quantity or for quality; the planners can merely guess at what the industry may be expected to produce. What actually happens in the Soviet Union is that the planners steadily increase the quotas required from different industries and at the same time encourage a system of 'socialist competition' between factories in the same industry. Factory managers who surpass their quotas are rewarded with high salaries, prestige, and promotion; while those who are less successful in driving their workers are penalized. Though, however, such methods produce increases in quantity, they do not provide for any control over quality. 'Socialist competition' is not genuine competition, since factories do not compete with each other in pleasing the consumer; each factory is assured of a market for its products. The inevitable result is a ruinous sacrifice of quality. Judging both from the reports of expert observers and from the 'self-criticism' of the Russians themselves, one of the most conspicuous characteristics of Communist industry is, by contrast with capitalism, the low-grade and slovenly quality of its products and the large proportion of them which are entirely useless. It may plausibly be argued that Russian Communism has been more wasteful than capitalism at its worst, and that a considerable part of the terrific sacrifices exacted from the Russian people in the building of an industrial system has been stultified. For this situation the only remedy available to Communism is more stringent control from the top, but such control is perhaps worse than the disease. With increasing frequency in recent years factory managers who have produced damaged goods have been accused of deliberate sabotage, linked with

Trotskyite plotters and Japanese and German spies, and shot. A system which can enforce efficiency only by shooting the inefficient is not likely to produce any genuine efficiency. Terror destroys initiative and reduces men to an unquestioning obedience. The result is that factory managers confine themselves to a blind fulfilment, by any means whatever, of the quotas assigned under the national plan, refuse to shoulder any personal responsibility, and never venture to adopt a new idea or to try out a promising experiment.

The Russian system is still in a state of transition, and its final achievement cannot be judged from its present performance. In the pursuit of efficiency the Russian government is being driven inexorably to abandon its original faith in equality and free co-operation, and to adopt practices little different from those prevalent in a monopolistic capitalism. In order that responsibility may be fixed, the various industrial units are acquiring a greater independence; and in order that efficiency may be increased, any attempt to achieve economic equality has been rejected. The collective farms are allowed to sell a part of their products directly to the consumer and to keep the proceeds, the result being that farmers living in rich soil are able to make larger profits than those less favorably situated. The trusts controlling the different branches of industry are exercising a greater initiative in their buying and selling operations and are rewarded when they show profits. The salaries of managers appear generally to be about ten times as large as the average wage of their workers; and if they invest a part of their earnings in government bonds, they receive a high rate of interest. The most probable end of Communism is a system which will differ from a monopolistic capitalism chiefly in that the beneficiaries of the system will derive their privileges from managerial salaries and from government bonds rather than from titles of ownership. From the viewpoint of the working class, the differences between the two systems would appear to be unimportant. When a government which has a monopoly of propaganda educates the workers into the belief that they are the ruling class, and that their comrades in other countries are slaves, they may eventually come to believe it. Yet there is no reason for supposing that work in a Communist factory is different from work in a capitalist factory. In either case the determination of wages and hours belongs to the authorities; in either case workers are liable to dismissal if they are slow or inefficient or if they oppose the policies adopted by their superiors; and in either case control over the 'surplus value' which they produce belongs to their employers. And though, under Communism, this surplus value might theoretically be used to provide social services for the workers, it has in practice (as under capitalism) gone either to finance the building of new capital goods and new war material or to reward a privileged class. In view of the powers enjoyed by the bureaucracy and the lack of adequate democratic control, there is no good reason for expecting that this inequality in the distribution of wealth will not continue to increase. Under Communism there is no large-scale unemployment and no leisured *rentier* class; but these advantages are nullified by the superior productive efficiency of capitalism.

IV. COMMUNISM AND WAR

THE final advantage claimed for Communism is that it will mean the abolition of war. Capitalism, it is alleged, leads inexorably to war; the capitalists of different nations compete with each other for profits in colonial areas, and this competition causes imperialist conflicts. Communism, on the other hand, by ending production for profit, removes the economic causes of war, and will eventually create a world-state in which the different nationalities will live in harmony. The hope that the victory of Communism will mean the final abolition of war has always been one of the most effective arguments in its favor. The association of war with private capitalism deserves, however, a more critical examination than left-wing writers have usually given it.

Much Marxist literature might lead one to suppose that war was a peculiar product of the capitalist system. History does not, however, support this supposition. War has existed since the dawn of history, whereas capitalism is a comparatively recent invention. The epoch of capitalism, instead of being more warlike, has on the contrary been more peaceful than the epochs which preceded it. If it has increased the menace of war, it has done so, not by making wars more frequent, but by increasing so enormously the wealth and power of mankind that war, when it does occur, is incomparably more destructive. During the golden age of capitalism — the century from 1815 to 1914 — there were two periods, from 1815 until 1854 and from 1871 until 1914, without any major war between European powers. These were the two longest periods of peace which Europe has enjoyed since the fall of the Roman Empire. The wars which occurred between 1854 and 1871 were, moreover, caused, not by the capitalist classes but by the policies of Napoleon III and of Bismarck, neither of whom can be identified with the interest of capitalism; while even the World War of 1914–18, however much the imperialist rivalries of Great Britain, France, and Germany may have contributed to it, was not directly provoked by those rivalries, but by a conflict between two powers — Russia and Austria — which were still, to a large degree, in a pre-capitalist stage of development.

The peace which Europe enjoyed throughout most of the nineteenth century was not accidental. Capitalism at that period was associated with liberal politics and with a free-market economy, and of all social systems this is the only one which is inherently unwarlike — a fact which was appreciated by its most ardent advocates (such as Richard Cobden) and considered by them to be a strong argument in its favor. Nor was this argument disputed, at that time, by the enemies of the system; even Karl Marx never suggested that the economics of capitalism would lead to any kind of war except the class war between the international bourgeoisie and the international proletariat.[9] When, on the other hand, war was praised, it was done so by military and landowning castes or by romanticist intellectuals, who maintained that the preoccupation with trade and profits made men timid and ignoble and sapped their manhood.

A common-sense view of the problem shows that the logic of the Cobdenite position is unassailable. There are three conditions which, separately or in combination, may lead to war: war may occur when one nation, or its dominant class, is likely to gain more by defeating another nation and seizing its possessions than by peacefully trading with it; when a dictatorial government, threatened by domestic discontent, wishes to strengthen itself by means of an aggressive foreign policy; and when the sense of national or collective unity is stronger than the sense of individual liberty and self-interest or than loyalty to some universal religious or humanitarian ideal. It follows that to prevent war it is necessary to promote international trade and the division of labor on an international scale, in order that all nations may become economically interdependent; to create democratic governments; and to strengthen individual freedom and the sense of the unity of the human race. Progress along these lines would make possible the formulation of a system of international law, which the majority of the nations of the world would be pledged to enforce. This is the only true solution to the problems involved in the use of force in international affairs. Force is necessary and justifiable — internationally as well as nationally — when it is exercised in accordance with law, in order to impose fixed penalties for fixed offences; it is wrong only when it is lawless.

A world of economically interdependent, free, and democratic nations was the aim of the liberal free-market capitalism of the nineteenth century. If this system had become world-wide — as in the nineteenth century seemed likely — major wars would have become impossible.[10] Capitalism causes war only when it abandons the free market and becomes associated with high tariff barriers and with other restrictions on international trade. The abandonment of the international division of labor makes it less advantageous for nations to remain at peace, while attempts to monopolize raw materials or to exclude foreign competitors from the trade of colonial areas provides a direct incentive to war. It must be realized, moreover, that economies cannot be gained from large-scale mass production unless it can command a large market. The United States has a sufficiently large internal market to make such production profitable without foreign trade; but none of the nations of western Europe enjoys this advantage. The search for foreign markets by European capitalism is due not only to the overproduction and the underconsumption which have so frequently characterized private capitalism, but also — and perhaps chiefly — to the need to make full use of the mass-production methods of modern technology. The only solution, therefore, to the economic — and ultimately to the political — problems of Europe is the establishment of free trade between the different European nations and the economic integration of the entire continent. Any rapid growth of trade barriers, such as has occurred since the World War, destroys the utility of the large mass-production plants by depriving them of foreign markets and increases economic and political maladjustments.[11]

Trade barriers thus constitute the chief economic cause of

war. A rivalry for foreign markets, such as is indeed inherent in capitalism, does not provoke war unless it is pursued by political and not merely by economic methods; trade rivalries within a free-market system result in a complicated inter-locking of interests which makes war unprofitable. Thus the mercantilism of the seventeenth and eighteenth centuries — a system under which European powers attempted to monopolize the trade of colonial areas — resulted in a series of imperialist wars; while in the twentieth century the growth of tariffs and of economic nationalism, and the attempts to achieve autarchy, make aggression inevitable. A peaceful autarchy is possible only in a country which contains within its own boundaries both all the raw materials which it needs and also a market sufficiently large to absorb the products of mass-production industries — a condition to which no exist-ing economic units except the United States and the Soviet Union even approximate. The attempt to achieve autarchy within any smaller area leads to the seizure by force of arms of countries which have valuable raw materials and — by ending the international division of labor and hence destroy-ing all the economic advantages of peace — makes such sei-zures profitable even when they are not necessary. The willing-ness of other countries which possess such raw materials to sell them is no remedy, since autarchies find it difficult to acquire the foreign exchange with which to buy.

It is undeniable that during the past half-century the de-velopment of capitalism has been accompanied by a growth of trade barriers; and the political power enjoyed by certain capitalistic groups probably made such a growth inevitable. Free trade will always cause hardships for certain economic interests; those interests will demand political protection from foreign competition; and one trade barrier will lead inexorably to others. There are, however, two considera-tions which Marxists are apt to overlook. In the first place, what causes war is not capitalism but trade barriers, and any system which abolished the private ownership of industry but continued to impose trade barriers or to aim at autarchy would present similar economic inducements to war. And in the second place, it is not merely the privileged classes alone but all sections of the population who are likely to benefit by successful aggressive or imperialistic policies. The support which the working classes gave to their own governments during the World War was not due merely to treacherous leadership, to patriotic sentimentality, or to stupidity; it was caused by their realization that if their country were defeated, their own standard of living, as well as that of their employers, would suffer.

The aggressiveness of Fascism is not caused merely by the fact that it is capitalistic. The factors which are supposed to make capitalism warlike — overproduction and underconsumption, and the consequent need to expand exports and restrict imports — do not apply to Fascism. When Fascist governments endeavor to expand their exports, it is not in order to dispose of a surplus, but in order to obtain foreign exchange with which to buy necessary imports. As a result of armaments and public works there is no overproduction in the Fascist states. The primary economic cause of Fascist imperialism (as distinguished from its political and ideological causes, which are perhaps equally important) is that Fascism is a planned economy which aims at autarchy, but which has an inadequate geographical basis. It should be realized that any form of planned economy (Communist as well as Fascist) must reduce its reliance on foreign trade to a minimum — partly for military reasons, and partly because foreign trade cannot be planned except on a very restricted barter basis — and must aim at autarchy. The Nazis need the iron of Czechoslovakia, the oil of Rumania, and the wheat of the Ukraine in order to make themselves more completely self-sufficient and to enlarge the internal market which mass-production technique requires. And it is not merely the German capitalist class but the German people as a whole who are likely to gain by successful Nazi aggression; inclusion of more raw materials within the German autarchical system means an improvement not only in capitalist earnings but also in the general standard of living.

The international free market has now disappeared, and its restoration in any visible future appears to be impossible. The general abandonment of economic liberalism reinforces the claims of Communism to be the one practicable method of establishing world peace.

Communism professes to aim at a world-state; but can one consider a unified world Communism as even remotely possible? Efficient bureaucratic planning of the economy of the entire world; subjection of all races and nationalities to a single international dictatorship; equalization of living standards throughout the world, countries with rich natural resources and developed industries being placed on a level with the poverty-stricken populations of Asia: this is what a Communist world-state would involve. Is it probable that there are human minds capable of planning a world-economy, or that the various sections of the human race, with their different historic traditions and economic standards, could ever be persuaded to consent to it? Consider, for example, the problems which would be presented by the unification under a single government of a rich nation like the United States with a poor nation like China or Japan. An equalization of the standard of living would be impossible, since the people of the United States would never agree to such a sacrifice. On the other hand, it would be equally impossible for one nation to remain rich and another poor, since the consequent rivalries and hatreds would be incompatible with any genuine unity. The only alternative solution would be the export of capital and of capital equipment, on profitable terms, from rich countries to poor countries; and how this would differ from the practices of nineteenth-century imperialism, and why it should not result in similar evils, it would be difficult to say.

Far more probable, however, is not a single world Communism but a series of national Communisms. Communism, if it triumphs at all, can scarcely be expected to sweep the world, or even a single continent, at the same time. Any Communist victory is likely to occur within a single country, as happened in Russia; and such a national Communism would then proceed to adopt a unified planned economy, to withdraw from the world-market, and to inculcate among its citizens an exclusive loyalty to its own institutions. The immediate effects of Communism would be to increase international disunity and to stimulate national separatism. Communism proposes to create world-unity, not, like economic liberalism, by moving toward it, but by moving away from it. Is it conceivable that national Communisms, having first organized themselves as single totalitarian systems, would afterward proceed to unite with each other? Or, as Communist theorists maintain, that if Great Britain or the United States adopted Communism, it would immediately — in defiance of all its national and economic traditions — proceed to merge itself with the Soviet Union, Stalin becoming the dictator of the joint republics or stepping aside in favor of Harry Pollitt or Earl Browder? The road to internationalism does not run through nationalism — a fallacy which was held by many nineteenth-century liberals and which has already been sufficiently discredited. The only method of achieving international harmony is to weaken the authority of the national state and to strengthen the liberties of the individual.

But if Communism is unlikely to achieve international unity, what reasons are there for supposing that it will abolish war? Marxists suppose that war benefits only a privileged class, but this is not true. As long as different parts of the world differ from each other in their natural resources and in the living standards of their populations, the inhabitants of the poorer countries would — in a world of autarchies — have economic motives for war. As, moreover, the mineral resources of the world decrease, the struggle to obtain control over them will become more intense. A Communist Germany would have the same economic motives as a Fascist Germany for acquisition of the natural resources of southeastern Europe. A Communist Japan would have the same economic motives as a Fascist Japan for expansion into China. Communism, so long at least as it operated in a partly capitalist world, would be able to find analogous reasons for intervening beyond its boundaries; it would intervene not to protect the Aryan race but to protect the proletariat — as the Soviet government soon after its establishment intervened in Georgia and sent an army into Poland, and as today it suppresses separatist movements among its minority races. Communism, moreover, like Fascism, creates authoritarian dictatorships which may need the prestige of aggressive foreign policies. Is it conceivable that, in a world divided into autarchic dictatorships, the inhabitants of the richer areas would voluntarily surrender their advantages and lower their own standard of living for the benefit of their less fortunate neighbors? The only reason for expecting Communism to be peaceful is that its ideology is pacifistic; unlike Fascism, it accepts war only as a means to an end; it does not glorify war as good in itself. As, however, the Marxists themselves have taught us, an ideology of peace is unlikely permanently to be effective if both economic and political forces impel men to war. The Soviet Union has already abandoned its internationalism and begun to stimulate an aggressive nationalistic patriotism, of a kind which, in the event of a European war, may easily degenerate into imperialism. The only permanently effective preventive of war — impossible as, under present conditions, it may be — is that of nineteenth-century economic liberalism: international free trade, the international division of labor, freedom of immigration, and the export of capital from richer nations to more backward areas.

V. THE RIVAL AUTHORITARIANISMS

THE kingdom of freedom of the Marxists means, therefore, neither freedom nor equality nor prosperity nor peace. All that it can offer to mankind is the abolition of some of the grosser economic and racial inequalities which exist under capitalism, a greater degree of order and economic security, and that release from personal responsibility which men are sometimes driven to desire when society seems to be in danger of complete disintegration.

If, however, the free market is destined to be replaced by an authoritarian economy — and twentieth-century society is in some danger of a fatalistic acceptance of this idea — is an authoritarian Communism so markedly superior to an authoritarianism of big business that men should sacrifice their lives and expose society to a prolonged revolutionary struggle in the hope of achieving it?

American industrialists have always resented any kind of political control, and have insisted that they could manage the economic affairs of the nation much better than the government could do it for them. In recent years some of them have put forward plans of 'industrial self-government,' the essence of which is that industry should be allowed to integrate itself on a monopolistic basis and should then proceed to fix prices and regulate production. Some of these industrialists might perhaps like to end political interference once and for all by themselves taking over the government; and if the leaders of American democracy prove to be incapable of ending unemployment and preventing large-scale depressions, it is likely that demands for some kind of identification of politics with business may win considerable support. Let us suppose that big business constitutes itself the American government and proceeds to plan the economic system. Could such an arrangement function successfully?

The substitution of economic planning for *laissez-faire* cannot stop halfway; once a government begins to interfere with the mechanisms of the free market and with the flexibility of prices and earnings, it finds itself inexorably compelled to increase its control over the economic system. Free-market methods cannot function in an economy which has become partly authoritarian. A business dictatorship would probably begin, as did both Mussolini and Hitler, by promising freedom to the individual businessman; but as has happened both in Italy and in Germany, it would be forced, in order to prevent economic crises, steadily to extend the authority of the state over every element in the economic system. Any such dictatorship must inevitably end by creating a unified and totalitarian state capitalism, under the control of a bureaucracy. Under such a system there would be no equality and no freedom, even for the individual businessman. Entrepreneurs and corporation managers would be required to obey the price-fixing and wage-fixing decrees of the dictatorship; independent trade unions would disappear; labor would be shifted from one occupation to another at the will of the authorities; the right of free criticism would be severely restricted; and the bureaucratic and *rentier* classes would receive enormous earnings, most of which — in order to prevent the system from being clogged with excess savings — they would be required to spend on their own consumption. Once individual freedom had disappeared, however, there would be no theoretical reason why the system should not function without any

disastrous breakdowns. Any fool, it has been said, can govern
with the aid of bayonets. And as Hitler has shown, no
extraordinary wisdom is needed to abolish unemployment
with the aid of machine guns. The difficulties of capitalism
are due to the right of free choice enjoyed by individuals —
to the right of *rentiers* to hoard their savings, of entrepreneurs
to raise their prices, and of trade unions to resist wage reductions. But an integrated monopolistic group, who combined
political and economic power and who had complete control
over prices, wages, and production, would be able to insist
that industry should give jobs to the unemployed, that all
savings should pass immediately into circulation, and that
the available purchasing power should be roughly equal to
the prices of the goods offered for sale.

In order, however, to make the economy of capitalism work
successfully, it is necessary to prevent surplus money from
flowing to the top of the system and staying there. Either
consumption must be increased and savings diminished, or else
savings must be taken over and spent by the government. To
prevent overproduction and unemployment, and to maintain
the flow of profits and dividends, a business dictatorship would
therefore be compelled either to raise working-class wages or
to assume control (through loans and taxes) of the savings
of the business classes and use them for public works. The
Marxists argue that no capitalist group would ever consent
to either of these things, and therefore that such a system is
unworkable and would collapse. It is true that such policies
would run counter to all capitalist tradition, and that a capitalist class would be extremely reluctant to accept them. But
it must be realized that the adoption of such a program would
be quite compatible with the continued enjoyment of luxury
and power by the capitalist classes. And if, as the Marxists
argue, a refusal to adopt it would mean economic collapse,
and eventually a revolution, it seems highly improbable that

a business dictatorship, when confronted by economic realities, would not display enough intelligence to make the necessary concessions. As Fascist experience has shown, one cannot predict what such a dictatorship would do by considering how businessmen have customarily behaved in a free-market economy or what slogans its leaders would probably adopt before they assumed power. Given, therefore, even a small degree of economic realism on the part of its ruling officials, a capitalist dictatorship would prove itself an economic possibility.[12]

Such a system might loosely be described as Fascism, but it would differ from the Fascism of Germany and Italy. In Germany and Italy power belongs, not to the business classes, but to the petty bourgeois adventurers, cranks, criminals, minor intellectuals, and poets and artists *manqués*, who constitute the Fascist bureaucracy. American businessmen would appear to have learned from German and Italian experience that if they assist a Fascist Party into power, they will end by becoming the prisoners and the victims of the monster which they have helped to create. A business dictatorship would be free from some of the wilder insanities of European Fascism. Nor can one assume that such a dictatorship would involve itself in war. It would doubtless adopt an aggressive imperialism toward Latin America; but the belief of Marxists that capitalists like wars, and are always plotting to bring one about, has never had much foundation in fact, and has been notably disproved by the pacifism of the right-wing parties in Europe during the past half-dozen years. Wars are apt to end in bankruptcies and revolutions. Fascist aggression in Europe is due to a number of factors, most of which would not be reproduced in the United States: to the humiliation of the Treaty of Versailles; to the need for more raw materials and a more extensive system of autarchy; to the pathological romanticism of the Fascist leaders and the Fascist ideology; and to the fact that the building of armaments presents fewer practical difficulties than the building of other public works and that the armaments must afterward be justified by being used. An American business dictatorship might use force to impose economic subjection upon South America; but it would be unlikely to engage in any major conflict or to destroy itself through war.

From the viewpoint of the average American, how great would be the difference between the rule of a privileged Communist bureaucracy and the rule of a privileged business bureaucracy? To the groups immediately concerned — to the American Communist Party on the one hand, to Wall Street bankers on the other hand — the difference is, of course, a matter of life and death. A business dictatorship means poverty, imprisonment, and death for Communists; a Communist dictatorship means poverty, imprisonment, and death for bankers. The rival groups will endeavor to persuade the American people that their conflict is about fundamentals, involving the preservation or destruction of civilization itself. But to the ordinary American the resemblances between the two authoritarianisms are, perhaps, as important as the differences. Under either system there would be order without freedom, and security without equality; and under either system power and privilege would belong to a ruling hierarchy. A Communist dictatorship would presumably have the advantage of an initial prejudice in favor of equality and humanitarianism, though — judging from the Russian experience — these prejudices would not survive twenty years of totalitarian bureaucratic control. By abolishing the *rentier* class, and by establishing racial equality, it would, moreover, destroy some of the worst injustices of the present system. On the other hand, a business dictatorship would begin with a greater practical experience in the control of the economic system, and — a fact of considerable importance —

would not require a revolution and a civil war in order to achieve power. Actually both systems would end as single consolidated state trusts, and the economics of the planning process would soon become almost identical, no matter which set of officials were doing the planning. The only important economic differences would be that a business dictatorship would probably pay somewhat larger salaries to its industrial managers and (while assuming control over all money not spent on consumption) would continue to pay large incomes to the *rentier* class. These differences may seem to be considerable, but whether they are important enough to fight a civil war about is dubious. The appetite for luxury and extravagance has its limits; and American industry, under totalitarian control, could afford to support the propertied classes in the style to which they are accustomed and still pay a living wage to the remainder of the population. The only really fundamental choice which confronts modern society is not a choice between two rival brands of authoritarianism, but a choice between any kind of authoritarian economy and an economy which preserves the right of individual free choice.[13]

V. The Marxist View of Life

V. The Marxist View of Life

I. THE MATERIALIST INTERPRETATION OF HISTORY [1]

MARXISM is not only a political program, it is also a philosophy; and its adherents claim that, in addition to showing men how to satisfy their economic and social needs, it also provides the only true solution to many of those metaphysical and scientific problems which perplex those thinkers whose minds are limited by a bourgeois ideology. From this confidence in the all-embracing validity of Marxist theory is derived the unquestioning fanaticism which so often characterizes Marxist practice. Communists believe in the dogma of a proletarian revolution because they believe that this dogma is a necessary deduction from a *Weltanschauung* which is so true and so comprehensive that it can be adopted with a kind of religious faith. They are, moreover, under no necessity to defend the Marxist view of life by intellectual argument or to answer intellectual criticisms; sceptics need not be confuted, they need only be condemned on the ground of 'bourgeois' prejudice. As the disciples of a new religion base their faith on an immediate knowledge of reality through divine revelation, as the exponents of the Nazi gospel appeal to a racial way of thinking to which non-Aryans have no access, so Marxist intellectuals (even when, like Marx and Lenin, they have never belonged to the proletariat) claim that their view of life is true because it is 'proletarian' and that their critics fail to apprehend it because they are 'bourgeois.'

The Marxist ideology is represented as being wholly rational and wholly scientific; but its rationality is not of a kind which commends itself immediately to the disinterested intellect. A purely rational doctrine, indeed, never provokes intolerance or fanaticism among its adherents; men are inspired to kill and to persecute for a set of beliefs only when those beliefs go beyond scientific proof and are partly mystical or incomprehensible. This has been the history of all religions, and the Marxist type of mind is religious and not scientific. In reading those dreary metaphysical pronunciamentos which appear to be the chief theoretical productions of the Soviet Union — pronunciamentos largely devoted to fulsome tributes to the genius for philosophy displayed by Comrades Lenin and Stalin and to harrowing accounts of the decay of culture alleged to be in process in the capitalist nations — one finds it difficult to reduce the Marxist view of life to any clear or logical propositions, free from contradictions and non-sequiturs; Marxism, one learns, teaches that the human will is free and is also determined; that truth is absolute and is also relative; that the future can be predicted, yet that novelties may occur; that progress is absolute, yet that degeneration is possible; and that the proletarian revolution is both inevitable and not inevitable.[2] Marxism, in fact, instead of solving those dilemmas which present themselves to 'bourgeois' intellectuals, merely asserts each horn of each dilemma as equally true, and bridges contradictions by means of those comforting but meaningless verbal incantations which constitute the philosophy of dialectical materialism.

Yet, though much of the Marxist philosophy consists only of metaphysical jargon, that philosophy is by no means valueless. Both the materialist interpretation of history and the dialectical philosophy contain considerable elements of truth; but those truths do not support the deductions which Marxists attempt to build upon them.

The materialist or economic interpretation of history, which accounts for the behavior and the ideas of groups and classes in terms of their material interests, provides a fruitful method of explaining social movements. Individuals may violate the interests or the ideologies of their class, but sociology can ignore the eccentricities of individuals; like physics, it can base itself on statistical probabilities. The reduction of idealistic pretensions to terms of class greed is apt to seem brutally cynical, since political groups are often unconscious of the economic motives which govern their behavior; but the effectiveness of the economic interpretation of politics abundantly justifies itself in experience.[3] If, however, the argument of the two previous chapters is valid, this interpretation does not support the Marxist faith in the necessity of Communism. The class groupings and economic tendencies of capitalism do not point to a proletarian revolution; and if such a revolution did occur, it would create a privileged class with economic interests distinct from those of the proletariat. The belief of Communists that in the Soviet Union privilege and inequality will disappear can be defended only by denying that economic and class interpretation of society which they apply to capitalism.

But though the Marxist interpretation of history is, in its broad outlines, true, it has also ambiguities and limitations which are of considerable importance with reference both to the understanding of present society and to the practical tasks of social reorganization. Marxism teaches both that men make history and that history makes men; and while both these propositions are partly true, it is obvious that, since they contradict each other, they cannot both be completely true. Marxists do not, however, define and interpret these propositions in such a way as to limit the applicability of each of them alone and to show how they are to be reconciled with each other. By asserting each of them, in different contexts, as an absolute truth, they conclude both that future social development is determined and can be scientifically predicted, and also that social development will be in accordance with the needs and wishes of mankind. Arguing that history makes men, they declare that Communism is inevitable; arguing that men make history, they declare that whatever is inevitable must also be desirable. This double line of defence provides them with an answer to any kind of criticism. In reality, however, history does not wholly make men, from which it follows that the future is not wholly determined; and men do not wholly make history, which means that what happens is not necessarily what men want to happen. A more precise definition of the two contradictory premises upon which the Marxist interpretation of history is based will undermine the foundations of Marxist dogmatism.

An ambiguity of this kind is apparent in the very words 'materialist interpretation of history.' These words can mean two quite different things. They can mean that the mental attitudes and the behavior of human beings are determined by material conditions; that 'social existence determines consciousness'; and that, as the *Communist Manifesto* declares, 'man's ideas, views, and conceptions, in other words, man's consciousness, changes with every change in the conditions of his material existence.' Or, on the other hand, they can mean that the most important human needs are material needs — for food, clothing, and shelter — and that human beings are motivated primarily by their desire to satisfy those needs. According to the first interpretation, it is possible to predict how any individual will think and act if one has sufficient knowledge of his natural and social environment; one can then argue that the course of historic development is determined; that Communism must follow capitalism; and that a new proletarian culture will replace bourgeois culture. Unfortunately, this belief in the material determination of consciousness makes it impossible to formulate any absolute truths or values; all ideas are relative to material environments, and there are no universal standards by which one cultural system can be regarded as better than another. According to the second interpretation, on the other hand, it is possible to evaluate different societies; one society is better than another if it satisfies human needs more adequately. This interpretation, however, admits a considerable element of contingency into history, and it suggests the criticism that not all human needs are economic, and that some of them may not even be material. There is a similar ambiguity in the formula, borrowed by the Marxists from Spinoza, that 'freedom is the recognition of necessity'; this can mean either that the human will is determined and that freedom means the recognition of this fact, or that human beings become free to do what they choose to the extent that they recognize those elements in their environment which are imposed by necessity.

On several occasions Marx explicitly declared that what he meant by the materialist interpretation of history was that men were motivated by material needs. His purpose, he explained, was to show that the primary needs of human beings were economic, and to make men conscious of those needs. He wished 'to make the time fully understand its struggles and its wishes.' 'We merely show the world for what it is really fighting, and the world must become self-conscious whether it will or not.... Our motto must therefore be: "Reform of the consciousness, not by dogmas, but by analysis of the mystical consciousness, of the consciousness which is not fully clarified, whether it be religious or political."' 'History,' he explained, 'does not use man as an instrument to fulfil its own purposes, as if it were a person apart. History is nothing else than the activity of man pursuing his own aims.' [4] From this viewpoint Marxism may be regarded as a kind of social psycho-analysis; as the analyst clarifies the consciousness of the individual, in order that he may become aware of the sexual urges which — repressed into the subconscious — have been influencing his behavior in a disguised form, so the Marxist explains society to itself in order that men may understand how social forces are determined by economic needs. The analyst, however, does not impose any particular course of conduct upon his patient; once the patient understands himself, he is capable of moral autonomy. Similarly an understanding of how economic factors influence social development does not necessarily involve any particular set of values or plan of action.

Yet much Marxist doctrine really implies that the behavior of human beings is governed by material conditions and that social development is determined. In spite of the claims of Marxists to be 'dialectical materialists,' they frequently talk in terms of mechanistic materialism, attributing all mental attitudes to material causes. Marx himself tended to view history as a kind of prearranged stage performance, in which the different classes and nations had their own rôles to play; and he became most irrationally contemptuous of any group which seemed to be missing its cue. He was, for example, perpetually denouncing the German bourgeoisie because they failed to do their duty by destroying German feudalism — a failure which would, in turn, delay the predestined destruction of the German bourgeoisie by the German proletariat.

If we adopt the view that 'history is nothing else than the activity of man pursuing his own aims' — and it is only on this assumption that it is possible to discuss history profitably at all — then it is obvious that the economic interpretation is not all-embracing. Its limitations become apparent as soon as it is applied to the motivation of individuals. The economic needs are the most fundamental, in the sense that they must be satisfied first; but they are by no means the only human needs, and as civilization advances and mankind acquires a greater power over nature, they become relatively less important. Individual behavior is governed, not only by a need for food, clothing, and shelter, but also by the various manifestations of the sexual instinct and by a craving for power; egoistic impulses are normally modified by a desire for social approval and for self-justification in terms of an objective ideal; and on the higher levels of culture intellectual curiosity and aesthetic pleasure begin to function independently. The cruder and more vulgar exponents of Marxist doctrine frequently interpret all individual behavior in terms of economic interest; but the inadequacy of this kind of materialism, which renders inexplicable the self-sacrificing idealism of such men as Marx and Lenin themselves, needs no demonstration.

Interpretation of human behavior is, moreover, complicated by the fact that most human needs, even when they are not economic, involve some degree of control over nature, and that any concrete human act is usually the resultant of several different kinds of motivation. Activity which was originally economic, and which appears to retain a purely economic character, may be pursued for motives which are not economic at all. A millionaire engaged in doubling his fortune is not governed by a desire for food, clothing, and shelter, or even — in most instances — by a desire for money for its own sake; his motivations are probably a complex mixture of a desire for power, a desire for social approval and applause, a desire to live in surroundings and to possess objects which will give him aesthetic pleasure, and a feeling that by adding to the wealth of the community he is being of service to it. Human energy constitutes a single stream, which begins with the satisfaction of man's material needs and then passes on to the moulding of man's environment into forms which will flatter his love of power and satisfy his aesthetic sensitivities. It is easy to regard it as wholly economic because there is nowhere any sharp differentiation between the economic, the egoistic, and the aesthetic; yet as culture advances, there is a gradual qualitative change in the objects which man pursues, and while at one extreme they are wholly economic, involving merely the preservation of life, at the other they become wholly aesthetic. Actually most human behavior involves a combination, in varying proportions, of material and idealistic motives, and even when men work directly for food, clothing, and shelter, they hope to acquire objects which will give them an aesthetic as well as a physical satisfaction.

An instructive parallel can be drawn between the method of Marx and that of Freud. The achievement of each man was to take one of the primal impulses of human nature, to show how it assumed disguised expressions in idealistic sublimations and ideological superstructures, and thereby to make men conscious of their real needs and desires. Each man can be criticized for denying all independent reality to aesthetic and intellectual constructions, and for interpreting all human activity in terms of a single basic physical urge. In Freud the sexual impulse, and in Marx economic need, are given such broad meanings that they almost lose their specifically sexual and economic characters and become identified with the undifferentiated flow of human vitality.

The fact that economic motivations are limited can often be ignored when one is studying capitalism; but it becomes important when one begins to consider programs of social reorganization. Marxists, for example, judge societies in terms of economic progress; they assume that the growth of collective wealth means the increase of human happiness and the development of culture; capitalism is better than feudalism because it is more productive, and Communism will similarly surpass capitalism. This assumption is not necessarily true. Man's economic needs are very elastic, and a low level of economic productivity may (as in the Italy of the Renascence) be associated with a high cultural achievement. Man does not necessarily require freedom in order to satisfy his economic appetites; but personal freedom is essential for all non-economic activities; and there is more freedom in a society where private property is widely distributed, and (as in the city-state) political power is decentralized, than in a society, whether capitalist or Communist, which is characterized by large-scale industry and a strong central government. Nor would the abolition of economic conflicts automatically prevent conflicts of other kinds; love of power and sexual jealousy are, under capitalism, associated with property rights, but this does not mean that they would disappear if property rights were abolished.

Marxists tend to overestimate the importance of the economic needs because they are the only ones which can easily be accounted for in a materialistic philosophy. The need for food, clothing, and shelter and for the satisfaction of sexual appetite are obviously material and nothing more. But the desire for formal beauty, for intellectual understanding, and for all the poetic subtleties which may become associated with a sexual relationship cannot, in any reasonable sense of the word, be called material; they grow out of physical and practical needs, but they gradually acquire an ideal character. And while the physical needs are limited and finite, ideal needs are insatiable. What is important is not whether one interprets their origins materialistically, but whether one believes that their proper sphere of activity is in the material world; whether one supposes that the function of man is to renounce the world and seek communion with the supernatural or to reshape the world and human society into forms which will increasingly harmonize with human ideals. Religion is the enemy of progress only when it preaches resignation to preventable evils. Since, however, it is difficult to trace aesthetic, intellectual, and humanitarian idealisms to any material cause, Marxists are apt to deny their existence. That materialistic philosophers have often been idealistic in their personal conduct proves only that men are inconsistent; a consistent philosophical materialism implies materialism in the more vulgar sense of the word also.

Though, however, Marxists frequently misinterpret the actions of individuals, the Marxist method has much validity when applied to society; and the individual consciousness is always conditioned, though not wholly determined, by social forces. Society exists primarily in order that men may satisfy their economic needs, and economic factors determine the form of social organization and have the greatest influence on the accepted code of values and beliefs. Human behavior is not governed by economic needs to the extent that the Marxists believe, but it is conditioned by cultural patterns, by ideologies, which have their roots in the economic system and in the interests of the dominant class. The non-economic activities of individuals occur within an economically determined framework; and human nature, which is basically everywhere the same, assumes quite different cultural expressions. Men inherit a series of instinctive and emotional tendencies, and these tendencies acquire their concrete content and their directives from the economic and social system. All men have the same physical needs, but the precise mode in which these needs find fulfilment varies in different societies. Similarly, the desire for social approval, for aesthetic pleasure, and for a rational understanding of the universe are natural human traits; but concrete social ideals, aesthetic tastes, and religious and philosophical beliefs are socially determined. The personal motives of a millionaire may not be economic, but the form which they assume is the result of an economically determined social system. In the Middle Ages equivalent motivations would probably have produced a crusader or an archbishop. A volunteer who dies in an imperialist war may be sacrificing himself in a spirit of the purest idealism; yet the social situation in which he found himself can be explained only in economic terms.

Society, moreover, not only gives concrete directives to human emotions; it also interprets them. Man is an animal who acts from deliberation and not directly from instinct; his behavior is determined, not by his needs, but by those needs as they are interpreted by the intelligence. He has no innate knowledge of what it is that he really wants; he has to discover his own needs either by learning from others or by a process of exploration through trial and error. Different cultural systems will impose upon individuals different interpretations of their desires. Sexuality, for example, is a normal human trait; but if society discourages its overt manifestations, the individual may remain unconscious of it; it may influence behavior in a disguised form which is given a non-sexual interpretation. The emotions associated with it have, moreover, received different interpretations in different cultures. The medieval poets regarded love as an indication that human desires were infinite and could be satisfied only by an infinite object; men really wanted God, and carnal love was an illusion. Modern man, instructed by the psycho-analysts, is apt to interpret the same emotion in opposite terms: carnal love is the reality and love of God the illusion. Different cultural systems have, moreover, adopted different standards of values, and given encouragement to different human traits. Under the feudal system loyalty and courage were the most important virtues, among the early bourgeoisie business integrity, and among the Communists the comradeship of the proletariat. Medieval society regarded avarice as a vice and a taste for solitary meditation as a virtue; bourgeois society reversed these judgments. A fanatical belief in one's own divine mission might create a saint in the Dark Ages or a Fascist dictator in twentieth-century Europe; in the eighteenth century it was considered to be a proof of insanity.

The importance of the social ideology in conditioning the behavior of individuals has been recognized by Marxists, particularly by Engels in those well-known letters in which he denounced the disciples of Marx who traced all individual activity directly to economic causes.[5] 'What these gentlemen all lack,' he declared, 'is dialectic. They never see anything but here cause and there effect. That this is a hollow abstraction, that such metaphysical polar opposites only exist in the real world during crisis, while the whole vast process proceeds in the form of interaction (though of very unequal forces, the economic movement being by far the strongest, most elemental, and most decisive), and that here everything is relative and nothing is absolute — this they never begin to see.' 'According to the materialist conception of history the determining element in history is *ultimately* the production and reproduction in real life. More than this neither Marx nor I have ever asserted.... The economic situation is the basis, but the various elements of the superstructure ... also exercise their influence upon the course of the historical struggles and in many cases preponderate in determining their *form*. There is an interaction of all these elements in which, amid all the endless *host* of accidents (i.e. of things and events whose inner connection is so remote and so impossible to prove that we regard it as absent and can neglect it), the economic movement finally asserts itself as necessary.... We make our own history, but in the first place under very definite presuppositions and conditions. Among these the economic ones are finally decisive. But the political, etc., ones, and indeed even the traditions which haunt human minds, also play a part, although not the decisive one.'

In spite, however, of the eagerness of Marxists to destroy bourgeois ideology and to create a new proletarian ideology, they do not, in general, attach sufficient importance to ideological influences. In any society there are certain cultural presuppositions, certain climates of opinion, which condition the personality of the individual and which provide the nuclei round which his sentiments become organized. To a large extent the behavior of the individual is governed by the prejudices which he acquires from society; and Marxists habitually underestimate this element of irrationality in human affairs. Both privileged classes and oppressed classes often fail to act rationally; traditional mental attitudes make them partially blind to their own real interests. Hence, for example, the victories of Fascism. It follows that any reforming movement ought to adapt itself to the dominant ideology; it ought to base itself on the appeal to historic traditions. This tactical necessity was not (until 1935) recognized by the Marxists, who consistently flouted every one of the dominant nationalistic, religious, and moral prejudices of mankind.

Thus, while an ideology may originally be determined by economic factors, it afterward reacts back upon its economic basis; and as Engels pointed out, society must be studied in terms, not of a chain of economic causes and ideological effects, but of perpetual interaction. And though the influence of economics upon ideology is no doubt considerably stronger than the reverse influence, it becomes, in practice, difficult to assign priority to either factor. All that can profitably be asserted is that the beliefs of a society and its economic organization will tend to be in harmony with each other; and that when there is antagonism, one or both of them will undergo modification. According to the Marxists the ultimate dynamic element which causes social change is economic; as the economic system becomes more productive, the social structure and the prevalent ideology must change also.[6] This conception ignores the fact that economic changes also have causes, and that such causes may be political or ideological. There is no law of automatic economic development; when the economic system becomes more productive it is because human beings have adopted new ideas. Of all civilizations only one — that of western Europe — has applied science to industry; and that achievement was the result of a number of interacting causes, one of which was the security against arbitrary governments enjoyed by the people of Great Britain, while another was that the Christian religion had regarded the material world as rational and comprehensible to the human intellect. Similarly, Marxism itself was no automatic product of the nineteenth-century economic system; its basic attitudes were derived from the European cultural tradition, in the moulding of which Christianity played a dominant rôle. And while one can, if one likes, trace Christianity back to the economic and class system of the ancient world, that system was itself ideologically influenced. The chain of interaction is, in reality, endless, and to ask which factor came first is meaningless.

The most important deduction to be drawn from these considerations is that the future is unpredictable and that men are influenced by ideas to a much greater degree than the Marxists have ever admitted.[7] The economic interpretation imposes certain limits upon social behavior. Groups and classes never consciously act against their interests; no privileged group, for example, forfeits its privileges without a struggle. But one cannot predict the behavior of men merely by considering their interests. Human interests are not merely economic, but are more complex; how men interpret their interests depends upon ideological influences; and what course of action men will consider to be most likely to advance their interests is something which can never be predicted with any certainty. The course of events, therefore, is governed, not by economic factors alone, but by a combination of economic interests with ideas; and ideas belong to the realm of imponderables. It is true, as the Marxists insist, that an idea is powerless unless it expresses an interest; but it is also true

that an interest does not govern conduct until it becomes formulated in an idea. By considering society in economic terms,
one can lay down certain possible lines of development; but
which of them is actually adopted depends upon ideas. And
it is for this reason that, although Marxism is invaluable
as an aid in interpreting the past, its adherents have almost
always proved themselves wrong in their predictions of the
future. In studying the past, one can show how economic
factors have influenced behavior; but in predicting the future,
one must attach more importance to imponderables than
Marxism allows. Thus, for example, by looking back over
the devious course of British foreign policy since 1931, one
can explain it in terms of the class interests of British Toryism;
yet it was by no means inevitable that the British Tories
should have chosen to build up Fascism as a counterbalance
to Communism. They might have realized, as did a few of
their leaders, that the Nazi movement would be a more formidable threat than Communism to the British Empire and have
acted accordingly. Even from the viewpoint of British im-
perial interests, British policy has been incredibly stupid; and
there is nothing inevitable about stupidity. Similarly, it is
by no means inevitable that the proletariat should choose
Socialism as the doctrine best adapted for advancing their
interests, nor is it inevitable that a property-owning class
should, in a time of economic crisis, succumb to that moral
corruption which expresses itself in Fascism. The prediction
record of the Marxists is, in point of fact, almost one hundred
per cent wrong; and such successes as they can claim are not
proofs of any genuine perspicacity. Marx, for example, is
alleged to have predicted the Russian Revolution. It is true
that he believed, at one period of his life, that the workers
might achieve power first in Russia. It must be added, however, that on other occasions he cherished similar hopes with
respect to three or four other countries, and that throughout

his life he believed the proletarian revolution to be imminent. Such recent predictions of the Communists as are alleged to be proofs of superior insight are mostly of a similar nature. The outbreak of a European war would, for example, be in accordance with Communist predictions; but it must be pointed out that the Communists have been predicting a war in the near future ever since 1919.

The most important error of the Marxists is, however, not their failure to emphasize the constant interaction between economic and ideological factors, but their insistence that all aesthetic and intellectual creations are mechanistically determined by the economic and social system. Instead of merely showing how scientists, artists, and philosophers are conditioned by their social environment — a truth of considerable significance — they argue that all cultural manifestations are nothing more than expressions of some particular ideology. History, in other words, makes men; and its counterpart — that men also make history — is ignored. This attitude is intellectually indefensible, and it has the effect of provoking intolerance and obscurantism.

Scientific work is always conditioned by the environment of the scientist. Certain social systems encourage scientific investigation, while others do not. The problems which the scientist undertakes to solve are often suggested by economic factors. Galileo was stimulated by seventeenth-century engineering, Newton by the calculations of probability made by insurance societies, modern scientists by modern technology. But the fact that scientists often deal with problems which are socially determined does not mean that the answers to those problems are also socially determined. What the technologist wishes to do is decided by society, but the correct method of doing it is dependent upon processes of nature which remain the same under all societies. Marxists, nevertheless, declare that not only the problems of the scientist but also the natural laws which he discovers are socially determined. They argue that Newton's cosmology was a reflection of seventeenth-century absolutism and Darwin's evolutionary theory of nineteenth-century bourgeois competition.[8] If this argument is valid, then it follows that the Newtonian and Darwinian hypotheses were to that extent untrue and should be revised; it does not mean, as Marxists appear to believe, that there is no such thing as objective truth and that scientific truths vary in different social systems. Marxists, nevertheless, insist that in some mysterious way there will be a proletarian science which is different from bourgeois science. Soviet scientists have developed such absurdities as proletarian mathematics, Leninist statistics, and even Stalinist medicine. If, however, all ideas are socially determined, then it follows that all those ideas which Marx borrowed from his bourgeois predecessors are valueless and that Marxism itself is a mere product of the nineteenth-century economic system and has no objective value. To argue, as Marxists occasionally do, that the viewpoint of the proletariat is truer than that of the bourgeoisie because the proletariat is a revolutionary class is to argue in a circle. How — unless we begin by assuming the truth of Marx's investigations — are we to know that the proletariat is revolutionary? The real value of the Marxist approach is that, by making men conscious of their social biases and prejudices, it facilitates the discovery of objective truth; like the discoveries of Copernicus and Einstein, it enables the observer to become aware of the extent to which his observations are deflected by his own viewpoint. But to argue that when society changes, the laws of nature also change is nonsensical.[9]

The Marxist view of science leads, moreover, to another and even more dangerous deduction. If all human activity is a product of economic needs, then the task of science is to solve the practical problems presented by industry and technology. From the fact that bourgeois scientists have frequently dealt with problems suggested by practical needs, Marxists argue that all science is applied science and that there is no such thing as disinterested intellectual curiosity. In the Soviet Union the prevalent tendency has been to regard pure science as a bourgeois prejudice and to expect scientists to harness themselves to the industrial system — an attitude which resembles that inculcated in Nazi Germany. In reality, however, the destruction of pure science must mean the eventual stultification of applied science. A number of the more important discoveries which have had practical utility have, in point of fact, resulted from investigations which were undertaken with no practical end in view. To deny the existence of intellectual curiosity is, therefore, not only a form of barbarism; it is also the end of scientific progress.

A similar inability to distinguish between social conditioning and social determination characterizes the Marxist approach to art. All aesthetic creation reflects the ideas and social forces of its time; but not everything in a work of art is a product of the social system. The aesthetic experience itself, the laws which govern the formal organization of works of art, and the recording of universal human emotions which recur under any social system are independent of economic factors. The Marxist approach can tell us much about a work of art, but it can say nothing about its aesthetic value; and the greater the value of the work, the less amenable it is to the categories of Marxist criticism. Art which is third-rate or purely commercial can be explained almost wholly in Marxist terms; but Marxism can tell us very little that is significant about great art. A great artist takes his material, his art-forms, and a system of ideas from his own time; but he is great to the extent that he transcends his own social environment, recording experiences which are human and not merely feudal or bourgeois and imposing upon them an aesthetic organization governed, not merely by the rules of good taste prevalent in his own age, but by the aesthetic sense common to all mankind. According to the canons of Marxist criticism, art can have no permanent value; since it expresses merely some particular social ideology, it becomes merely of historical interest as soon as society has changed. Thus, Dante is feudal and Shakespeare (according to the Marxists) is bourgeois; from which it would appear to follow that there is no reason why Communists should read either of them. But what Dante and Shakespeare took from their own time is what is least important about them. The enduring significance of the *Divine Comedy* is not that it embodied the Catholic philosophy of the Middle Ages, but that, using that philosophy as a framework, Dante was able to record the greatest variety of human experiences and to evaluate them in terms which are not only Catholic but also universal. For the non-Catholic reader the theological structure of hell, purgatory, and heaven is merely an aesthetic symbolism; the universal meaning of the *Divine Comedy* is that human beings are damned — in this world as well as theologically — when they are the victims of their own passions; they are in process of redemption as long as they struggle for harmony and self-mastery. Similarly, the value of *Hamlet* does not lie in its portrayal of a particular social situation; the situation, so far from being bourgeois, belonged to that more primitive stage in human development when vengeance was still the duty of the individual. The greatness of *Hamlet* is its study of a type of human experience which recurs in different contexts in any society. The concrete conditions which determine the specific objects of human activity and the environment upon which human beings must act are socially determined; but the basic human emotions and types of experience are invariant.

The theory that all art is socially determined leads Marxists to an even more harmful consequence: from the fact that the artist reflects his age, and from the assumption that he does nothing else, they deduce a standard of value. It is the artist's duty, they declare, to be revolutionary, and he is good to the extent that he fulfils this duty. Such an assertion shows a complete misunderstanding of the nature of art. The business of the artist is to convey life as he himself has experienced it, to record what he finds significant and valuable in the world which he inhabits and in his own emotional apprehension of it; the greatness of the art depends upon the comprehensiveness and the insight of the experience, and upon the honesty, the technical mastery, and the precision with which the experience is recorded. The artist's function is not to inculcate any particular mode of behavior, whether moralistic or political, it is to enlarge our knowledge of human nature and its possibilities, to make us more fully conscious of our own emotions and of the kind of world in which we live, and thereby to give us the kind of insight which enables us to act with wisdom, as free, self-governing individuals. In a revolutionary age the experience of artists will usually reflect a spirit of revolution; but this does not mean that artists must necessarily take sides, they may well recognize the tragic clash of values involved in a revolutionary struggle; nor does it mean that the aesthetic significance of their work depends upon their adherence to a correct ideology. The dogma that good art is always revolutionary has led Marxist critics to perform the most extraordinary operations upon some of the masters of the past. Since Shakespeare was a great writer, and since the rising class in Shakespeare's age was the bourgeoisie, they assume that Shakespeare must have expressed a bourgeois ideology; he is great, they say, because embodied that ideology so comprehensively (though why a spokesman of the early bourgeoisie should be of interest to us remains obscure); and they proceed to torture his text in the effort to prove that the mainspring of his work was a hatred of feudalism. Artists of the present day are exhorted to express a proletarian viewpoint; their duty is to heighten the revolutionary consciousness of the masses. It is not impossible that a great artist should convey life as seen by the proletariat, or should deal with contemporary revolutionary struggles; but the artistic process cannot be forced. In the last resort the artist can record only his own experience; and the forced and mechanical adoption of an ideology can result only in artistic dishonesty. To suggest, moreover, that art is good to the extent that it arouses the masses is to imply that a popular song, a stirring moving picture, or a Communistic success story may be the highest kinds of art. Such an exhortation applies really not to art at all, but to commercial writers, who in capitalist countries inculcate a bourgeois ideology and who, if revolution came, could as easily transform themselves into propagandists for Communism. The result of this attitude is that the Communistic writers of the United States, torn between their own sense of artistic integrity and their belief that they ought to arouse the masses, have for the most part relapsed into a troubled silence; while in the Soviet Union the greatest artists have been similarly tongue-tied or — the fate of the two most talented post-revolutionary poets — have committed suicide, and enormous financial rewards accrue to those commercial writers who devote themselves to proclaiming the greatness of Stalin and the glories of the Five-Year Plan.[10]

The Marxist denial of the enduring significance of great art and science, and of the possibility of disinterested intellectual and aesthetic creation, is accompanied by another and even more fundamental denial: that of the existence of any universal categories of morality.[11] All value judgments are regarded as dependent upon some particular economic and social system. What Marxists fail to recognize is that there are two quite different kinds of morality. Morality means, in the first place, a system of ethical prohibitions, regulating such matters as property and sexual relationships and having as its purpose the ordering and preservation of society. There is no sharp distinction between this kind of morality and, on the one hand, written law and, on the other, the accepted code of manners and social customs; in savage societies, in fact, the three are identical. Morality in this sense is a product of social conditions, and changes when society changes; thus one can appropriately speak of feudal morality, bourgeois morality, and proletarian morality. Morality means also, however, that ordering and disciplining of the emotions, that achievement of self-harmony and self-control, that recognition of the independent rights and reality of other men, which has been recognized in all ages as the finest fruit of civilization. To the extent that human beings achieve this second kind of morality they transcend the laws and prohibitions of society, both accepting them and also becoming capable of judging them. Obedience to the law, as Saint Paul proclaimed, is bondage; but by passing beyond the law, men achieve moral autonomy, they become free. Freedom, in fact, is both a necessary condition and a result of true morality; and it is for this reason that the proper function of all political and economic organization is to create conditions in which human beings can live freely, responsible to themselves. The bases of this kind of morality — self-awareness and self-control, and acceptance of other men as ends and not as means — are not socially determined; they are true for all societies and all ages, and the philosophical and religious thinking of the past has an enduring value to the extent that it recognizes them. Such a recognition of the nature of the human ideal, and of the rôle of political organization in making possible its realization, provides, indeed, the only standard of evaluation by which different social systems can be advocated or rejected.

The doctrine that all ideas and all values are socially determined leads, on the other hand, to the destruction of individual freedom and to the tyranny of the collectivity or of its embodiment in a dictator. Only the belief in objective rational truths and moral values can preserve freedom; for it is only through the right of appeal to objective standards that men can judge the actions of their government and resist them when they believe them to be wrong. Freedom, in the last resort, depends upon the independence, the vigor, and the enlightenment of the conscience of each individual. If standards of right and of rationality vary in different societies, and are mere products of a social system, then the individual loses his right of appeal, the independence of his conscience is undermined, and he can be compelled to conform to whatever the state chooses to recommend. The belief in the relativity of all standards is common to both Germany and Russia; and in each case its logical result is the complete subordination of the individual to the collectivity. Good is what, in the one case, serves the interests of the Aryan race as embodied in Hitler; what, in the other case, is in accordance with the will of the proletariat as embodied in Stalin. This growth of moral relativism is the most alarming tendency in both the theory and the political practice of the modern world; and though it is the Fascist states which have carried it to its most pernicious extreme, it originated — it is worthy of remark — with the Marxists.[12] By interpreting all cultural phenomena in terms of class struggle, by explaining all the beliefs of every individual by his rôle in that struggle, by proclaiming that any means whatever are justified in achieving the end, and that the only predestined historic end is the conquest of power by the proletariat, Marxism subordinates man to the march of history and ennobles tyranny, dishonesty, cruelty, and mass murder. And since the collectivity is an abstraction and only individuals are real, Marxism, by enthroning a collectivity, must also create individuals who can embody and interpret the will of that collectivity. The conquest of power by the proletariat becomes, therefore, the conquest of power by an individual whose function is to represent the march of history and to destroy the right of any other individual to criticize or oppose it.

II. DIALECTICAL MATERIALISM [13]

THE philosophy of dialectical materialism, like the economic interpretation of history, contains elements of truth; but its chief function in the Marxist cosmology is to provide a metaphysical proof of the inevitability of Communism. The need for such a proof, as an additional support for the politics of Marxism, is a result of the Marxist view of history.

The Marxist interpretation of history, as we have seen, denies the possibility of objective judgments of value. All standards of value are expressions of some particular social system or class interest; and different classes will evolve different ideals between which there can be no reconciliation. The only standard which, in the Marxist system of thought, can claim universality is that of economic productivity; different societies can be judged according to their efficiency in satisfying man's economic needs. The validity of such a test is, however, open to dispute. The mere provision of food, clothing, and shelter is not enough to satisfy human beings; and if they were the only human needs, mankind would never have advanced far beyond an animal level. The more important activities of human beings in civilized societies can be explained only in terms of non-economic motives; and the function of social organization is not only to preserve human life, but also to satisfy and control the desire for pleasure and power and to make possible aesthetic and moral development. If this is admitted, then it follows that judgments of value can be based only on a more elaborate conception of human nature and human needs than can be found anywhere in the Marxist gospels.

In practice, Marxists do not lay too much stress on the economic standard of value. They prefer to evade the problem of value judgments by insisting that Communism is inevitable. Partly by means of metaphysical doctrine, and partly by an analysis of the economics of capitalism, they endeavor to show that the victory of the proletariat, and the consequent creation of a Communist society, are objective necessities which can be scientifically predicted. They assume, moreover, that the real is the rational, and that all human values are derived from objective social conditions; and they believe in the existence of a law — which is presented as scientific, but which is, in reality, very mystical — according to which constant development, the future being always better than the past, is an objective necessity. It follows that there can be no distinction between what must happen and what ought to happen. Communism is desirable because it is inevitable, and inevitable because it is desirable. Social processes are sometimes explained in terms of metaphysical and economic forces of which human beings are merely the instruments; at other times it is implied that the economic needs of human beings are the original dynamic force in history, and that Communism is inevitable because it means the satisfaction of those economic needs. This combination of contradictory viewpoints is an essential part of Marxism, and one of the chief sources of its strength. Emphasis on desirability alone would provoke arguments as to whether Communism was actually better than other systems; emphasis on inevitability alone would lead to a fatalist passivism. By fusing both conceptions, at a sacrifice of logical coherence, Marxism provides itself with an answer to any kind of criticism.

The economic arguments for the inevitability of Communism have been discussed in a previous chapter. The metaphysical arguments will be examined in this section. It has sometimes been doubted that Marx himself placed any faith in these arguments; but they were undoubtedly used by Engels, and afterward by Lenin, and they have become a part of orthodox Marxist apologetics.[14]

The Marxist philosophy of dialectical materialism originated as an attempt to reconcile materialism and idealism. The materialism of the eighteenth century, with its belief in mechanistic determinism and its conception of the human mind as the passive recipient of sense impressions, had been unable to explain the capacity of the mind to distinguish between truth and error, to organize sense impressions into systems, and to change the world through creative activity. It had, moreover, failed to account for the appearance of novelty, of genuine change, in natural processes. Such difficulties had resulted in the growth of German idealism, which had taken as its starting-point the activity of mind and — in contrast with the mechanists who had interpreted mind materialistically — had explained the capacity of the mind to discover truth by interpreting matter idealistically. Marx and Engels attempted to combine these two attitudes. They abandoned idealistic interpretations of the universe, denying the existence of God and regarding mind as a product of matter; but at the same time they retained the idealistic belief in the activity of mind. Human beings were not merely the mechanically determined products of natural processes; they were also capable of creative action upon the world. Such a conception did not solve any of the theoretical problems involved; it merely ignored them. That the mind had evolved out of matter and was dependent upon the physical structure of the brain was a plausible hypothesis; but how it had acquired its capacity for independent judgment remained mysterious. These difficulties were, however, brushed aside by Marx as of no practical importance. Man proved the truth of his ideas by testing them in practice. To say that Marxism teaches the unity of theory and practice is merely a truism, since all philosophical systems do this; theory always influences practice, and any practice always implies a theory. What Marxists mean when they define Marxism in these terms is that theory is subordinated to practice.

The Marxists, however, have not been content with this pragmatic attitude. They have also retained from the idealism of Hegel a number of metaphysical doctrines which are incompatible with materialism. Hegel emphasized the weaknesses of mechanistic determinism — in particular, its inability to account for novelty and growth — and used them as arguments for idealism. The universe was supposed to be the expression of a divine mind, and the laws of thought were also the laws of things; by examining mental processes one could thus arrive at a genuine understanding of material realities. According to Hegel the universe was a unity whose parts were in constant movement and were constantly interacting upon each other. In studying movement and change the human mind discovered contradictions, and these contradictions were objective realities; the universe was built out of pairs of opposites. Change was real; and since the universe was the expression of a divine mind, change could be viewed eulogistically, as development. Such changes were of two kinds: a change in quantity might become a change in quality; and two opposites might be synthesized into a higher unity. The human mind arrived at truth by synthesizing opposite conceptions, each of which was partially true; and this 'dialectical' process was characteristic also of the divine mind by which matter was animated. Thus, the chief dialectical laws were those of interaction, of the unity of opposites, of novelty, and of development.

When Marx, according to his own statement, turned the dialectic right side up and interpreted it materialistically, there was no longer any justification for assuming that the laws of thought could be used to interpret nature. Obviously the doctrine that mind is material cannot mean that mental and physical processes are identical; there is still a difference between psychology and physics, just as there is between organic and inorganic matter.[15] The Hegelian dialectic continued to have a negative value; the weaknesses of mechanistic materialism which had been emphasized by the idealists still existed. But the positive doctrines of Hegelianism no longer had any justification. Thus the real significance of the dialectical laws, when they are combined with a materialistic philosophy, is that they formulate those situations where chains of cause and effect cannot be discovered. They do not supersede the traditional forms of logic or provide us with a new and superior scientific method; on the contrary, in so far as they still have meaning, they define the limitations to scientific method. Instead of enabling us to predict the future, they show under what conditions the future cannot be predicted. They apply, not to objective realities, but to the methods by which the human mind apprehends those realities. Beyond this they degenerate into mystical verbiage. It is, however, precisely in this mystical verbiage that Marxism discovers its metaphysical arguments for the inevitability of Communism.

The method of science is to isolate phenomena and thereby to discover invariable sequences of events; in so far as the scientist is successful, he makes possible prediction and control. Scientific method necessarily assumes a belief in determinism, because events which do not have sufficient causes are not amenable to scientific treatment; but to believe that all events must necessarily be determined is to make an assumption which goes beyond factual proof and to erect a method into a dogma. The discovery of invariable sequences of events is impossible to the extent that situations are characterized by interaction. When a number of different forces are all interacting upon each other, one cannot isolate any chains of cause and effect; events may still be determined, but it is a practical impossibility to show how the determinism operates. In the natural sciences the interaction is often small, and a sufficient degree of isolation can usually be artificially created for experimental purposes. This has proved to be difficult in certain branches of modern physics; the physicist cannot isolate for purposes of study the movement of an electron because there is an interaction between the electron and the flash of light which the physicist uses in order to study it. This has been hailed by the Marxists as a proof of the scientific value of dialectical materialism. But dialectical materialism does not enable scientists to surmount the difficulty; it merely provides them with a set of phrases for stating the fact that such a difficulty exists. Similarly, dialectical materialism does not make possible any rigidly scientific sociology. In sociology any isolation of chains of cause and effect is impossible. Different individuals, classes and nations, factors of economics, politics and ideology, are all constantly interacting upon each other; interferences by independent geographical (e.g. droughts) and biological (e.g. births of men of genius) factors are always frequent. Sociology, therefore, can never become an exact science. Every phenomenon must be studied in relation to the total situation, and our reading of events must be based not so much on scientific method as on a capacity to grasp the meaning of a situation, of a kind which is more intuitive than logical. The dialectical law of interaction, instead of making possible a new kind of science, is thus a warning against any excessive use of scientific method in human affairs. In practice — and this was a meaning frequently given to it by Lenin — it means reliance on common sense rather than on theory.

The law of the unity of opposites means partly that in attempting to describe movement and change the human mind arrives at contradictions, and partly that natural phenomena can sometimes be analyzed into opposing forces. The former of these meanings has reference merely to certain verbal paradoxes. Thus, when an object is moving, it both is, and is not, in a particular place at a particular moment; or when a man is becoming bald, there is a moment when he can be described as both bald and not bald. Such contradictions, which have fascinated metaphysicians since the time of Zeno and have occasionally (as in the case of Bergson) been made the basis of a mystical philosophy, are merely tricks of verbal legerdemain. Marxists love to emphasize them, but they have no practical importance; the opposites are in the human mind, not in the external world.[16]

Having thus, by playing tricks with language, acquired a belief in the universality of opposition, the Marxists then plunge into the study of the natural sciences and of history, and proceed to find opposites everywhere. It is true that opposite forces can sometimes be distinguished at work in nature; this is an objective fact and not a verbal paradox. But there is no reason, except in Marxist mysticism, for asserting that all phenomena are unities of opposites; whether they are or are not is a matter for investigation. In practice, most phenomena, both in nature and in society, can be analyzed not merely into a single pair of opposites but into a much larger number of different forces. It is merely a metaphor to apply the word 'opposite' to many of the contradictions which Marxists discover with such profusion in nature — to the 'opposition' between life and matter, for example, or between animals and their environments. Marxists frequently become intoxicated with a mystical passion for discovering opposites everywhere and appear to be wholly incapable of distinguishing between mental operations and objective natural processes. Engels, for example, believed that the fact that two minuses made a plus was an example of a dialectical process actually at work in nature. But the fact that $a - bc + b^2$ is another way of saying $a - b(c - b)$ tells us nothing about the external world. The reason for this insistence upon the universality of the unity of opposites is, of course, that it provides Marxists with a justification for viewing capitalist society as a conflict of opposites. As matter consists of positive and negative electricity, so capitalism consists of the bourgeoisie and the proletariat. But the assumption that the same laws apply to both politics and physics, in addition to being untrue, does not even support the conclusions which Marxists deduce from it. In physics opposites combine to form higher unities; in politics, according at least to the Marxists, one opposite will destroy the other. The phrase 'unity of opposites' is conveniently vague, and is used in Marxist literature to describe both the unity of opposites in nature and the opposition of opposites in society. Lenin discovered a class struggle — i.e. a 'conflict' between positive and negative electricity — in every particle of matter, and used this fact as an argument for Communism.[17] But if we are to deduce our politics from our physics, it would seem that we should be Fascists rather than Communists. Negative electricity does not destroy positive electricity; matter is composed of the two together, in perpetual 'conflict.' This resembles the Fascist theory of the state.

The Marxist emphasis on the appearance of novelties has a negative value, in that it involves a denial of materialistic determinism. The universe cannot be wholly explained in terms of mechanistic causation; genuine change is possible. Thus, quantitative changes may become qualitative; when water reaches a certain degree of heat it changes into steam. Of greater significance is the fact that a whole, such as living organism, may be more than the sum of its parts. Matter, organized in a certain way, becomes a living creature; a living creature operates in accordance with laws which differ from those which apply to the matter of which it is composed. At some period in the history of the earth, life, one must suppose, emerged out of dead matter; at various stages in the evolutionary process mutations have occurred, bringing into existence new species; until finally man appeared, a creature qualitatively different from other animals. Dialectical materialism does not, however, enable us to understand such changes nor can they be predicted unless we have had previous experience of them; dialectical materialism merely states the fact that such changes have occurred. The manner in which matter becomes organized into new compounds and acquires new properties remains mysterious. Marxism endeavors to explain novelty and growth by means of its doctrine of opposites. A thesis is negated by its antithesis, which is followed by a negation of the negation; in other words, by a synthesis. A seed dies, and from its death springs new life. Such statements have no scientific value; they are merely metaphors, which explain nothing. They do not enable us to predict what novelties will be like or when they will occur. The Marxist belief that dialectical materialism makes it possible to predict novelties is, in fact, a contradiction in terms; if an event is a genuine novelty, it is, by definition, unpredictable. The original core of truth in the Marxist verbiage of thesis, antithesis, and synthesis was the fact that the human mind often discovers truth by synthesizing contradictory ideas. This process can also be traced occasionally in the pendulum swing of action and reaction between opposing intellectual tendencies in society. But it cannot be applied either to nature or to the material development of society unless one believes, with Hegel, that a divine mind is immanent in the universe and that the laws of thought are also the laws of things. Marxists use the doctrine of novelties in order to prove that capitalism will change in Communism. But if, as Marxists believe, the Communist revolution means a qualitative change in social development, then it cannot be predicted; if, on the other hand, as it is reasonable to suppose, it does not involve any such qualitative change, then (as was argued in the previous chapter) it would not produce all the beneficial consequences which Marxists have expected.[18]

Similarly dependent upon belief in a divine mind is the dialectical law of development — a law which, according to Lenin, is 'absolute.' This Hegelian conception was an inheritance from the Christian tradition, with its belief in history as the working-out of God's plan for the salvation of humanity. Hegel was influenced in particular by certain mystico-heretical doctrines, which originated with the Book of Revelation, were elaborated by the Montanists in the third century, were transmitted to a number of heretical sects in the Middle Ages, and were revived in Germany during the Reformation. According to these doctrines history would end in a terrestrial millennium, an Age of the Holy Ghost, when men would obey the impulses of God in their hearts, and laws and institutions would become unnecessary. In other words, the state would wither away and mankind would enter the kingdom of freedom; but this Christian kingdom of freedom could be achieved, not by economic changes, but only by a qualitative change in human nature brought about by divine grace. For a materialist, however, such a change in human nature can be regarded only as a utopian fantasy, and there can be no absolute law of development. A materialist has no objective standards by which he can measure growth and decay; he can assess events only in human terms which have no cosmic validity. Development, moreover, can be absolute only if time is limited; an endless development is impossible; if time is infinite, then cosmic processes must be cyclic. Actually Marxists judge development by the standard of economic productivity. This, however, is a human value which can claim no metaphysical support; and since the only justification for such a standard is the assumption that human behavior is primarily governed by economic need, there is no reason for supposing that development of this kind is inevitable. Economic growth is dependent upon the mental capacity of human beings to find methods of satisfying their needs; it may, therefore, be thwarted by destructive conflicts and by a failure of human intelligence to reconcile them. Similarly, it may be prevented by objective natural conditions. The raw material available in the world is limited, and may eventually be exhausted. The only basis for a permanent civilization is that men should put back into the earth as much as they take out of it; and it is possible that industrialism may be a mere temporary phase in human history, and that when the supply of metal, fuel, and timber has been exhausted, and a large proportion of the earth's surface has been reduced to desert by soil erosion, mankind will be driven back to a much more primitive way of life. The course of human history has not hitherto been characterized by any unilinear development. On the contrary, a dozen different civilizations have advanced up to a point and then degenerated. Progress is possible, but it is by no means inevitable; and whether it occurs is not determined by any dialectical laws but is contingent on human intelligence.

In so far, therefore, as the dialectical philosophy is true, it offers no support for Communism; and in so far as it serves to justify Communism, it is not true. It is true that the universe is characterized by interaction, and that natural and historic processes exhibit certain discontinuities which cannot be described in terms of mechanistic causation. It is not true that the universe is composed of pairs of opposites, that these opposites tend always to become synthesized into higher unities, and that development is absolute. It is true that society can be analyzed into a number of different interacting forces, that the clash of these forces must produce constant changes, and that such changes may be qualitative and dialectical and not merely quantitative and mechanistic. But there is no metaphysical justification for dividing society into a single pair of opposites — bourgeoisie and proletariat — or for assuming that their conflict must produce the higher synthesis of Communism.

VI. The Spiritual Basis of Progressivism

VI. The Spiritual Basis of Progressivism

IF ONE considers the Marxist movement in terms only of the doctrines which it preaches, then it is impossible to understand why it should exercise such a compelling power over the minds of men. A metaphysics which declares that the future is determined, a sociology which traces all human ideals and aspirations to a basis in material needs, an economics which is riddled with the most elementary fallacies and with predictions which have not been realized — how is it that such a system can have inspired the pertinacious and self-sacrificing heroism with which Marxists have fought Fascism in Spain and Austria and have faced torture and execution in the prison camps of Mussolini and Hitler? What motive caused such men as Marx and Lenin themselves to abandon comfort and respectability and to choose poverty and obscurity in exile? Whatever elements in human society may be accounted for in Marxist terms, there is one phenomenon for which Marxism offers no explanation: the behavior of the Marxists. As long as one judges the Marxist movement only through a logical examination of its intellectual principles, the keystone of the entire system is missing.

The question of motive has been persistently ignored in Marxist literature; yet unless one answers this question, the whole left-wing movement becomes unintelligible. And when this question is satisfactorily answered, it provides a standard by which the Marxist program can be judged and, in part, condemned.

Marx himself sprang from a prosperous German bourgeois family, and was given a university education by his parents, who expected him to become a lawyer. At that time, however, German society was fermenting with the ideas put in

circulation by the French Revolution; the abolition of absolutist monarchies and of the powers of the feudal landowning
caste, the creation of a liberal society which would establish
the rights of man, the realization of freedom and democracy —
these were the hopes of the younger German intellectuals.
After leaving the university, Marx devoted himself to revolutionary activity, on behalf of those liberal-bourgeois doctrines
which German progressives had acquired from Great Britain
and France. He soon discovered, however, that the bourgeois
program had its limitations, and that its practical aims were
much narrower than its ideals. In theory it proclaimed a universal freedom and equality, but in practice it was restricted
by the economic interests of the bourgeois class; its freedom
meant chiefly a freedom to buy in the cheapest market and sell
in the dearest; and when it spoke of equality, it thought of
equalizing the self-made man of money with the landed aristocrat. The bourgeois liberalism of Great Britain and France,
which had begun as a universal human idealism, was becoming identified with the viewpoint of the merchants and the
manufacturers. Within the framework of the society created
by the bourgeois revolutions was developing an industrial
society under which a propertyless class were chained to labor
in the factories. The bourgeois nations might have established
representative government, guaranties of civil liberty, and the
equality of all men before the law; but the ideals of bourgeois
society were merely a mockery to the hundreds of thousands
of wage-slaves in the coal mines and the cotton mills. To this
problem Marx found an answer in the ideas propounded by
the French Utopian Socialists, Saint-Simon and Fourier, who
had declared that industry ought to be owned co-operatively
by the workers instead of by private entrepreneurs. But
whereas the Utopians had merely advocated Socialism as a
desirable ideal, without considering the struggle which
would be necessary in order to overcome the opposition of the

capitalist class, Marx declared that only the workers themselves, by revolution, could achieve the Socialist ideal. Two
revolutionary movements, and not one only, were needed in
such countries as Germany; first the bourgeoisie must overthrow feudalism, and afterward the proletariat must transform a bourgeois society into a Socialist society. And having
adopted this faith in a proletarian revolution which would
bring about Socialism, Marx fused it with the philosophy of
perpetual dialectical development which he had acquired,
during his university career, from a study of Hegel, and proceeded to an examination of the English writers on political
economy, and in particular of Ricardo, in order to find an objective justification for it.

Throughout this mental evolution the determining element
was Marx's acceptance of the ideals of the eighteenth-century
liberal enlightenment, the ideals of human liberty and equality. He had found corroboration for these ideals in a critique
of religion, though it is important to realize that the only
kind of religion which he investigated was that passivistic
pietism which was encouraged by the German reactionaries
under the aegis of the Holy Alliance and which taught men
to endure poverty and oppression in this world in order to be
rewarded in the hereafter. And having concluded that this
promise of happiness in heaven was a delusion, that such beliefs were merely a reflection of an evil social system and were
deliberately inculcated by privileged classes in order to keep
the masses from rebellion, and that religion was the opium
of the people, Marx declared that 'man is the highest being
for man,' and consequently that 'all conditions must be revo-
lutionized in which man is a debased, an enslaved, an abandoned, a contemptible being.' [1]

This humanistic idealism was the mainspring of Marx's
career. 'It is our business,' he declared, 'to order the empiri-
cal world in such a way that man shall have truly human ex-

periences in it, shall experience himself to be a human being.'
And it was because the proletariat under capitalism was degraded to a sub-human mode of life that Marx became a
prophet of revolution. According to the doctrines which he
adopted, Marx could not, without inconsistency, adopt an
attitude of moral indignation; the bourgeoisie were limited
by the viewpoint of their class, and their activities were
determined by their position in the social structure. The
Marxist interpretation of history justifies everything and can
condemn nothing. But Marx never became a genuine Marxist.
He was faithful always to a nobler and more universal idealism
which his own theories negated; and his writings are shot
through with a bitter hatred of the injustices and wicked-
nesses of capitalism. It is its Hebraic passion for social justice,
and not its dreary and often fallacious chains of reasoning,
which has made *Das Kapital* the bible of twentieth-century
revolution.

Marx, however, never idealized the proletariat. It was
precisely because the proletariat had become less than human
that Marx was a revolutionist. In the proletariat, he declared, 'the human being has lost himself'; 'the withdrawal
of all humanity, and even of the semblance of humanity, has
been practically completed.' Paradoxical as it may appear,
the purpose of all Marx's career was to abolish the proletariat.
He recognized, however, that whatever oppressed classes receive as a gift, as charity, does not benefit them. The proletariat could be humanized only by itself, through its own efforts. Only the inspiration of a social ideal and the struggle
to achieve it, with the discipline and the heroism which such
a struggle produces, could regenerate the workers and transform them into human beings. But 'when the proletariat is
victorious, it has not thereby in any way become the absolute
aspect of society, for it is only victorious inasmuch as it
abolishes itself and its opposite.' [1]

The doctrines with which the Marxist movement has become identified — the dictatorship of the proletariat, the abolition of private property in the means of production, centralized planning of the economic system, the steady increase of economic productivity — are, in reality, not ends in themselves but merely instrumental. They are the means which Marx proposed for the realization of a humanistic society. He acquired them through a fusion of Hegelian metaphysics, English economics, and French Utopian Socialism. But what is fundamental to Marxism, and what supplies the driving-force to the whole left-wing and progressive movement, is the hope of creating a society in which all men shall live as human beings and shall have truly human experiences. And in fighting for this ideal modern progressivism is the heir of whatever is valuable in the civilization of the past, for the humanistic ideal is the essence of the religious and philosophical tradition of western Europe.

The slogans which were adopted by the liberal revolutions of the eighteenth century — liberty, equality, fraternity: life, liberty, and the pursuit of happiness — were attempts to define this ideal; but they did not express it fully because their emphasis was mainly negative. Early liberalism thought primarily of protecting the individual against arbitrary governments. It did not find it necessary to guarantee rights which were positive as well as negative; it spoke — in America — of the pursuit of happiness, but what this phrase meant was never translated into concrete realities. The true purpose of twentieth-century progressivism is to complete liberalism by giving it a positive as well as a negative content. The positive meaning of liberalism is that the individual shall have the opportunity fully to realize himself as a human being. This self-realization can be achieved only through work. It is a frequent modern tendency to suppose that conditions of labor must necessarily be inhuman; and that the individual can achieve a full humanity only in his hours of leisure. The en-slavement of man to the machine is defended on the ground that it makes possible a high standard of living and a short working day. This attitude is sometimes expressed by Com-munists as well as by defenders of capitalism, and it can be found in the writings of Marx himself, who declared that 'the realm of freedom ... lies beyond the sphere of material production in the strict meaning of the term,' and that 'the shortening of the working day is its fundamental premise.' [2] But a system which allows men to be human only when they are not working is fundamentally inhuman; leisure is sub-ordinate to work, and its chief purpose is to serve as a prepara-tion for it. It is impossible to split human lives into two com-partments; human life is essentially a unity, and if men are slaves in their work, they will be slaves also in their leisure. A truly human mode of existence is one in which men can ex-press themselves in work, performing tasks which they have themselves chosen, of which they cannot be deprived without their own consent, in the successful performance of which they can find pleasure and pride, and through which they can be of service to society. The various physical and psychological needs which govern human nature — the need for economic support, the need for social approval and esteem, the need for aesthetic pleasure and creative self-expression, and the need for service to an ideal — cannot be separated from each other without depriving men of their humanity; and the only truly moral activity is the activity in which all of them are satisfied at one and the same time. A human society is a society in which all men are guaranteed the right to work, and in which through work they can satisfy their spiritual needs in addition to obtaining economic support. Such a society embodies the principle of functionalism; every individual, by freely pursuing his own chosen activity, contributes to the welfare of the whole, and no individual capable of work is condemned to inaction or to tasks which are unnecessary or socially harmful. The fundamental evil of modern capitalism is that it deprives men of their right to express themselves in work. The worker is merely the instrument of the economic machine; he has no control over the conditions of his labor; his work serves to enrich a small leisure class rather than to benefit the whole of society; and he is subject to dismissal and unemployment whenever the workings of the system and the will of his employer so decree. The spiritual meaninglessness of the life to which they are subjected, rather than poverty and inequality, is the cardinal grievance of the proletariat.

Modern capitalism is, however, not a fulfilment of the ideals of eighteenth-century liberalism. The early liberals failed to give the doctrine of natural rights an explicit positive content only because, before the growth of large-scale industry, such explicitness was unnecessary. The ideal of *laissez-faire*, as it was first formulated by Adam Smith, assumed a society in which the ownership of property was widely distributed. Manufacture would be carried on by small producers, each of whom would express himself in his work because he was the owner of it. The ideal of *laissez-faire* meant that government should no longer grant privileges and monopolies to corporations or impose regulations restricting the freedom of the small producers. *Laissez-faire* thus meant economic democracy; and the deduction that large-scale corporations should be immune from democratic control is a grotesque perversion of the original doctrine.[3] A similar perversion has been the history of all the natural rights of the early liberals. According to John Locke and to the American Constitution, men possess rights to life, liberty, and property. The true meaning of this doctrine is plain; men cannot enjoy a truly human existence unless they are guaranteed against arbitrary deprivations of life and liberty and unless they are owners of property. Of these three rights the most fundamental is the right to property. Property means economic self-support. Only by the ownership of property can men fulfil themselves in work. If men are without property, they are slaves, no less than if they are subject to execution or imprisonment at the arbitrary will of the government. To interpret the right to property, as was done in the nineteenth century, as meaning merely that a corporation has a right to make a profit on its investments, is an astonishing misinterpretation of the ideals of John Locke and Adam Smith and Thomas Jefferson. The right to liberty does not mean that some men may enslave others; it means that all men shall be free. Similarly, the right to property does not mean that some men may monopolize property; it means that all men shall own property. Since the decline of the small producer and the growth of large-scale industry, however, the right to property must be redefined. Under modern conditions it means that all men have a right to a job, and that a job constitutes a property right.

In rediscovering the positive content of the liberal ideals, however, Marxism has forgotten their negative significance; and these are equally important. Men have a right to work at tasks which will promote the welfare of society; but they have a right also to be free from any kind of arbitrary interference. A truly human existence is impossible without freedom of occupation (the right to choose one's own work), without civil freedom (the right to be immune from punishment except for crimes which have been proved by due process of law), and without intellectual freedom (the right to form one's own opinions through a free study of different viewpoints, and to express them freely, both in speech and in writing). The greatest danger of twentieth-century civilization is that the insecurity and the spiritual emptiness of life under capitalism may make men willing to sacrifice these negative freedoms in the hope of finding, under a dictatorship, a positive self-fulfilment. Such a positive self-fulfilment, of however perverted a kind, is offered by all the totalitarian states, Fascist as well as Communist. The purpose of the Nazi movement — the domination of the world by force — is evil; but it is at least a purpose which gives some kind of meaning to the lives of the German people, and in the pursuit of which unemployment can be abolished and each individual can be assigned a function to perform. And democracy can defeat the totalitarianisms only if it can create a society which is genuinely animated by the pursuit of a civilized way of life and in which each individual can be of service to the whole.

Freedom, in the full sense of the word, is both negative and positive, and without it there can be no genuine morality. The free man is the man who is responsible to himself, choosing his own way of life, paying the penalty for his own errors, and learning from his own experiences. It includes a freedom to make mistakes, provided that one is not protected from the consequences of them; and it is therefore incompatible with paternalism, or with governmental control which goes beyond the negative function of preventing men from injuring each other. Only in a free society can men transcend the morality of the tribe, which means merely obedience to laws and regulations, and achieve that truly moral existence which means autonomy, self-awareness, and self-control. To believe in freedom does not mean to idealize human nature or to deny the weaknesses and follies of human beings. But it does mean the belief that all men are capable of moral growth, and that such growth is impossible except under conditions which encourage it. In proportion as men are free, or struggle to become so, they become worthy of freedom; the exercise of responsibility, under conditions which require courage, pertinacity, and self-sacrifice, can evoke those qualities even in men who have seemed the most degraded. Slavery, on the other hand, makes slaves; and whenever men have been required to live as slaves, and have accepted such a rôle instead of fighting to become free, they have always seemed to be incapable and unworthy of freedom.

Freedom and morality are qualities of the individual and not of the collectivity. Only the individual has a moral sense or a sense of responsibility; only individuals can evolve new ideas or make new discoveries. The moral and intellectual standards of men in a group are always lower than those of man as an individual. The individual is capable of sacrificing himself to the group, but the group is governed only by self-interest and is incapable of altruism. The individual may be a reformer, but the group is necessarily conservative; and when it changes, it does so only under the leadership or at the instigation of individuals. The only proper purpose of group organization is to enlarge the freedom of the individual; and any doctrine which, like both Communism and Fascism, denies the moral autonomy of the individual and subordinates the individual to the collectivity, is fundamentally inhuman. To say this is not to deny that individuals can fulfil themselves only through co-operation and through service to society; it does not mean any romantic exaltation of the individual ego. But there is an essential difference between free co-operation and the forced co-operation of the totalitarian states. Free co-operation means that individuals may freely associate themselves with co-operative organizations of their own choosing, and may freely leave them at their own discretion. Free co-operation means a minimum of centralized control and a maximum of local and functional self-government. The difference between free co-operation and forced collectivism is an example of that change of quantity into quality which is emphasized in the Marxist philosophy. When a group of men work together in a common task there is both freedom and co-operation. But when the principle is extended to an entire nation and an entire economic system, a qualitative change occurs; freedom disappears, and a bureaucratic dictatorship becomes necessary. True freedom is possible only in a pluralistic society, not under Communist totalitarianism.

The creation of a political and economic system which will reconcile the freedom of each with the freedom of all is a practical legislative task, which was partially achieved in the eighteenth century and which must be undertaken afresh in the changed conditions brought about by the Industrial Revolution. But morally and ideally there is no incompatibility between them, since those individuals who are the most free themselves are the most willing to encourage freedom in others. Domination over others, or interference with the rights of others, is always pathological. It is impossible to become free oneself, governing one's own behavior and accepting responsibility for one's own actions, without expecting, and indeed demanding, that others should display a similar capacity for autonomy and self-responsibility. The wish to rule and the wish to be ruled are the obverse and the reverse of the same psychological weakness; and both are equally repugnant to the free man. This is the basis of the revolutionary ideal of equality. The principle of equality does not involve any denial of the need for leadership, of the obligation of those who have greater abilities to exercise greater responsibilities. In a truly functional society men should exercise different functions according to their capacities; in the words of Thomas Jefferson, there should be 'an aristocracy of virtue and talent.' The meaning of equality is that each person is an end in himself; that all persons should be permitted to develop their talents as far as they are capable; that no man or woman should be treated as a mere instrument for increasing the wealth, the pleasure, or the power of others. Equality is incompatible with any caste system or with hereditarily determined class divisions; yet even a caste system which assigns a social function to each individual may be a less fundamental denial of the principle of equality than a system which proclaims equality, but which nevertheless allows one group to be used as an instrument for the enrichment of another. Medieval Europe recognized, however inadequately, a functional principle; and the society of the Middle Ages gave a greater recognition to individual dignity, and hence came closer to a genuine equality, than the society of twentieth-century industrialism.

The humanistic ideal cannot be deduced by processes of reasoning from any philosophy; it is a fundamental datum of the human consciousness, prior to all processes of reasoning and all philosophies. In the words of the Declaration of Independence, it is self-evident. It dominated the thinking of Marx so completely that he never became critically aware of it; and he proceeded to construct a philosophical system which omitted to account for it or to make it explicit. Marx acquired it from the intellectual climate of his time, which was that of liberalism. His whole work was built on the intellectual premises laid down by liberalism. It was in terms of the fundamental liberal doctrines that he criticized the society of bourgeois liberalism and demanded the construction of a new kind of society. The liberals of the eighteenth century had in their turn, however, derived their view of life from the European tradition to which they belonged; and the basic doctrines of that tradition came from the Jewish and Hellenic philosophies which had been combined in Christianity. The roots of European civilization are the Jewish doctrine of a God who governs all mankind and who requires righteousness and social justice, the Aristotelian doctrine of goodness as the fulfilment in an organic harmony of all the potentialities of human nature, and the Christian doctrine of the infinite value of every human soul. These doctrines have been the animating forces of European civilization; and from them are derived the liberal and Marxist faith in freedom and equality. The belief that the universe is basically rational and can be understood by the human mind; the belief in the unity of the human race and the denial of any doctrines of tribal, racial, or caste supremacy; the belief that goodness means moral growth under conditions of freedom and not obedience to any coercive code of rules; the belief that all men are ends in themselves and may not be used as instruments, and that each man should respect the free individuality of others by doing as he would be done by: these beliefs, which are the unstated assumptions upon which Marxism is based, are the cardinal beliefs of Christianity; and they are what chiefly distinguishes the tradition of European civilization from other traditions, such as that of India, which have partially denied them. Marxism, therefore, is a derivation from Christianity; and should properly be regarded as a Christian heresy.

It is, perhaps, unnecessary that a humanistic morality should be validated by means of a theology or a metaphysic; moral intuitions are prior to philosophical rationalizations, and a theology is merely an attempt to construct a picture of the universe which will give those intuitions their proper weight and will find a plausible explanation for them. Since, however, it is the nature of men to demand explanations and not to accept the existence of mysteries, there is danger that the decay of organized and dogmatic religion may lead to the growth of dogmatic materialistic philosophies; and any form of dogmatic materialism is incompatible with a genuine human freedom. The values which govern men's conduct and their view of the universe and of man's place in it are intimately connected; and the only values which can be justified in terms of a consistent materialism are wealth, pleasure, and power. For these, which are egoistic satisfactions, other individuals become instruments and not ends in themselves; and even if the satisfaction is to be enjoyed by the collectivity and not by separate individuals, it remains true that the individual as such has no rights and is merely an instrument of the collectivity. A materialistic philosophy is incapable, therefore, of becoming the basis of a free society; either each individual seeks egoistic satisfactions at the expense of others, or the individual will be subordinated to the egoism of the collectivity. The denial of rights to the individual in the Soviet Union, and the belief that individuals may be sacrificed whenever the interests of the collectivity appear to require it, are necessary consequences of the materialism of the Marxist philosophy. And if the inhabitants of the Soviet Union are still capable of moral energy and self-sacrifice, it is because of those aspects of Marxism which were taken from the Christian tradition: its assumption, derived from Christianity through liberalism, that freedom and equality are good; and its metaphysical faith, derived from Christianity through Hegel, in a necessary development toward a kingdom of freedom. The belief in the value of free individual development requires a spiritual interpretation of the universe; and though such an interpretation need not be formulated in a dogmatic religion, it must, at least, not be prohibited by the inculcation of a dogmatic materialism.

Although, however, it is impossible to deduce the value of freedom by processes of scientific reasoning, that value triumphantly justifies itself in its consequences. A free society, which gives independence to all the individuals in it, releasing and stimulating their moral energies, is superior to a slave society by any test which anyone might wish to apply. The purposes which a slave society sets before itself, and which it uses to justify its slavery, can always be attained more completely by a free society. Only a free society can achieve economic progress. The enormous technological development of the past hundred and fifty years is the direct result of the economic freedom created by the doctrine of *laissez-faire*. It is true, as the Marxists insist, that the bourgeoisie created *laissez-faire*; but it is a more significant truth that *laissez-*

faire made possible the growth of the bourgeoisie. The Industrial Revolution originated in England because England, since the Middle Ages, had been the freest country in the world. Only a free society can achieve cultural and intellectual development. Those rare periods of intellectual activity which have been responsible for whatever degree of civilization mankind has hitherto attained — the age of Periclean Athens, the age of the Italian Renascence, western Europe between the end of the Wars of Religion and the rise of the totalitarian states — have always been characterized by an emphasis on individual freedom. In the last resort a free society is superior to a slave society even in military strength and efficiency. A slave society may create a smoothly functioning military machine; but it does not have the same resources of individual energy and initiative, it cannot easily replace its leadership or maintain its morale, it is less able to evolve new methods of warfare, and when its machine encounters unexpected difficulties, it may succumb to sudden and total disintegration.

It is true that recent developments present the greatest threat to freedom since the present cycle of civilization began; but that is not because totalitarianism is superior to freedom. The totalitarian states are living parasitically upon the achievements of the free societies. All the technological methods which are being developed in Russia, all the scientific instruments of warfare which are being constructed for the German military machine, were invented by the citizens of free societies — by British and American scientists, and by German and Jewish scientists before the advent of the Nazis. Neither Nazi Germany nor Communist Russia has made any important contribution to human knowledge. The peculiar danger of the present situation is that the totalitarian society of the Fascists, by adopting the most advanced scientific methods and by subordinating all its energies to the single end of military power, may be able to acquire a military superiority over the free societies for a period long enough to crush them. Over a long period the greater capacity of the free societies for developing leadership and maintaining morale, and for making scientific and technological progress, will always give them the victory. But whether democracy will be able to survive for a period long enough to capitalize on its advantages is at present doubtful.

Freedom, therefore — in the fullest meaning of the word, not in the meagre and negative sense in which it is enshrined in the constitutions of bourgeois democracy — is the proper object of all political and social organization, and a necessary prerequisite for economic and intellectual progress. The belief in freedom is what gives moral energy to Marxism and to the whole left-wing movement in the modern world. That belief, however, is not made sufficiently explicit in the Marxist philosophy; a genuine freedom cannot be achieved in any society which is based on the principles of dialectical materialism, or which creates a totalitarian system, subordinates the individual to the collectivity, and establishes the rule of a dictatorial bureaucracy. The Marxist movement has adopted means which are incompatible with its real ends, and those means have then been erected into dogmas and themselves given the status of ends. The task of the progressive movement is to maintain the moral idealism, the enthusiasm for freedom and human development, which have characterized the Marxists; but to elaborate an economic program and a political strategy which will not make that enthusiasm futile.

VII. An American Program

VII. *An American Program*

I. AGAINST FANATICISM

ANYBODY who accepts the Marxist diagnosis of the maladies of the contemporary social system, and who is not blinded to realities by a fanatical confidence in the inevitability of a proletarian revolution, must necessarily succumb to an extreme pessimism. The possibility of a proletarian revolution in the United States is so small that it can be dismissed from serious consideration. A majority of the population must be classified as belonging to the middle class, among whom Marxism is incapable of winning any considerable support. Only one-third are industrial workers, and even among the industrial workers a large proportion are inhibited by ideological or practical reasons from accepting a revolutionary program. The only conceivable effect of any important development of revolutionary sentiment in the United States will be to stimulate the growth of a fanatical reaction, to weaken democratic processes and respect for civil liberties, and to bring about some form of Fascist or big-business dictatorship. For this reason the propagation of revolutionary Marxism does more harm than good and should be abandoned by all liberal-minded persons.

Even, moreover, if one were to assume that a proletarian revolution is a practical possibility, it is still difficult to view the future with any optimism. The Russian economic system is undoubtedly free from the more obvious weaknesses of capitalism, and in course of time it may conceivably achieve a reasonable efficiency. But the operation of it involves the rule of an all-powerful bureaucracy, the denial of individual freedom, and the indoctrination of the entire population into a remarkably dreary and irrational philosophy of life. Communism is a much nobler and more humane political creed than Fascism; but it is almost equally hostile to that free play of the intelligence which any genuine cultural development requires. If we accept the familiar Marxist doctrine that Communism and Fascism are the only alternatives before us, and that if we reject one then we must accept the other, it is difficult not to feel that mankind must, in either case, enter a new Dark Age, and that the freedom, the tolerance, and the intellectual growth which have characterized western Europe and the United States during the past two or three centuries have been merely a brief interval of sunlight in an otherwise dark and melancholy history.

Yet from a common-sense view an attitude of pessimism and defeatism is, in the United States, completely absurd. This country has everything which is needed to achieve a satisfactory economic system and a civilized way of life. It is the one major power which can hope to solve its problems without war, without revolution, and without dictatorship. It is true that the European nations are confronted by problems which are perhaps beyond peaceful solution. The vital need of Europe is continental unity — the obliteration of national boundaries and the integration of the different national economies into a single system; and the achievement of European unity, within any visible future, is probably beyond the wit of man to accomplish. Fortunately, however, Americans are not yet required to settle the difficulties of that unhappy continent. The question of foreign policy which at present confronts the American people — whether to take a militant part in opposing Fascism in Europe or to concentrate on solving America's internal difficulties, whether to increase trade relations with European nations in the hope of promoting world peace and an ultimate world economic unity or to decrease foreign trade and thereby to strengthen the stability of the American economic system — is one of the most important and complex questions which the United States has ever been required to answer. This problem is, however, not relevant to the present discussion. Whatever part America chooses to play in world politics, it is obvious that the primary danger of Fascism is at home and not abroad. Fascism is a disease which is liable to attack any society which is not healthy and vigorous; and the only way by which it can permanently be defeated is to build an economic and social system under which men can live prosperously and contentedly.

For the creation of such a system the United States has every material and psychological prerequisite. She is already by far the richest nation in the world, both potentially through the possession of raw materials and actually through her industrial system. She has within her own boundaries a large majority of the mineral and agricultural products which are needed by modern technology. She has such a large internal market that most of her industries do not require any considerable foreign trade. She surpasses every other nation in the development of science and technology and in the general level of education. She has a population habituated to optimism and enterprise and, in the main, to tolerance, whose spirit has never been broken by defeat in foreign war or by any destructive internal catastrophes. She inherits a revolutionary tradition of freedom, equality, and democracy, these ideals being written into the two documents with which her history as an independent nation begins. She has no relics of feudalism, no aristocratic ruling class, no privileged military or clerical caste, and no habits of regimentation or of obedience to an absolutist government. It is apparent that in the present historic epoch the task of preserving civilization will devolve primarily upon the United States. And it is obvious that if the United States succumbs to totalitarian barbarism, it will be the most remarkable example of the folly of the human race which has ever been recorded in the annals of history.

What is required is a rational approach to the practical problems of social engineering and the avoidance of any form of fanaticism. The fanatic is one who brings a religious intolerance to questions which need a scientific weighing of possibilities and a spirit of tolerance and compromise. In times of social stress fanaticism is often regarded as a virtue. But the fanatic, being capable of seeing only one side of a question, is usually blind to important facts; and he invariably provokes a corresponding fanaticism on the opposite side. Fanaticism thus makes democracy impossible. The art of democratic politics is the art of compromise; different groups with different interests must be brought together in support of a common, and limited, program. Tolerance and compromise are regarded by fanatics (both Communist and Fascist) as proofs of weakness, of lack of principle. It is true that a fanatical belief in some system of dogmas makes tolerance impossible; but history is strewn with the ruins of grandiose ideological constructions which once caused men to persecute and kill each other, and which survive only as proofs of the extraordinary follies of which the human race is capable. In reality, tolerance springs, not from lack of principle, but from adherence to the most fundamental of all moral and political principles — respect for the freedom and the right to self-expression of every individual. This principle is the spiritual basis of democracy; and for this reason there are certain attitudes — attitudes which threaten democracy itself — toward which tolerance would be suicidal. The right of a constitutionally elected government to govern, the right of a minority to carry on propaganda by peaceful methods, and the equality of all men and all races before the law — toward any forces which threaten these principles there can be no tolerance or compromise whatever. But with the exception of these fundamental matters, there are very few political disputes in which there are not valid arguments on either side; very few political groups are wholly selfish or wholly blind to wider interests; and the task of statesmanship in a democracy is to find a solution for each dispute which embodies whatever is sound in the arguments of each party to it. All disputes about matters of practice are capable at least of compromise, if not of a genuine reconciliation. The only arguments which are irreconcilable are arguments about ideas. Men only begin to shoot each other when they see immediate disagreements in terms of rival ideological systems. Civil wars are caused, not by disputes about dollars and cents, but by conflicts between capitalism and Communism, religion and atheism, the ideal of proletarian dictatorship and the ideal of racial imperialism. It is because the fanatic sees every dispute in terms of these irreconcilable ideologies that he is so dangerous. In the last resort, fanaticism can settle problems only by the appeal to force. But whenever force is invoked, its results (no matter which side is victorious) are likely to be very different from the hopes of those who first appeal to it. Force means dictatorship and terrorism; and all history proves that dictatorship and terrorism invariably endure long after the need for them has passed.

The error of the fanatic is that he believes in the possibility of a short-cut to a better society. But all social changes are necessarily gradual; men are creatures of prejudice and habit, and no elements in society change more slowly. The nations which today are democratic have achieved democracy only by a slow evolution extending through centuries. The foundations of English and American democracy were laid in the Middle Ages; it required a hundred years — from the Revolution of 1789 to the Boulanger episode and the Dreyfus case — to habituate democracy in France. When a society has a government which (like that of France in the eighteenth century) dams up the normal flow of change, a revolution is needed to overthrow it; but the real accomplishments of a revolution are always smaller than appears on the surface. A revolution can overthrow a decadent social system; but the creation of a new system is always slow. The France of Napoleon I, of Louis Philippe, of Napoleon III was not so markedly different from the France of Louis XIV.. Yet because changes are slow, it does not follow that they are not real. They may occur almost imperceptibly, but after any prolonged period of peaceful and gradual development a glance backward, which shows how change has accumulated, is often startling. Fanaticism, on the other hand, by attempting to accelerate the natural rate of change, often ends only by provoking a stubborn conservatism.

The history of the United States presents a significant case-study in the effects of fanaticism in the Abolitionist movement. In the eighteen-thirties and forties there appeared a well-meaning but misguided group of idealists, who were obsessed by the evils of slavery, who refused to understand the very genuine problems of the white race in the South, and who demanded immediate and total abolition. The result was the provocation of a corresponding fanaticism among the Southern whites, which precluded any peaceful solution of the problem and which led to the secession of the Confederacy. It is probable that economic causes would eventually have brought about the abolition of slavery by peaceful means. It is certain that the fanaticism of the Abolitionists resulted in a destructive civil war and in the ruin of the entire South; and that, by permanently embittering racial relations (during the Reconstruction period), it not only failed to establish that racial equality at which it aimed, but actually made its attainment slower and more difficult.

Almost every nation in the world today is in danger of becoming divided into two hostile armed camps. These pages are written in the conviction that there are more resemblances between the two extremist groups than either of them is willing to admit, and that the victory of either would, in the long run, have similar consequences; that the middle way, the way of gradual change, is not only the way which civilized people will prefer to follow, but also the only way by which it is possible to make any genuine progress; and that since both the champions of capitalism and the champions of Socialism are partly right and partly wrong, an enlightened program of reform will embody features out of both systems. In the following pages an attempt will be made, very tentatively, and in no spirit of dogmatism, to suggest how such a program should be constructed.

II. THE PRINCIPLES OF LIBERALISM

THE proper objective of a program of reform is to create conditions under which, in Marx's phrase, 'man shall have truly human experiences' and can live as a free, self-responsible individual. This objective is not achieved under capitalism as it exists today, nor can it be achieved by any form of Marxist Socialism. Capitalist democracy guarantees, at least on paper, those negative freedoms which are enshrined in the Bill of Rights, but it denies to a large section of the population that positive freedom which consists in self-expression through work. Marxist Socialism endeavors to remedy the primary evil of capitalism, but it does so only by subordinating the individual to the collectivity and to the bureaucracy in which the interests of the collectivity are supposedly embodied. A program based on the belief in freedom will, therefore, run counter to the conventional line of demarcation between capitalism and Socialism; from some points of view it will appear as Socialist, from others as reactionary. Such words are merely convenient ways of referring to very complex realities; and when, through frequent use in certain emotional contexts, they become charged with emotional associations, it is very easy and very dangerous to be led astray by them. The label which one chooses to attach to any particular political proposal is usually determined, not by a desire for scientific accuracy, but by one's political intentions. Political words very rarely remain emotionally neutral; some of them acquire favorable emotional connotations, while others are used mainly as terms of abuse. In reality, however, a pure capitalism and a pure Socialism have never existed; every social system is a compound of several different tendencies. What is usually meant by the word 'capitalism' is the economic system which prevailed in England and the United States in the nineteenth century, while by 'Socialism' is meant what is happening in the Soviet Union or what might conceivably happen in some other country which adopted similar principles. But a system mainly capitalist always contains elements of Socialism, and Socialist Russia contains elements of capitalism. Nor do nineteenth-century England and contemporary Russia exhaust the possibilities of social organization. Various other permutations and combinations can be made out of the elements of a social system.

In passing, it may be remarked that one powerful institution which cannot be labelled as either capitalist or Socialist is the Catholic Church. The economic program of the Church emphasizes the value of private property and is therefore opposed to Socialism; it is, however, also opposed to capitalism in its insistence on the right of the workers to belong to trade unions and to receive a living wage, its hostility to the stock-exchange manipulations of financiers, and its belief that certain industries, which are too important to be owned by private persons, ought to be socialized. The reason for the Catholic attitude is significant; the basis of the Catholic program is the belief that what is important is the religious salvation of the individual and that economic freedom is an essential prerequisite of it. The political activities of the Church are also governed by other considerations, in particular by a desire to maintain its own power and independence as an institution, it being assumed that men cannot find salvation without the Church's guidance; and for this reason it has often (as in Spain and Mexico) supported political groups which are opposed to economic freedom. The political practices of Catholics are, moreover, often very different from the political principles of Catholicism. Nevertheless, any economic program based on the belief in individual freedom will be similar to the program set forth in the encyclicals of Leo XIII and Pius XI and to the writings of such contemporary Catholic liberals as Jacques Maritain and John A. Ryan.[1]

For Americans, however, it is unnecessary to seek guidance from Europe. One of the greatest advantages enjoyed by the United States is that it was organized as a nation on liberal principles and that its whole national tradition is that of liberalism. The principles of a free society were fully grasped by the fathers of the American Republic, in particular by those of them who organized the Democratic Party in order to oppose the European policies of Alexander Hamilton and whose intellectual leaders were Thomas Jefferson and John Taylor of Caroline. The proper task of twentieth-century Americans is to apply the doctrines of Jefferson and Taylor to an industrialized society. Americanism is a word which every political party now tries to appropriate; and while the German-American Bund depicts George Washington as an American *fuehrer*, the Communist Party claims Jefferson and Lincoln as forerunners of Lenin. The American Way is, however, a phrase which, in spite of its misuse at the hands of capitalist politicians and sectarian fanatics, has a genuine meaning; and what it means is freedom and equality.

The most marked political characteristic of eighteenth-century Americans was their suspicion of governmental authority. Government was, at best, a necessary evil; and unless the people were on their guard, there was always danger that governmental officials would begin to claim tyrannical powers and to develop into a parasitical bureaucracy living idly at the taxpayers' expense. In Jefferson's words, 'eternal vigilance is the price of freedom.' The proper function of government was to prevent men from injuring each other; and this function should be performed by the enactment and enforcement of general laws, not by positive and specific acts of administration. The power of the executive branch of the government, in other words, should be restricted to an irreducible minimum. In order, moreover, to ensure democratic participation and control, all authority should as far as possible be decentralized. It was for this reason that Jefferson upheld the rights of the states against the federal government; he also wished to limit state powers for the benefit of township and county governments.

The doctrine that the preservation of freedom requires that governmental authority should be limited and decentralized is as true as it ever was. The growth of direct government administration of economic affairs, which today characterizes every country in the world, means everywhere the decay of individual freedom. The only economic system under which it is possible to ensure either freedom or stability is the system under which the necessary control of individual activities is performed partly by general laws and partly by the automatic processes of the system itself, not by specific acts of administration. An economic system should be as nearly foolproof as possible; in other words, the controls should, as far as possible, be automatic, and the successful functioning of the system should not require any unusual ability or disinterestedness in the officials of the government. Politicians can frequently achieve high office merely through ability to make speeches and through cleverness in the management of men; and that office-holders should also be idealistic and should have an understanding of economics is something for which we may legitimately ask but which can never be guaranteed. This is an important argument against any kind of planned society.

The perils of bureaucracy are fully apparent in the totalitarian states. A rapid growth of bureaucratic power is, however, visible also under the form of what has been called the 'crisis state' in the democratic nations, in particular in Great Britain, France, and the United States. The instinct which causes many Americans to view the crisis state with suspicion is healthy. Government participation in economic matters tends to be cumulative; every intervention to remedy a maladjustment causes maladjustments elsewhere, and leads to more intervention. The more the government interferes with economic activities, the more such interferences become necessary. The ability of the government to grant economic favors makes economic groups desirous of controlling the government; and economic rivalries become transformed into struggles for political power. Efficient governmental regulation cannot, moreover, be performed by democratic methods, neither can it be performed by a legislative body. This is particularly true in the United States, where the members of the Congress have always tended to be the political representatives of special local and economic interests, and where legislative intervention in economic matters has always involved a series of bargains and horse-trades between different pressure groups at the taxpayers' expense. In the United States the only official who represents the national interest, and not some special group, is the President; and efficient regulation of economic life can be performed only by the President and by those officials who are under his control. An American planned society would necessitate a dictatorship by the executive. Yet the argument that, in order to achieve a successful planned economy, it is necessary to make the President into a dictator, while entirely true, is unlikely to convince Americans. They will prefer to abandon the notion of economic planning.

Yet, while those who oppose the growth of bureaucracy are faithful to the American tradition, they appear to be in considerable danger of forgetting that the cause of this growth was the complete breakdown of the economic system and that the New Deal represents an attempt to cure intolerable evils. The kind of system which prevailed in America before 1929 is unworkable, and any attempt to restore it can result only in the same disastrous consequences. The answer to this problem is to change the rules which govern economic activity; to work out a new kind of system, under which the controls will be automatic and government intervention can be reduced to a minimum, but which will not mean periodic crises and depressions and permanent poverty for one-third of the nation.

The original economic basis of American democracy, and in particular of Jeffersonianism, was the widest possible distribution of private property. Each individual was independent of political and economic pressure because, as a property-owner, he was dependent upon himself alone for his own livelihood. In the eighteenth century this meant a society of small farmers. The Jeffersonians believed, moreover, that all wealth was produced by human labor, and that those who consumed without producing were living parasitically upon the labor of others. Their chief political objective was to prevent the growth in America of any parasitical class; for this reason they opposed Hamiltonian finance, which meant the creation of a *rentier* class who lived at the taxpayers' expense from government bonds and which encouraged the development of other financial devices enabling stock-exchange manipulators to juggle wealth into their own pockets. America was free from those forms of parasitism which prevailed in feudal Europe; but she was in danger of developing a new parasitical class of her own. She might, in the words of John Taylor, fall under the rule of an 'aristocracy of patronage and paper.' The chief economic principles of the Jeffersonians, therefore, were that each man should own the means of his own livelihood, and that no *rentier*, bondholding, or other parasitical class should be permitted to develop.

Jefferson, however, lived before the Industrial Revolution, which created a wholly new kind of society. The growth of large-scale industry has destroyed the old kind of private property; where corporations are involved, all property is now co-operative and not individual. Moreover — and this is its vital characteristic — an industrial society is necessarily dynamic. If equilibrium is to be maintained, nothing must interrupt the flow of goods and services and the circulation of money. New industries constantly develop, and old ones become obsolete, so that the wealth and labor of the nation must be constantly redistributed.

The only method by which such a system can be controlled automatically, without bureaucratic regulation or compulsion, is the method of the free market, as worked out by Adam Smith and the early classical economists. The essence of the free market is the utmost flexibility of prices and earnings. An increase in the demand for any commodity means an increase in prices and earnings, so that new capital and labor are attracted into the production of it; a decrease in the demand means a decrease in prices and earnings, and capital and labor seek other fields. As was emphasized in an earlier chapter, the automatic operations of the free market constantly redistribute labor according to the needs of society, yet no compulsion is exercised directly upon any individual.

Any interference with the flexibility of prices and earnings prevents the automatic functioning of the free market and makes bureaucratic regulation, and finally dictatorship, inevitable. To attempt directly to equalize wages means that labor is no longer automatically redistributed in accordance with social needs, and must eventually necessitate compulsion; if individuals are no longer attracted into understaffed occupations by the magnet of higher wages, they must be shifted into them by coercive governmental decree. To attempt directly to fix prices means that the price-system will no longer indicate what articles are being produced over or under the needs of the consumer; eventually governmental planners must undertake the responsibility of deciding what forms of industry are socially desirable or needed by the public.

The free-market system is the direct economic equivalent of political freedom and equality; and it is no accident that political and economic liberalism grew up in close association with each other. This interdependence still continues; it is impossible to destroy the free market and to establish an authoritarian economic system without also destroying political freedom and democracy. Under a free-market system each individual is free to choose his own occupation; and the only compulsion upon him is that, if he chooses an activity for which there is little social need, he must be willing to accept low monetary earnings. Under a free-market system what is produced depends upon what the consumer is willing to buy; the majority vote of the public, as determined by their purchases, determines the distribution of productive resources, just as it determines political power. Under any authoritarian economic system, moreover, the system is master of the individual, and its operations cannot be changed without a revolutionary overthrow of those who control it. In a free-market system, on the other hand, the individual can, if he wishes, separate himself from society (by, for example, adopting subsistence farming); and the operations of the system can be constantly improved by the democratic method of educating the consumer.

It has become customary to describe the free-market system as chaotic and to emphasize the superior merits of economic planning. The free-market system is chaotic only in the same sense as democracy is chaotic by contrast with dictatorship. In reality, the free-market system serves the public much more completely than could ever be done by economic planning. All those delicate and inconceivably complex economic operations which satisfy the needs of the consumer in a modern society could not possibly have been planned, even by the most superhuman group of planners. They have developed, by a kind of organic growth, as a result of the rewards which are offered to any individual who can anticipate a new consumer demand or satisfy an old one more efficiently than has been done hitherto. It would be easy for some catastrophic political convulsion to destroy this economic organism; it would be quite impossible for any group of authoritarian planners to reconstruct it.

Certain considerations are habitually forgotten by the advocates of planning. In the first place, a free society is necessarily an imperfect society. Freedom includes a freedom to make mistakes, to act contrary to the interests of society, and to disagree with one's fellow citizens. The belief that society can become perfect has always involved, as a necessary corollary, the belief that the individual should be merely an instrument of the collectivity. In the second place, it is impossible to construct a system which will not involve hardships for individuals. Under any system industries will become obsolete, mines will become exhausted, and occupations will become overcrowded; whenever this happens, workers will find that their skills have become useless or that they must move from one part of the country to another. In the third place, mistakes will be made under any system; men will fail to anticipate consumer demand correctly and will develop industries above or below the economic need for them. The difference between a free-market system and a planned system is not that a planned system makes fewer mistakes; on the contrary, its mistakes are likely to be more numerous, since the planners do not have sufficient personal inducement to plan wisely. The difference is that under a planned system the penalty for mistakes is paid, not by those who make them, but by the whole society; the public must accept whatever goods the planners choose to give them, even though they might have preferred goods of some other kind or of a better quality.

The case for economic *laissez-faire* is irrefutable. Yet almost all the advocates of *laissez-faire* appear to be totally blind to the realities of the present situation. They ruin their own case by identifying *laissez-faire* with what actually happens under capitalism. Opposing any government interference with industry, they become defenders of monopoly, stock-exchange manipulation, low wages, excessive profits, the business cycle, and periodic crises and depressions. It is, however, plain to everybody but Wall Street bankers and professors of economics that the operations of uncontrolled capitalism have become intolerable. And since, in theory, any maladjustment in a free-market system ought to disappear automatically through the operations of supply and demand, it is obvious that practice has not corresponded with theory. Something prevents the controls from functioning. Our task is not to restore capitalism of the old kind by merely putting a stop to government interference, but to construct a new kind of *laissez-faire* system under which the controls will be genuinely effective.

The idea that, under *laissez-faire*, the government exercises no control over economic activities is untrue. *Laissez-faire* is not something which comes into existence of itself whenever the government leaves business alone; it is an ideal which has never yet been fully realized, and the means of its realization is the legal structure created by the government. The essence of *laissez-faire* is that the government guides economic life through general laws, not by specific acts of intervention; and how the system works depends upon the kind of legal structure within which it must function. It is the government which determines the rights of property-owners and the terms under which corporations may acquire charters. The United States, since the Civil War, has had a legal structure which has favored *rentiers* and monopolists at the expense of the remainder of the population; but it is also possible to create a *laissez-faire* system which will favor workers and farmers at the expense of *rentiers* and monopolists. It is, for example, essential to a *laissez-faire* system that the earnings of a particular industry should fluctuate in accordance with social needs; but it is by no means essential that those earnings should be divided between workers and stockholders in the proportions which have hitherto been customary. It is essential to a *laissez-faire* system that when the need for an industry decreases, those who work in it should be induced to look for other occupations by lower earnings. It is by no means essential that an industry should be allowed to force its workers to look for other employment, and meanwhile to shift the burden of supporting them onto the backs of the taxpayers, by dismissing them from its payroll. A legal structure under which each industrial corporation was obligated to provide, at whatever level its financial capacity allowed, for all its workers until they found employment elsewhere would not involve any violation of the principles of the free market.

In two important respects, moreover, the controls which regulate a free-market system have ceased to function automatically; and in these two respects government action of some kind has become essential. In the first place, monopolistic industries are immune from competitive pressure to reduce prices; government action to reduce monopoly prices is therefore necessary. In the second place — and this would appear to be the most important element in the whole economic problem — the rate of interest is partially immune from those operations of supply and demand which regulate prices. Without government intervention the rate of interest cannot fall below a certain minimum, and that minimum is, in modern society, higher than what the economic system requires. The government must, therefore, intervene in order to force down the rate of interest.

III. WHAT IS TO BE DONE?

THE formulation of a progressive program can be undertaken by three different methods. In the first place, one can examine capitalism as it exists today in order to discover its basic economic weaknesses, and can then ask what changes are needed in order to create an economic system which will function more efficiently and more smoothly. In the second place, one can define one's conceptions of a desirable social order, based on the ideals of freedom and equality, and can inquire in what ways capitalism has most notably violated those ideals. In the third place, one can examine the economic interests and political psychology of the various underprivileged classes, and can then proceed to recommend a plan of action which will have an equal appeal to all those classes and which will, therefore, be capable of winning the support of a sufficient majority of the electorate to be politically possible. The thesis of this section is that each of these methods leads to the same results, and that, from whatever point one begins one's investigations, one will arrive at the same two cardinal defects in the present order. There are two key features of the capitalist system where changes of a radical nature will be found to be imperative. The first of these is the unearned income which accrues to the property-owning classes, and the second is the status of the wage-earner in industry. The two main items in any progressive program should be to reduce the share of the national income which goes to the *rentier* class, and to give the worker in large-scale industry the status of a property-owner.

The most obvious economic weakness of capitalism is its inability to operate at full capacity. Even before 1929 American capitalism was using, at most, only eighty per cent of its equipment (this is probably a very favorable estimate); while since 1929 its inability to put to work the productive resources of the nation has been catastrophic. Idle money accumulates at the top of the social system; idle men accumulate at the bottom; and without radical changes in the functioning of the system, there is no way by which the money and the men can be brought in contact with each other.

Accumulations of idle money necessarily mean economic depression. As was stated in an earlier chapter, the total income of the nation during a given period is roughly equal to the total value of its production, and there can, therefore, be no deficiency of purchasing power as long as that income is being spent; if, on the other hand, money is hoarded in the banks, or if it merely circulates among the propertied classes (through stock-exchange speculation), instead of being invested in new capital goods or used to buy new consumers' goods, industry will be unable to operate at full capacity.

The main cause for the accumulation of savings is the inequality in the distribution of the national income. Almost all saving is done by the richer classes, who habitually spend on consumers' goods only a relatively small fraction of their incomes. According to the economic theory by which the capitalist system supposedly operates, these savings should automatically be invested in industrial expansion; and this was what normally happened during the nineteenth century. At that period it was necessary to encourage saving, in order to increase the productive resources of the community; and a high rate of interest was economically justifiable. Today, on the contrary, we have reached a point where a much slower rate of increase in capital equipment is desirable, and where the chief need is not to encourage saving, but to stimulate consumption. The only purpose of industrial expansion is to produce more consumers' goods, and such expansion will not be profitable unless the consumers' market can absorb these additional goods. The owners of capital will, therefore, be unable to find profitable investments for their savings unless consumption is increasing to a corresponding degree. Any growth in savings must be balanced by an equivalent growth in consumption. This, however, will not occur if the distribution of the national income is grossly unequal.

The inequality of incomes is, moreover, growing larger. Dividends and interest must be paid on the accumulations of invested capital; and as industry enlarges its capital equipment, and as men are replaced by machines, a larger proportion of the cost of each commodity will accrue to capital and a smaller proportion will represent wages. This tendency, which is inherent in capitalism as it now operates, was particularly rapid during the prosperity period of the twenties. In the value added by manufacturing, for example, that proportion which was paid out as wages and salaries dropped between 1921 and 1929 from 57.5 to 48.6 per cent, while the proportion which accrued to the various forms of ownership rose correspondingly from 42.5 to 51.4 per cent. While the wages and salaries paid by American industry during these years rose by 35 per cent, the earnings of capital increased by 76 per cent. The total value of the invested capital of the nation, consisting of public and private long-term debts, short-term debts, and the stocks of corporations, and representing claims to interest and dividend payments, amounted in 1930 to some three hundred and thirty-six billion dollars, a figure somewhat larger than the entire national wealth. These claims to unearned income have, moreover, been increasing much more rapidly than has production; in other words, the share in the total national income which accrues to the *rentier* class has been constantly growing larger. Long-term debts, which amounted in 1930 to one hundred and sixteen billion dollars, had increased by 219.8 per cent since 1912; during the same period the national wealth had increased by only 76.7 per cent, and the national income by only 94 per cent. Such figures mean that, without radical changes in the functioning of the economic system, it is a mathematical necessity that the income of capital should increase more rapidly than the income of labor, that savings should, therefore, increase more rapidly than consumption, and that economic depressions should, in consequence, grow more frequent and more catastrophic.[2]

For this condition the remedy which has most frequently been propounded — the raising of working-class wages — is inadequate. A large proportion of the claims to unearned income represent fixed debt charges, which industrial managers cannot alter. The owners of industry will always compensate themselves for any increase in wages by a corresponding increase in prices; and experience has shown that when wages rise, prices rise even more rapidly, the final result being a contraction of the consumers' market and an increase in unemployment.[3] The only ultimate solution is a drastic reduction in the claims of the property-owning classes to unearned income — a solution which sooner or later, either by peaceful or by revolutionary methods, will prove to be unavoidable.[4] Such a reduction can most easily be effectuated partly by drastic limitations on the right of inheritance, such as will gradually wipe out a large proportion of these capital claims, and partly by reducing all rates of interest and all stockholders' dividends. Changes of this kind can be accomplished only by political action and will, of course, be bitterly opposed by the privileged classes.

Excessive saving is not, however, the only economic weakness of capitalism. Almost equally significant is the fact that semi-monopolistic industries (and almost all the more important American industries are semi-monopolistic) have no sufficient incentive to pass on to the consumer the benefit of technical improvements, and that their most usual tendency is to restrict production rather than to reduce prices. The result of any technical improvement which is not accompanied by any considerable increase in production is that men are thrown out of work. According to the economic theory of capitalism these men should be absorbed into other industries; but this theory implies that the technical improvements are accompanied by price reductions, and that consumers have more money to spend on other goods. Without price reductions all the gains of the improvement accrue to capital, there is no enlargement of the consumers' market, and the consequent unemployment is likely to be permanent. Under monopolistic conditions technological unemployment is, therefore, a very likely occurrence.[5]

That industry must somehow be compelled to increase its production and lower its prices is generally admitted; but how this can be accomplished remains obscure. Any re-establishment of genuinely competitive conditions has been proved, during the fifty years which have elapsed since the first antitrust law, to be impossible; while price-fixing regulations by the government are difficult to make and still more difficult to enforce. Some different approach to the problem must, therefore, be discovered. The basic right enjoyed by industrialists which makes it possible for them to restrict production is their right to dismiss their workers when they find it profitable. What this means is that they can transfer to the government and the taxpayers the obligation of providing for their workers whenever they choose to do so, retaining the power, if they choose to exercise it, of hiring them again at a later date. The appropriate remedy is to make this practice impossible. If a job in corporate industry constituted a property right, so that the worker could not be deprived of it (except for legally proved misconduct) without his own consent, industrial managers would normally find it profitable to keep their workers fully occupied and would, therefore, expand production; and in order to sell their products, they would be compelled to lower their prices.

The notion that a job ought to constitute a property right, which is today in process of becoming the creed of the most important section of the American working-class movement, the C.I.O., may prove to be one of the most significant contributions made in the twentieth century to politico-economic theory — as significant, perhaps, in the economic sphere as were the eighteenth-century ideas of liberty and equality in the sphere of politics. It is, of course, revolutionary in its implications, and a prolonged struggle, partly political and partly on the trade-union front, will be necessary in order to secure legal recognition for it. But though such an idea is anti-capitalist, it is also, to an equal degree, anti-Communist. What it implies is that each industry should be the property, not of the state, but of the individuals who work in it; and that the relationship between different industries should be regulated, not by centralized planning and control, but by the mechanisms of the free market.

The application of such a principle must, of course, be accompanied by measures for ensuring full employment, since otherwise, if an industry were unable to dismiss its workers, it might be reluctant to give new jobs. And it would involve the abandonment, on the part of the workers, of claims to fixed wage and salary schedules. Wages would henceforth fluctuate in accordance with the earnings of the industry, rising when business was good and falling when those earnings decreased. The responsibility for the movement of labor from one industry to another, in order to meet changes in demand on the part of consumers, would, under such a system, belong to the individual workers and not to industrial managers. In other words, if the economic need for a particular industry decreased, its managers could not, as at present, dismiss their workers. Since, however, the earnings of the workers would decrease, they would themselves have a sufficient inducement to seek other jobs.

A consideration of the economics of capitalism leads, therefore, to two conclusions: that if the American economic system is to function with any reasonable efficiency, it will become necessary to diminish the claims of the capital-owning classes to unearned income; and that the most effective solution to the problems inherent in monopoly is the enforcement of a new conception of property rights which would give job-security to the working class.

If, however, we consider in what ways capitalism has most notably violated the ideals of freedom and equality, we shall arrive at identical conclusions. The cardinal moral defects of the present system are its inequality and its insecurity.

Economic equality is justifiable to the extent that higher earnings represent a reward for genuine services to the community; and according to the theory of the free-market system the correlation of rewards and services should be automatic. The profits of the entrepreneur who develops a new industry can be defended as a legitimate reward (even though such persons have often been considerably overpaid); and there is no reason why high earnings should not continue to accrue to individual entrepreneurs and to industrial managers. In earlier periods, moreover, savings represented genuine abstinence, which could appropriately be encouraged by means of a high rate of interest. No such defence can, however, be offered for the dividends of the contemporary *rentier* class, who invest their savings merely because they are unable to spend them in any other way; or for the wealth which is obtained through stock-exchange manipulation. For the inequality which arises from unearned income there is today no possible justification; and its existence not only causes economic crises and depressions, but also poisons the whole social system.

If the earnings of the *rentier* class are a violation of the ideal of equality, the workers' lack of job-security represents an equally fundamental violation of the ideal of freedom. Genuine freedom belongs only to the person who can choose his own occupation and who enjoys economic security. It becomes impossible if the free market is abolished, since coercive authority over the distribution of labor must then be exercised by the state; but it is equally impossible for the worker under capitalism, as long as he is subject to dismissal at the will of his employer and can have no assurance that, if he loses one job, he can find another. Freedom is dependent upon the ownership of property; and the worker can achieve freedom only by acquiring a property right in his occupation.

The third test which must be applied to any progressive program is that of political possibility; it must be capable of winning equal support both from the working class and from the farmers and the middle classes, promising them immediate economic benefits and harmonizing with their prevalent mental attitudes. Such a program will necessarily diminish the power and the wealth of the privileged classes; and as the Marxists have insisted, no privileged group ever forfeits its privileges without a struggle. It does not, however, follow that such a struggle must always be fought by violent or revolutionary methods. The correct deduction is that the only way to overthrow a privileged class is to mobilize against it every other element in the population. This means that any progressive program in the United States must be so framed as to appeal equally to all the different underprivileged groups. Any policy, on the other hand, which tends to benefit one of these groups at the expense of the others, and which, therefore, prevents them from uniting with each other, is likely to be defeated.

Inability to win political support is the cardinal weakness of all attempts to restore the kind of *laissez-faire* system which was supposedly characteristic of the nineteenth century. The kind of economic liberalism which demands the dissolution of monopolies, the restoration of competition, and the abolition of the tariff and of other government aids to industry, is politically impracticable. It requires a strong and impartial government, yet at the same time it cannot win support from any large section of the electorate; its government is to be a kind of *deus ex machina*, coming down out of the clouds to enforce economic sanity upon the human race. Unfortunately, however, governments come from below and not from above, and a program which benefits nobody in particular will not be supported by anybody in particular.[6] The assumption that a *laissez-faire* system is impartial and does not favor any particular class is, moreover, untrue. The United States in the nineteenth century had a *laissez-faire* system keyed for the benefit of big business. What is recommended in this chapter is a *laissez-faire* system keyed for the benefit of the working class, the farmers, and the middle classes.

The problem of finding a common platform upon which these classes can unite is the key problem of modern politics, and the failure to find such a platform has been responsible for every defeat of progressivism during the post-war years. In combination, these classes constitute an overwhelming majority of the electorate. It has, however, been singularly difficult to persuade them to form any political union except on the purely negative basis of defending democracy against Fascism.

The primary economic interest of these groups is to secure a different distribution of the national income. They have most frequently attempted to obtain this by the method of directly increasing their own earnings. The workers have demanded wage increases; the farmers have demanded increases in the prices of agricultural commodities. Wage and price increases tend, however, when carried too far, to contract the market instead of expanding it, and to provoke rivalries and antagonisms between the different underprivileged groups; while as long as the owners of industry are able to counterbalance any rise in costs by also increasing their selling prices, there is no redistribution of the national income. The ultimate effect of such policies is to increase the economic maladjustments within the system and to make political cooperation between workers and farmers more difficult, as has been fully exemplified during the past six years. Under a progressive government the working class, owing to its superior capacity for organization, usually obtains, or at least appears to obtain, the major share of the benefits; and the result is that farmers and other small property-owners swing back to conservatism. This was the primary cause for the Republican victories in the United States in 1938 and for the disintegration of the Popular Front in France. Some different approach to the economic problem must, therefore, be adopted.

The growth of proletarian Socialism has, moreover, made it appear that the ideals of the worker are fundamentally different from those of the small property-owner. The working-class movement has tended to become identified with the repudiation of private property in the means of production and with the belief that the entire economic system must be collectively owned and planned. The farmers and the petty bourgeoisie, on the other hand, are pronounced individualists, who are anxious to retain their status as owners of private property and who have always been reluctant to accept even a mild degree of co-operation or of government regulation. Working-class Socialists have been in the habit of despising the small property-owners as a retrograde class, and have accepted co-operation with them only with very considerable reservations; while the small property-owner is unlikely to ally himself with any working-class movement if he feels that he will be used merely as an instrument for the establishment of a proletarian dictatorship and that his ultimate fate will be similar to that of the kulaks in the Soviet Union. The ideal of proletarian Socialism is thus a barrier to the creation of an effective progressive movement.

The only fruitful approach to the political problem is to begin by inquiring what the working class and the farmer and petty bourgeois classes have in common with each other, and to elaborate a political strategy on that basis. What they have in common, first of all, is an interest in diminishing that share of the national income which accrues to capital; and any reduction in rates of interest and in other forms of unearned income would tend to benefit both groups equally. The farmers and the petty bourgeoisie are, and throughout American history always have been, a debtor class; and though they have most frequently sought relief from their economic burdens by raising the prices of their products, they would gain even greater advantages by a lowering of the rate of interest on mortgages and bank loans. Since the colonial period the most fundamental division in American politics has been the division between debtor and creditor groups; and a policy designed to assist debtors by reducing all interest rates would be in accordance with a long American tradition. Such a policy would, however, be of equal advantage to the working class, although it would affect them more indirectly. By diminishing that part of the income of industry which is paid out as interest on bank loans and as dividends to stockholders, it would make possible either a decrease in prices which would benefit all groups of consumers or an increase in wages which would not be accompanied by any increase in prices. Direct reductions in the income of the capital-owning classes would, therefore, unlike wage and price increases, benefit all under-privileged groups at the same time.

Equally important in the formation of a progressive politics is the question of ideology, which has often proved to be an insuperable obstacle to any farmer-labor combination. The assumption that the real aim of the working-class movement is the socialization of industry is, however (if the argument of this book is valid), unfounded. The real interest of the workers is to secure for themselves a property right in the industry for which they work. If this theory is accepted, then it becomes possible to define the aims of progressivism by means of a simple formula which has an equal appeal to the worker and to the small property-owner. That formula is that, as far as possible, every man should own the means of his own livelihood. No farmer or small businessman should undergo expropriation; no small property which is operated by its owner need be disturbed. The worker should, however, acquire a co-operative property right in industry, similar to the individual property right which the farmer has in his land. Society would be pluralistic, allowing a great variety of forms of ownership; but it would restrict the power of creditor groups to collect unearned income; and it would affirm the right of every individual to own property, of one form or another, in the means of production.

IV. THE RATE OF INTEREST [7]

THE program suggested in this chapter must now be examined in more detail.

Capital may be invested in two different ways. There is the capital which is contributed by the owners of an enterprise, who expect repayment in the shape of profits and dividends, and which is represented by stocks; and there is the capital which is lent by a bank or some other credit institution and which must be repaid in full. When apologists for the present system speak of capital, they usually mean capital of the former kind, which is risked by those who invest it. Actually, however, a larger proportion of the invested savings of the community consists of loan capital. In the three hundred and thirty-six billion dollars of capital claims existing in 1930, only about eighty-six billion dollars consisted of stocks, the remainder being all loan capital. This section will be concerned mainly with loan capital rather than with risk capital.

From the viewpoint of abstract justice there is no reason why loan capital should earn any interest at all — a fact which was generally recognized in the Middle Ages. The right of private property should mean, at most, that property cannot be arbitrarily confiscated; it should not include a right to collect an annual five or ten per cent on it. Abstractly, it would be as reasonable for the owner of money to pay somebody else for the trouble of looking after it for him as to expect payment for allowing somebody else to have the use of it.

The medieval prohibitions against usury broke down during the fifteenth and sixteenth centuries for good and sufficient reasons. Capital was scarce; and in order that industry might develop, it was necessary to promote the increase of capital by offering special encouragement to the practice of saving. Interest became, therefore, a reward for abstinence. No other device would have made possible that vast growth in the productive resources of mankind which has taken place during the past four hundred years. The present economic crisis in the United States is due primarily to two reasons: in the first place, the capital equipment of the country is now so enormous that a decrease in saving has become desirable; in the second place, certain groups receive such large incomes that they are unable to spend more than a small fraction of them, so that during prosperity periods savings actually increase instead of decreasing. The result is an accumulation of idle money which is neither lent to industry nor risked by investment in industrial expansion.

According to the theory of the free-market system this situation should lead automatically to a fall in the rate of interest. It is assumed that those who own savings are always eager to lend them, and that competition will lower interest rates to a level at which business entrepreneurs and corporations are willing to borrow; as interest rates fall, the incomes of the *rentier* class will be diminished, the incentive to save will be weakened, and the surplus of savings will disappear. Unfortunately, there is a fundamental difference between money and a commodity; money is a universal symbol of value, whereas commodities have only an exchange value. When there is a surplus of some particular commodity, its owners will be willing to sell at a loss; but nobody willingly lends money at a loss. Rather than lend at an abnormally low rate of interest, the owners of savings prefer to keep them. There is, therefore, a minimum below which, without government intervention, the rate of interest cannot fall; and this minimum is higher than the rate which the economic system now requires.[8]

The situation is complicated by other factors. In the first place, the leading New York banks have, for more than thirty years, been in the habit of co-operating with each other.

As Woodrow Wilson declared, the greatest monopoly in the United States is the monopoly of money. The result is that rates of interest are not lowered through competition, and that small businessmen cannot borrow as easily as can big corporations with which the bankers are connected. In the second place, the rate of interest, even on loan capital, includes an allowance for risk; and when the risk is great, the rate of interest will be high. Those who most need to borrow — farmers and small businessmen — are thus required to pay the highest rates. The influence of risk becomes even more important during a depression. Recovery can be achieved only by a revival of investment, for which reason a lower interest rate is economically desirable; instead of which lack of confidence tends to make financiers reluctant to lend except at a higher rate. Since, moreover, the interest rate on any particular loan is fixed at the time of borrowing and is not afterward subject to alteration, debts which could be handled easily during prosperity periods become a crushing burden during depression.

The result of this peculiarity of the monetary system is that the richer a country becomes and the more it accumulates savings and capital resources, the more acute must be its economic maladjustments. But the remedy is not to establish government ownership of industry; it is to force down the rate of interest to the appropriate economic level. It is improbable, however, that this can be accomplished by any means short of direct government control of the banking system.

It is agreed that what is at present needed is a revival of investment; and the defenders of capitalism believe that this should be in the form of risk capital, invested in industrial expansion, and argue that what prevents this expansion is the policy of the Roosevelt government. They believe that the depression of the past ten years is merely a temporary setback in our economic progress under capitalism and not an epochal turning-point. To those, on the other hand, who (like the present writer) believe that no revival of capitalism of the old kind is possible, it does not appear that there could be any considerable investment of risk capital whatever government were in office. In the first place, an expanding capitalism requires an expanding consumers' market; the share of the national income which goes to the workers and the farmers must, therefore, be enlarged. The tendency of capitalism is, however, not to enlarge that share, but to decrease it; and without a very drastic change in the functioning of the system (of a kind which would inevitably destroy 'business confidence'), that tendency cannot be reversed. In the second place, even a considerable expansion of the consumers' market would not make possible any great expansion of capital investment. The growth of private business in the United States would appear to be approaching its economic limits. We already possess almost all the factories, machinery, and office buildings that we require, even with a considerably higher standard of living. With the stoppage of large-scale immigration and the falling birth-rate, the growth of population is rapidly tapering off and will soon cease altogether. Barring the discovery and development of some important industrial invention, comparable to the railroad and the automobile, the period of rapid expansion is almost ended; and capital will soon be required by private business for little except replacements.[9] In view of these economic conditions, and in view also of the political unrest which will continue to be their inevitable consequence, it does not appear that even the election of a Republican administration could bring about any considerable or permanent revival of investment in the form of risk capital. Savings will henceforth flow back into circulation, if at all, mainly as loan capital.

Since it is necessary to prevent savings from being hoarded, and since this now requires a lower interest rate than that at which the owners of savings are willing to lend, it would appear that the only ultimate solution is direct government control over the banking system. The federal government must act as intermediary between lenders and borrowers, gathering the accumulated savings of the country and passing them out at whatever rate of interest is necessary to ensure complete investment. This would, in point of fact, be the logical conclusion of tendencies which have been in process since the beginning of the depression; since the establishment of the Reconstruction Finance Corporation the federal government has been by far both the greatest borrower and the greatest lender in the country. But a much more drastic lowering of the interest rate, particularly for small borrowers, and a much more complete control over the whole process of banking, will be necessary before the tendency of savings to accumulate can be prevented.

To call such a measure the socialization of investment would be misleading. It is frequently alleged that government control of banking means government planning of the entire economic system. This, however, is untrue. It is not proposed that the government should itself determine where capital is to be invested; the initiative in contracting loans would belong (as at present) to the borrower, not to the government. Nor would the government acquire any share in the ownership of economic enterprises; all lendings would be in the form of loan capital, repayable in full, the risk being assumed by borrowers.[10] The government should act merely as intermediary between those who have savings to lend and those who wish to borrow. The fixing of the interest rate would be a matter of mathematical calculation, not of arbitrary decision; it would be fixed at whatever rate is necessary to equalize savings and borrowings.

It is, however, probable that a considerable proportion of

the accumulated savings would be borrowed by public or semi-public bodies rather than by private business. A low interest rate would be of very considerable assistance to farmers and small businessmen, but it is unlikely that all the available capital could be used by any form of private enterprise. Though, however, the growth of private business is nearly complete, there is a great need for capital investments of a kind which can be undertaken only by municipalities and other public bodies and by consumer co-operatives: investments, for example, in housing, schools, hospitals, roads, and public parks. The maintenance of full economic activity is probably dependent upon the maintenance of large-scale public investment of this kind.

During the past six years economists have begun to formulate the rules which should govern public investment, although they have not yet been adopted in practice. The ordinary budget of a government body, which ought to be kept in balance, should be distinguished from government borrowing for the purpose of creating tangible capital assets. Such assets need not bring in cash dividends directly; they may also, as with schools and measures for promoting public health, pay dividends indirectly, collectible in the form of taxes. Government borrowing which creates assets is not a cause for alarm, any more than is private borrowing for the purpose of increasing the capital equipment of an industry. The failure of the New Deal to make this distinction is one reason for the agitation over the failure to balance the federal budget; whether the budget is really unbalanced — whether, in other words, the government is borrowing to meet deficits or to create assets — it is impossible to say.

The purpose of a reduction in the rate of interest is to serve the ends both of prosperity and of justice — two objectives which are, in the last resort, identical. What is ultimately desirable, on both moral and economic grounds, is that all forms of unearned income accruing to individuals should disappear. The first step toward this end would be to lower the rate of interest on all forms of loan capital. The claims of stockholders to the profits of corporations should, however, be similarly reduced, and eventually — by means of drastic limitations on the right of inheritance — cancelled. Such measures should, of course, apply only to individual *rentiers* and not to institutions; a government which proposed to force down all interest rates would make special arrangements for maintaining the incomes of educational and philanthropic institutions.[11] Ultimately, at the end of one or two generations, it would probably be possible to bring down to zero the interest rate due to individual lenders — in other words, to abolish it. Entrepreneurs and corporation managers who could profitably borrow money would henceforth be required to pay back the full amount of their borrowings, but no more. Meanwhile, taxation of land values should similarly destroy any kind of unearned increment accruing to owners of real estate. Rent differentials represent a genuine economic cost; to erect a building in the middle of a city ought, on economic grounds, to cost more than to erect one on the outskirts; but it does not follow that this cost should become a profit for private owners instead of for the community as a whole. There is no reason for supposing that such changes would destroy freedom, private enterprise, or entrepreneurs' profits; but they would make it impossible for men to enjoy leisure unless they had themselves earned it. The incentive to save would still be considerable; and when a man retired it would be to live on his accumulated savings rather than on his dividends. Such a society would fulfil the ideals of the founders of American democracy, who were opposed, not to private property, but to the growth of a *rentier* 'aristocracy of patronage and paper'; and it would put an end to that long conflict between debtor and creditor interests which has filled

American history. The creditor group, though always a minority of the total population, has always been victorious because it has had economics on its side. But since 1929, for the first time, economics supports the debtor.

V. INDUSTRIAL DEMOCRACY

WE TURN now to the second item in the program recommended in this chapter — the suggestion that the worker in corporate industry ought to acquire a property right in his job. This suggestion has considerable affinities with those branches of the working-class movement which are represented by Syndicalism, Guild Socialism, and consumers' co-operatives. Of all the forms of revolutionary Socialism, Syndicalism is the healthiest because it alone has recognized the evils of state centralization and bureaucracy. Syndicalism has, however, been a rather ineffectual movement because its spokesmen have never succeeded in formulating clearly by what means they expected capitalism to be overthrown or how — without centralized control — the various working-class syndicates would preserve harmony with each other and be prevented from exploiting the consumer. The co-operative movement, on the other hand, has a more definite program, but its scope is limited. It can be of considerable value in improving the functioning of certain consumers' goods industries, but it cannot hope to win control of the big mass-production industries which form the backbone of American economy.

The chief theses of this section are, first, that one can plausibly imagine the American corporation developing into a kind of working-class syndicate or producers' co-operative, and that to bring about such a transformation ought to be a principal aim of American progressivism; and secondly, that the only possible way in which such producers' co-operatives can be prevented from injuring each other and exploiting the consumer is by the mechanisms of the free-market system, under which different industries compete with each and prices and earnings fluctuate in accordance with supply and demand.

There is, as yet, no general realization of the degree to which American corporations have already ceased to be private property of the old kind. American industrial enterprises normally pass through several clearly marked phases. They originate as small-scale private businesses, in which the manager is also the principal owner. If they are successful, they develop, partly by growth and partly through mergers with competitors, into large corporations with a number of stockholders; but the original owner usually retains control until his death or retirement. Finally, they become wholly impersonal institutions, in which control is vested in management and not in ownership; and when they reach this stage, they can no longer be regarded as private property at all. The three largest corporations in the country, for example, are American Telephone and Telegraph, United States Steel, and the Pennsylvania Railroad. Each of these institutions has tens of thousands of stockholders, none of whom owns as much as one per cent of the stock. The degree to which stock-ownership in these industrial giants is diffused is, of course, exceptional; yet even small corporations exhibit the same tendency. A corporation in which one person owns as much as one-third of the stock is today a rare exception. By legal theory corporations are still the property of the stockholders; but when stockholding is widely diffused, the holders are incapable of exercising any of the rights which traditionally belong to ownership. A stock represents merely a claim to a certain percentage of the earnings of the corporation; and even this claim can often be partially evaded by the management. The legal theory has become almost wholly fictitious. In reality, such a corporation as American Telephone and Telegraph or United States Steel is no more private property than is Harvard University or the Catholic Church. Almost all the rights of ownership now belong to management; and though management is supposedly responsible to the stockholders, whom it really represents it would often be difficult to say. In practice, it tends to be self-perpetuating and to be closely allied with the New York bankers.[12]

The logical conclusion of this evolution would be to regard a corporation as the property of those who work in it. The rights which are gradually being lost by the stockholders would gradually be acquired by the workers, and management would become their representative.

It is probable that most of the complaints which capital customarily makes against labor have considerable justification. That the workers ask for wage increases which, under existing conditions, industry cannot pay without reducing production; that they are apt to make demands at the most inconvenient moments; that they deliberately choose to work slowly and inefficiently; that strikes are intolerable interferences with the workings of the productive system — all this is, no doubt, partly true. Such behavior is, however, an inevitable consequence of the wage system, which divides the industrial population into two classes and which gives to one class all the rights and all the responsibilities; and only the abolition of the wage system and the sharing both of rights and of responsibilities can bring about industrial peace.

It is both reasonable and necessary that there should be workers willing to hire themselves out for the performance of specific tasks. A part of the labor force of the country must always be mobile, and it is probable that there will always be men who will choose mobility, in preference to tying themselves permanently to a particular job. But a system under which men who work for a particular corporation can have only the status of hired employees and can be subject to dismissal, at the discretion of the management, when they reach middle age, when new machinery is installed, or when stockholders' dividends begin to decline, is a fundamental violation of the ideals of democracy.

What is recommended in this chapter, as the most appropriate objective of working-class political and trade-union activity is, by a process of steady pressure, to bring about a gradual extension of the workers' rights in industry in the direction of job-security and of a partial control over policy. Meanwhile, the rights of stockholders should be correspondingly diminished; and wherever possible, management should be encouraged to regard the maintenance of permanent employment as its chief obligation instead of being secondary to stockholders' dividends. In return for job-security the workers would find it necessary to relinquish their claim to fixed wage and salary schedules; wages would fluctuate in accordance with the earnings of the corporation, so that the workers would have an incentive for increasing those earnings. Ultimately the worker would become vested with a property right, including both privileges and obligations, which could not be forfeited except for proved incompetence or misconduct. Such might be regarded as the appropriate end of the evolution of the American corporation; and given an intelligent trade-union leadership, a generally progressive trend in national politics, and an avoidance of any growth of either Communism or Fascism, it would seem to be within the limits of possibility.

Job-security is, however, not the final goal. What should be envisaged as the ultimate objective of the trade-union movement is complete workers' ownership of corporate industry. In other words, the claims of stockholders (other than those of non-profit-making institutions) should ultimately be wiped out (this, as was suggested earlier, can best be accomplished by limiting the right of inheritance); and industrial managers, instead of being the agents of the stockholders, would be responsible to the workers. Only such a system — and the achievement of it would obviously be slow and difficult — can properly be described as industrial democracy.

If this is accepted both as the most desirable objective of progressivism and as a realization of the true aim of the working-class movement, then a very considerable revision of traditional progressive ideas must be made. The general tendency of progressive intellectuals has been to regard state ownership and bureaucratic planning, and not workers' ownership and the free market, as their goal, and hence to consider any extension of governmental power over industry as good. From the viewpoint of this book governmental ownership of industry is a step toward the totalitarian state; and when it occurs within the existing system of property relationships, it usually has Fascist implications. As was argued in an earlier chapter, Fascism and Communism both end in centralized bureaucratic control of the whole economic system, and the only important difference between them is that Fascism maintains the incomes of the *rentier* class, whereas Communism expropriates them. It is not at all impossible that the property-owning classes should come to favor socialization as the likeliest method of obtaining returns on their investments — a phenomenon already beginning to be apparent in the case of the American railroads and of certain measures of British Conservative governments. The economic system may conceivably slide into Fascist totalitarianism by way of what has been called the 'socialization of losses'; and there is considerable danger that progressives may support such measures, in the belief that any extension of government control is good. Socialization should, on the contrary, be regarded as, in general, a reactionary step. The socialization of losses means that stockholders, in return for parting with stocks of dubious value, receive compensation in the shape of government bonds; while the workers, becoming employees of the government, have even less control over their wages and conditions of labor than they had before. The only genuinely progressive policy is, on the contrary, that each industrial corporation should be the property of those who work in it.

The second contention of this section is that a society in which industry was carried on by producers' co-operatives ought to maintain competition and the free market, and that a society so organized would be able to avoid the more blatant evils both of capitalism and of Communism.

As was argued in earlier sections, the free-market mechanism, under which prices and earnings fluctuate in accordance with supply and demand, is the only possible mechanism by which production can be regulated in accordance with the wishes of the consumers and individual freedom can be reconciled with social regulation. And there is no reason why producers' co-operatives should not compete with each other to the same degree and by the same methods as industrial corporations do under the present system. The optimum size of an industrial unit, from the viewpoint of economic efficiency, though probably rather smaller than that of such giants as United States Steel, is quite large; and most branches of production should probably, as at present, be controlled by a small number of units. Under present conditions these units make price agreements with each other, the result being that prices remain high and production is restricted. Though, however, industry is, to this extent, monopolistic, it is also partially competitive. There is a sufficient degree of competition to ensure high quality and to provide a check on inefficiency; and there is competition between different branches of industry — between, for example, gas and electricity, or between busses and railroads. Price stability, moreover, has advantages as well as evils; the cut-throat rivalries and price instabilities of extreme competition do more harm than good.

What is required, therefore, is not to enforce a greater degree of competition or even to abolish price agreements. What is necessary is to ensure that production should tend to increase and prices should tend to fall. This result would be achieved under a system where industries could not dismiss their workers, and where, in consequence, production could not profitably be restricted and any falling-off in the consumers' market could be met only by a decrease in prices. Since, moreover, there would be no obligation to pay stockholders' dividends, any expansion being financed by borrowing loans through the government, the workers would have the most direct incentive for maintaining and increasing the efficiency of their industry.

One important problem remains to be mentioned. Would not, it will be asked, the workers in each industry endeavor to maximize their earnings by restricting their membership? And would not workers' ownership prove, therefore, to be as selfish and as obstructive to the common good as stockholder and management ownership? To this problem there is a solution which is very simple, which is of vital importance, and which is capable of very broad application. Under a régime of industrial democracy each corporation should be required by law to accept the services of every competent and qualified worker who presented himself; the ultimate decision as to whether a worker had the necessary qualifications should, in cases of dispute, be vested in an impartial judicial body; and after a sufficient period of probation every such worker should acquire a property right in the industry. The only adequate solution to the problems of unemployment is to establish the principles that every man has a legal right to a job and that every man has a legal right to choose his own occupation. Under the present system, where industry is carried on in order to increase the profits of ownership, it is impossible to establish any guaranties against unemployment. Under an authoritarian system, on the other hand, whether Communist or Fascist, where earnings are no longer directly dependent upon supply and demand, unemployment can be abolished, but the government must assume dictatorial power over the distribution of labor. Both the right to work and freedom of occupation could, however, be assured under a system which combined the co-operative ownership of industry with the free market. Such an arrangement would make monopolistic policies impossible. If the workers in any industry attempted to restrict production and to keep prices high and thereby to increase their earnings above the general level, they would quickly attract new labor, which would mean a reduction in their earnings and would compel them to increase production and to lower prices. Governmental regulation of the price mechanism would, therefore, be unnecessary. Enforcement of such a principle would run counter to the monopolistic traditions of certain trade unions, particularly of the craft unions. Industrial unionism, on the other hand, would probably find it easier to accept.[13]

Under such a system permanent unemployment would disappear, and the principles of the free market would, for the first time, be fully realized.[14] The earnings of each industry would depend directly upon the factor of supply and demand, and could not be deflected by financial or monopolistic manipulations. It is probable that changes of occupation would be rare, and (except when the economic need for an industry was rapidly declining) it would be desirable that such changes should be discouraged; but new labor would be constantly attracted toward industries where earnings were high and away from industries where earnings were low. This, it should be observed, is what has always happened in occupations where private property of the old kind is still the rule. Any person can choose to become a farmer or a storekeeper, any qualified person can become a doctor or a lawyer, even though those occupations may already be overcrowded; and the already-existing farmers, storekeepers, doctors, and lawyers have no power to prevent them. This is, in fact, essential to the workings of a free-market system, in order that labor may always be distributed according to the needs of society. The same principle should be applied to the new kind of co-operative property represented by large-scale industry. The ultimate effect would be that the earnings of different occupations, while rarely being actually equal, would constantly tend toward equality, with the exception of those in which, owing to the need for unusual ability or for some special skill or training, or to unusually arduous or dangerous conditions, the demand for labor was always greater than the supply.

Co-operative property would never become universal, though it is probable that it would eventually cover some of those occupations, such as retail trade, which today are still partially individualistic. It is, for example, unlikely that farming would become co-operative (except in the marketing of its products). Co-operation is essential only in occupations where a number of men must work together on the same machine and in the same industrial process; and agriculture, even when it is mechanized, does not require such co-operation. Even the Soviet Union has found it necessary, for economic reasons, to abandon its policy of creating large-scale state farms and to allow, on its co-operative farms, a considerable degree of individual private ownership. The American farmer, in particular, has always been a pronounced individualist; and there is no good reason why he should be compelled to adopt co-operative methods against his will. We may assume, therefore, that the one-family farm would continue to be the normal type; and that the present difficulties of American agriculture would find their solution partly through the reduction of debt-burdens and partly through the absorption of the less efficient farmers into industry. Farming, moreover, ought normally to be a hereditary profession. The farmer has the responsibility not only of producing the nation's food supply, but also of conserving the quality of its soil; and the most satisfactory inducement for the performance of the latter function is that each farmer should have the expectation of handing down his land to his descendants.

A large number of service occupations and of small-scale industries producing consumers' goods should, moreover, remain individualistic. The most appropriate sphere for co-operative ownership is in the big mass-production industries whose products are standardized. Individual entrepreneurs hoping for profits should be permitted to experiment with new inventions and with new methods of satisfying consumer demands. Such entrepreneurs would normally finance their operations by borrowing capital through the government; and since they could obtain labor only by paying wages at least as high as the earnings obtainable in corporations, any government or trade-union regulation would be unnecessary. New industries which proved to be important and which grew into large-scale organizations would eventually be reorganized on a co-operative basis; but there is no reason why the exercise of initiative by entrepreneurs should be discouraged by unduly hastening this transformation. The economic system would, therefore, be pluralistic; the basic principle would be that men should normally own the means of their own livelihood, and this would involve a combination of private property and co-operative property.

Whether such a system should be regarded as socialistic or individualistic, as radical or as reactionary, is immaterial, except for purposes of political propaganda. Its main objective is not to destroy bourgeois liberalism, but to fulfil the promises implicit in it; not to abolish private property, but to elevate all men into property-owners, making universal those rights which, under the present system, are the prerogative of a small class. The appeal of Marxist Socialism lies, in the last resort, in the belief of its adherents that it is impossible to abolish poverty and unemployment by any other methods. The argument of this chapter is intended to show that this challenge is not unanswerable; and that it is possible to formulate a program which is more likely than is that of the Marxists to be politically effective, which is based on a sounder economics, and which would not destroy individual freedom or create a bureaucratic dictatorship.

Notes

Notes

Chapter II

1. Lenin declared in *What Is To Be Done?*: 'The history of all countries shows that the working class, exclusively by its own effort, is able to develop only trade-union consciousness; i.e. it may itself realize the necessity for combining in unions, to fight against the employers, and to strive to compel the government to pass necessary labor legislation, etc. The theory of Socialism, however, grew out of the philosophic, historical, and economic theories that were elaborated by the educated representatives of the propertied classes, the intellectuals. The founders of modern scientific Socialism, Marx and Engels, themselves belonged to the bourgeois intelligentsia. Similarly, in Russia, the theoretical doctrines of Social-Democracy arose quite independently of the spontaneous growth of the labor movement; it arose as a natural and inevitable outcome of the development of ideas among the revolutionary Socialist intelligentsia.' (See *The Iskra Period*, ii, 114, in Lenin's *Collected Works*.)

What may prove to be the verdict of history on Leninism was spoken shortly after the October Revolution by no less a person than Maxim Gorky, who was to become a dozen years later the canonized saint of Stalinism. Gorky, of course, knew Lenin intimately. Gorky said: 'Lenin as a "leader" and Russian aristocrat (certain mental traits of this defunct class are not alien to him) deems himself in the right to perform over the Russian people a cruel experiment, doomed to failure in advance. Exhausted and ruined by war, the people have already paid for that experiment with thousands of lives, and will now be made to pay with tens of thousands more.... This inevitable tragedy does not embarrass Lenin, slave of his dogmas, nor his sycophants — his slaves. Life, in all its complexity, is unknown to Lenin. He does not know the mass of the people, he has not lived with them; only from books has he learned how one can raise this mass on its haunches, and how one can most easily infuriate its instincts. The working class is for

Lenin what ore is to the metallist. Is it possible, under the existing conditions, to cast a socialistic state out of this ore? Apparently, it is not possible; yet — why not try? What does he risk, if the experiment should fail? He is working as a chemist does in his laboratory, with the difference that the chemist employs dead matter with results valuable for life, whereas Lenin works over living material and leads the revolution to perdition.' (See Alexander Kaun: *Maxim Gorky and his Russia*, 472.)

2. According to the *Communist Manifesto*: 'The lower middle class, the small manufacturer, the shopkeeper, the artisan, the peasant, all these fight against the bourgeoisie, to save from extinction their existence as fractions of the middle class. They are, therefore, not revolutionary but conservative. Nay, more, they are reactionary, for they try to roll back the wheel of history.' 'The individual members of this class, however, are being constantly hurled down into the proletariat by the action of competition, and as modern industry develops, they even see the moment approaching when they will completely disappear as an independent section of modern society, to be replaced, in manufactures, agriculture, and commerce, by overseers, bailiffs, and shopmen.'

Marx believed that the proletariat should make every effort to win the support of the poorer peasants, but he insisted that they should be treated, not as small property-owners, but as a rural proletariat, and that their land should immediately be collectivized. When feudal estates were confiscated, the workers must demand that the estates 'remain state property and be converted into labor colonies cultivated by the associated rural proletariat with all the advantages of large-scale agriculture, through which the principles of common property immediately obtain a firm basis in the midst of the tottering bourgeois property relations. Just as the democrats combine with the peasants so must the workers combine with the rural proletariat.' (See Marx's *Selected Works*, edited by Adoratsky, II, 166.)

Lenin, on the other hand, allied himself with the peasants on their own terms. After the Russian Revolution the land was legally state property, but for practical purposes it became the property of individual peasant proprietors. In the Land Code of 1922 the right of the individual peasant to the land which he cultivated was declared to be of unlimited duration.

3. Very occasionally Marx supported a movement for national liberation (most notably in the case of Ireland). Fundamentally, however, both Marx and Engels were German imperialists; and whenever German national interests were involved, they always found a reason for arguing that the cause of the international proletariat required the victory of Germany. The following quotations, which are taken from the writings, not of Adolf Hitler, but of Karl Marx, show how easily (as today in Russia) Communist internationalism can become a cloak for nationalist aggrandizement:

On Czechoslovakia: 'Dying Czechian nationality, dying according to every fact known in history for the last four hundred years, made in 1848 a last effort to regain its former vitality — an effort whose failure, independently of all revolutionary considerations, was to prove that Bohemia could only exist, henceforth, as a portion of Germany, although part of her inhabitants might yet, for some centuries, continue to speak a non-German language.' (*Selected Works*, II, 91.)

On the Danish provinces of Schleswig-Holstein: 'These countries, unquestionably German by nationality, language, and predilection, are also from military, naval, and commercial grounds necessary to Germany.' (*Selected Works*, II, 94.)

On another occasion Marx refers approvingly to 'the historical tendency and at the same time the physical and intellectual power of the German nation to subdue, absorb, and assimilate its ancient eastern neighbors,' and adds that 'this tendency of absorption on the part of the Germans had always been, and still was, one of the mightiest means by which the civilization of western Europe had been spread to the east of that continent.' (*Selected Works*, II, 120.)

In 1870 Marx supported the war policy of Bismarck, disapproving of the neutral attitude assumed by the German Socialist leaders, Bebel and Liebknecht. 'The German working class have resolutely supported the war, which it was not in their power to prevent, as a war for German independence and the liberation of France and

Europe from that pestilential incubus, the Second Empire.' (*Selected Works*, II, 471.) 'The French need a thrashing. If the Prussians win, the centralization of the state power will be useful for the centralization of the German working class. German predominance would also transfer the centre of gravity of the workers' movement in western Europe from France to Germany, and one has only to compare the movement in the two countries from 1866 till now to see that the German working class is superior to the French both theoretically and organizationally. Their predominance over the French on the world stage would also mean the predominance of our theory over Proudhon's.' (*Correspondence* of Marx and Engels, 292.)

Marx opposed the annexation of Alsace-Lorraine. His main reason, however, was that this would result in a Franco-Russian alliance which would be harmful to German interests.

In 1891 Germany seemed likely to be involved in a war with France and Russia. Said Engels: 'If we are victorious our Party will come into power. The victory of Germany is, therefore, the victory of the revolution, and if it comes to war we must not only desire victory, but further it by every means.' (*Correspondence*, 490.)

There are to be found in Marxism all the elements which were afterward to be combined, according to a different formula, in Naziism. This applies even to anti-Semitism. Marx rarely lost an opportunity of speaking contemptuously of Jews. See, for example, his reference (in *The Class Struggles in France*) to the power of the 'stock-exchange Jews' in France under Louis Philippe, and his constant application to his rival Ferdinand Lassalle (in his correspondence) of the nickname of Itzig ('Ikey').

4. The movement of real wages and the degree of inequality in the Soviet Union are difficult to fix with any precision, since the Soviet government does not publish any statistics on such questions — a fact which is in itself suspicious. It is, however, certain that real wages are very low and that inequalities are very considerable; and it is probable that the average real wage is smaller than it was before the first Five-Year Plan. The Soviet Union has made rapid progress in building heavy industry, but the consumption goods industries are still very backward; and as a result of the op-

position of the peasants to collectivization, the increase in food production has been negligible. Statistics on these questions can be found in Sir Walter Citrine: *I Search for Truth in Russia*; and in L. F. Hubbard: *Soviet Trade and Distribution*.

In 1937 the average wage of the worker was about 250 rubles a month. By 1939 the average wage had increased to between 280 and 290 rubles, but prices had also risen, so that the increase in real wages was inconsiderable. In estimating the average wage the salaries of managers and technicians are included (all Russians being either 'workers' or peasants), so that the average wage of the manual laborer is considerably smaller. In November, 1937, the Soviet government announced that it proposed to establish a minimum wage of 110-115 rubles; that this would involve an increase in its monthly wage bill of 50,000,000 rubles; and that the average increase per worker would be 19 rubles a month. It appears, therefore, that 2,500,000 workers (out of a total of 26,000,000 workers) had previously been receiving less than 100 rubles a month. The workers also receive various benefits other than wages, the value of which (according to Citrine) is not more than one-third of their wage; while their rent is fixed at a certain percentage (apparently ten per cent) of their earnings. For this rent, however, the worker usually receives only one room, with no plumbing; housing has been one of the most conspicuous failures of the Soviet Union, and the building of new houses has not even kept pace with the growth of urban population. To make allowance for these benefits the average wage of 1937 might perhaps be increased to 350 or 400 rubles a month.

In 1937 the ruble was the equivalent in purchasing power (calculated in terms of food prices) of between six and eight cents (by this date, it should be remembered, rationing had been abolished, and the workers were no longer given the benefit of especially low prices for necessities). A pound loaf of bread, for example, cost from 1.27 to 1.91 rubles; a quart of milk cost 2.17 rubles. The average wage of the Russian worker was, therefore, not more than 32 dollars a month, and the minimum wage was not more than 14 dollars a month. It should be remembered that almost all Russian women work, so that most families have two or more wage-earners. An exchange value of eight cents to the ruble appears, however, to be very favorable when clothing prices are considered. In Moscow in 1937 a pair of shoes cost from 150 to 300 rubles; a suit of clothes cost from 700 to 1200 rubles.

Real wages, though higher than in 1931 and 1932, appear to be still lower than they were in 1926, before the inauguration of the Five-Year Plan. In 1926 the average monthly wage was 52 rubles, so that monetary wages have increased five or six times. Prices have, however, risen at least ten times.

There are no adequate data as to the living standards of the peasants, but they are certainly lower than those of the workers. Hubbard calculates that in 1936 the average monetary income of all persons employed in agriculture was about 700 rubles a year. This figure does not, of course, take account of what the peasants produced for their own consumption.

In 1935 the salary of the manager in the factories visited by Citrine was usually 2000 rubles a month. At that time the average wage was 189 rubles a month, and the minimum wage was less than 100 rubles a month. Factory managers, therefore, earned about eleven times as much as the average, and about twenty times as much as did the 2,500,000 workers who belonged to the most poorly paid categories. The difference has certainly not decreased since 1935. Earnings of 8000 rubles a month are not unknown, while the Stakhanovist workers (who are able to perform their extraordinary feats because each of them has a corps of assistants) receive from 2000 to 4000 rubles a month.

The size of the privileged class in the Soviet Union — the class which earns relatively high wages and which consists of government officials, Red Army officers, factory managers, collective farm presidents, and Stakhanovist workers — is unknown, since the government prefers not to publish any statistics which might shed light on this subject. Most observers estimate it at about 5,000,000 (in a total population of more than 180,000,000). There are about 2,500,000 Communist Party members.

5. A number of the facts in this section are taken from F. Borkenau: *World Communism*.

6. With reference to Mexico this statement requires some qualification, since the Marxist ideology now has considerable influence in the Mexican labor movement. The Mexican government, however, repudiates State Socialism and Communism, and aims at the establishment of autonomous workers' and peasants' co-operatives. According to President Cardenas the Mexican Revolution 'departs from State Communism, because our people are not the kind to adopt a system which deprives them of the full enjoyment of their efforts, nor do they want to substitute the individual boss with the boss-state.' In Sweden there is a similar emphasis on the co-operative movement, though in the shape of consumers' rather than of producers' co-operatives.

7. In discussing such organizations as the Communist and Fascist Parties it is necessary to distinguish between (1) the class composition of the Party membership, and (2) the classes from whom the Party hopes to win support. With respect to (2) Communism and Fascism differ fundamentally; with respect to (1) there is considerable similarity.

8. The ideology of Fascism was largely created by such romanticist aesthetes and intellectuals as D'Annunzio in Italy and Nietzsche and Stefan George in Germany. Viewed in terms of intellectual history, Fascism marks the final stage in the romantic degeneration.

9. The question whether or not Fascism represents the economic interests of the capitalist class is often debated, but it does not have quite the importance which is attributed to it by Marxist writers. Marxists often argue that Fascism makes the capitalist class richer and the working class poorer; but it should be obvious that if it did merely this, it would quickly create an economic crisis, caused by a deficiency of purchasing power and by overproduction. Fascism has, however, shown itself able to avoid catastrophic economic crises; and no system can do this, whether it represents the capitalist class or not, without maintaining the purchasing power of the working class. Actually, Fascism makes the economic system work by spending a large proportion of the national income on armaments;

and both the capitalist class and the working class are better off in some respects and worse off in others. The capitalist class earn higher profits, but they must contribute a higher proportion of them to the state in taxes and loans; and their freedom to operate their industries as they would like is severely curtailed. The working class receive lower hourly wage rates, but on the other hand, unemployment has virtually disappeared; so that, though the individual employed worker must work considerably longer hours to receive the same wage, the total wage bill of the working class is appreciably larger.

10. In the elections of 1930 the Communist vote was 4,590,178; the Nazi vote was 6,406,397. In July, 1932, the Communist vote was 5,282,626; the Nazi vote was 13,745,781. During two years of acute depression, therefore, the Communists were able to gain only 700,000 votes, whereas the Nazi vote increased by more than 7,000,000. In November, 1932, the Communist vote was 5,980,539; the Nazi vote was 11,737,386. Thus the Communists gained 600,000, while the Nazis lost more than 2,000,000. It is arguable, however, that much of the Communist gain may have come from the Social-Democrats, who lost 700,000 votes. In March, 1933 (after Hitler had become chancellor), the Communist vote was 4,848,058; the Nazi vote was 17,277,180. The Communists had lost more than 1,000,000, the Nazis had gained more than 5,500,000. Since the votes of all other parties (except the Nationalists, who gained 120,000) were only slightly smaller than their votes in the previous election, it would appear that the Nazi gains came partly from new voters (of whom there were about 4,000,000) and partly from the Communists.

11. In April, 1934, Earl Browder was declaring that 'Roosevelt's program ... is a program of hunger, fascization, and imperialist war.... The New Deal is not developed Fascism. But in political essence and direction it is the same as Hitler's program.' 'Roosevelt, leading the present ruling class, finance capital, stands for degradation, hunger, misery, oppression, Fascism, war.' (See Browder's *Report* to the 8th Convention of the Communist Party, 20, 32.) In 1939 the same Earl Browder was a strong supporter of

the New Deal, and was denouncing Congress because it had refused to prepare for a war with Japan by fortifying the island of
Guam.

12. The articles of General Krivitsky published in the *Saturday
Evening Post* may or may not be reliable, though they contain nothing
which is intrinsically improbable. Evidence as to Soviet activities
in Spain is, however, accumulating. See, for example, the articles of
Luis Araquistain, a well-known Spanish Socialist leader of long
standing, published in the *New York Times*, May 19 and June 4,
1939.

Chapter III

1. Since the Communist Party of the United States now declares
not only that it does not now advocate revolution, but also that it
never did advocate revolution, it may be advisable to quote a few
sentences from the program of the Communist International (drafted
in 1928): 'The conquest of power by the proletariat does not mean
peacefully "capturing" the ready-made bourgeois state by means
of a parliamentary majority.... The conquest of power by the
proletariat is the violent overthrow of bourgeois power, the destruction of the capitalist state apparatus, ... and the substitution in its
place of the organs of proletarian power.' 'When the revolutionary
tide is rising, ... the Party of the proletariat is confronted with the
task of leading the masses to a direct attack upon the bourgeois state.
This it does by carrying on propaganda... and by organizing mass
action, upon which all branches of Party agitation and propaganda,
including parliamentary activity, must be concentrated. This mass
action includes: strikes; a combination of strikes and demonstrations;
a combination of strikes and armed demonstrations; and finally, the
general strike conjointly with armed insurrection against the state
power of the bourgeoisie. The latter form of struggle, which is the
supreme form, must be conducted according to the rules of war; it
presupposes a plan of campaign, offensive fighting operations, and
unbounded devotion and heroism on the part of the proletariat.'
(See *A Handbook of Marxism*, published in 1935; pages 990, 1036.)

2. For example, in John Strachey's *Coming Struggle for Power*, a book which is about everything except its title.

3. The factors which have most frequently caused the fall of monarchical or dictatorial régimes have been: (1) financial collapse (England in 1640, France in 1789, Spain in 1930); (2) defeat in war (France in 1814 and 1870, Russia in 1917, Germany and Austria in 1918); (3) senile decay of the dictator and failure to provide for the succession (Mexico in 1910). In every one of these instances the fall of a reactionary dictatorship was followed, not by a left-wing dictatorship, but by an attempt to establish parliamentary government and to guarantee individual freedom.

4. A careful analysis of the class composition of the population of the United States has been made by Alfred Bingham, who bases his figures on the Census of 1930. Bingham calculates that the employed population is divided as follows: businessmen 8 per cent; professional workers 7 per cent; farmers 16 per cent; white-collar workers 17 per cent; government employees 1.5 per cent; service trades 5 per cent; farm laborers 5.5 per cent; servants 5.5 per cent; industrial workers 34.5 per cent. Since 1930 there has been some decrease in the number of industrial workers. (See Bingham's *Insurgent America*, 233.)

5. The number of industrial workers reached its peak in the United States in 1919, and has since been declining not only relatively to the total population but also absolutely. In 1919 there were 9,039,000 industrial workers; by 1929 the number had fallen to 8,742,000. During the same period the population increased from 105,000,000 to 122,000,000.

6. It is not sufficiently realized that during a depression prices tend to fall more rapidly than wages, and that, in consequence, those workers who are able to keep their jobs are actually better off than during prosperity. In 1931, for example, hourly real wages in the United States were 6.2 per cent higher than in 1929. Real wages fell during 1932, but by 1934 they were again well above the

1929 level. The result of such a situation is a conflict of interest between the employed and the unemployed. In Germany during the same period the antagonism between the Social-Democrats and the Communists was largely a reflection of this employed-unemployed antagonism.

7. Some of the ideas in this section are derived from Selig Perlman: *A Theory of the Labor Movement*.

8. Establishment of complete political democracy was also the chief purpose of the Paris Commune. (See Max Nomad: *Apostles of Revolution*.) The notion that the objectives of the Commune were Socialist or — in the modern sense of the word — Communist was deliberately propagated by Marx in order to give prestige to the Socialist movement. Actually a majority of the Communards were Jacobins who believed in a political democracy similar to that imposed by Robespierre during the French Revolution; only a small minority were Marxists. As Marx himself admitted, 'the majority of the Commune was in no sense Socialist' (*Correspondence*, 387), and 'the International did not lift a finger to produce it' (*Correspondence*, 330). The singular importance which Lenin attached to the Commune was the result of Marx's misrepresentation of it.

9. *Das Kapital*, American edition of 1906–09, I, 14.

10. From the *Communist Manifesto; A Handbook of Marxism*, 27.

11. *Das Kapital*, I, 846.

12. Marxists sometimes attempt to defend the labor theory of value by asserting that it is not intended as an explanation of prices. But a theory of economic value which does not explain prices is highly metaphysical, and it is difficult to attach any meaning to it or say what purpose it serves. In reality, Marx believed that the labor theory of value explained prices, although prices did not always correspond exactly to values. He declared that 'price is the money-name of the labor realized in a commodity' (*Das Kapital*, I, 114),

and that 'the law of value dominates the movements of prices,' adding that the value of commodities 'is the centre of gravity around which prices fluctuate, and around which their rise and fall tends to an equilibrium' (*Das Kapital*, III, 211). The reason for the assertion that Marx was not trying to explain prices is that when Marx came to write the third volume of *Das Kapital*, he found that some of the theories which he had advanced in the first volume were inapplicable; in certain passages dealing with prices he had, in fact, virtually to abandon the labor theory of value altogether.

13. *Das Kapital*, III, 213.

14. *Das Kapital*, III, 265. No proof or further elucidation is offered for these assertions.

15. See *Das Kapital*, III, chapter 10.

16. *Das Kapital*, III, 244, 181, 186.

17. Strachey, however, lays more emphasis than Marx on the economic effects of a deficiency of purchasing power. By combining the falling rate of profit theory with the underconsumption theory, he deduces that capitalism has now reached a dilemma which it cannot surmount. The falling rate of profit requires that wages be reduced (Strachey declares, for example, that the immediate cause of the depression of 1929 may have been that wages in the United States were too high); on the other hand, low wages mean underconsumption and overproduction. If wages go up, capitalists cannot make profits; if wages go down, they cannot sell their goods.

18. There appears to be no adequate statistics as to long-term movements in the rate of profit. In any case such statistics would have little meaning, since (in spite of what Marx says) capitalists are interested primarily in the amount of profit and not in its rate; and the amount of profit has (with occasional setbacks) been increasing rapidly ever since capitalism started. Lewis Corey (in his *Decline of American Capitalism*, chapter 8) asserts that the long-term

tendency of the rate of profit is to fall; but the only statistics which he adduces in support of this assertion show that in 1923 the rate of profit was 9.2 per cent, in 1927 it dropped to 5.5 per cent, in 1929 it rose to 7.5 per cent, and in 1931 it dropped to a minus quantity. Obviously figures covering such a short period prove nothing. If Mr. Corey had chosen to begin at 1931 and end at 1936, he would have arrived at a completely opposite conclusion. Mr. Corey draws the Marxist conclusion that the fall in the rate of profit can be counteracted only by a decrease in wages. Yet the increase in profits between 1931 and 1936 was accompanied by an increase in wage-rates.

19. That oversaving was the primary cause of the 1929 depression has been shown in a number of publications of the Brookings Institution, and particularly by Harold G. Moulton in *The Formation of Capital*. Between 1922 and 1929 the total amount of savings put back into circulation through investment in production and in mortgages averaged between $5,000,000,000 and $6,000,000,000 a year; throughout these years the annual amount showed no marked increases or decreases. On the other hand, the total savings of the community were between $8,000,000,000 and $9,000,000,000 in 1923 and 1924, and had risen to about $15,000,000,000 in 1929. These surplus savings were either poured into the stock market and used to boost the prices of stocks or merely remained in the banks; in either case they did not go back into the productive system from which they had been extracted. The result, of course, was both that industry could not make full use of its productive resources even during the prosperity period, and ultimately that a crisis of overproduction and underconsumption occurred. The crisis was postponed until 1929 only by a rapid growth in the debt obligations of underprivileged groups (through, for example, instalment buying, and an increase in farm mortgages). The stock-market crash, by causing a sudden decrease in purchasing power, acted as the precipitant of the crisis.

An overwhelming proportion of the saving was done by the richest class, who — to a large degree — derived their incomes from interest, dividends, and rents, rather than from wages and salaries.

More than two-thirds of the total saving was done by the 2.3 per cent of the families who had incomes above $10,000 a year. The 59 per cent of the families who earned less than $2000 a year were responsible for only 1.6 per cent of the saving.

Mr. Moulton summarizes his conclusions as follows: 'The rapid growth of savings as compared with consumption in the decade of the twenties resulted in a supply of investment money quite out of proportion to the volume of securities being floated for purposes of expanding plant and equipment, while at the same time the flow of funds through consumptive channels was inadequate to absorb — at the prices at which goods were offered for sale — the potential output of our existing productive capacity. The excess savings which entered the investment market served to inflate the prices of securities and to produce financial instability. A larger relative flow of funds through consumptive channels would have led not only to a larger utilization of existing productive capacity, but also to a more rapid growth of plant and equipment.... At the present stage in the economic evolution of the United States the problem of balance between consumption and saving is thus essentially different from what it was in earlier times. Instead of a scarcity of funds for the needs of business enterprise, there tends to be an excessive supply of available investment money, which is productive not of new capital goods but of financial maladjustments. The primary need at this stage in our economic history is a larger flow of funds through consumptive channels rather than more abundant savings.'

20. For an admirable study of the functional weaknesses of American capitalism, based mainly on statistics from government publications and with a minimum of theorizing, see John M. Blair: *Seeds of Destruction*.

Chapter IV

1. See *Correspondence* of Marx and Engels, 517, 477; Engels's *Anti-Duhring*, reprinted in *A Handbook of Marxism*, 298.

2. See, for example, the interpretations of seventeenth-century

English history in John Strachey's *Coming Struggle for Power*, and
A. L. Morton's *People's History of England*.

3. Lenin's *State and Revolution* is reprinted in *A Handbook of Marxism*; see pages 757-59.

4. In order to anticipate criticisms, it should perhaps be pointed
out that every argument used in this and the following section has
been used many times before. Readers will find all these arguments
discussed in books written in defence of Communism: for example,
in the Webbs' *Soviet Communism*. They will find also, however, that
Communists have made no serious effort to confute them; they content themselves with arguing that Communism is better than capitalism; that it is less undemocratic, allows more freedom, satisfies the
needs of the workers more fully, and so on. Such arguments do not
constitute an adequate defence, since there is a third possibility which
Communists do not take into account: namely, to keep the free market, but to modify its workings in such a way as to create a much
greater degree of equality.

There is a direct connection between the deficiencies of Communist economic practice and those of Marxist economic theory.
The subject-matter of Marxist economics is the exploitation of labor
by capital; and Marxists have always assumed that once this exploitation had been abolished, the creation of a just and efficient
system would present no particular problems. But in reality the
same fundamental economic problems confront any society, whether
capitalist or Communist, which is based on the division of labor
and production for exchange. Economics is a science, and its subject-matter is (in the definition of Lionel Robbins) 'that aspect of
behavior which arises from the scarcity of means to achieve given
ends'; in other words, it deals with relationships of supply and
demand. And as long as human beings must work in order to satisfy
their needs, society must not only compel men to do their quota of
work (which was all that Lenin believed to be necessary), but must
also adopt some technique for measuring the relative necessity and
value of different kinds of work.

5. That Lenin believed in complete financial equality is apparent from the passages which have been quoted from *The State and Revolution*. Marx, in his *Critique of the Gotha Programme*, explained that immediately after the revolution each worker would be paid according to the amount of his work. The worker would receive 'a certificate from society that he has furnished such and such an amount of labor' and would then draw 'from the social stock of means of consumption as much as costs the same amount of labor.' 'The right of the producers is *proportional* to the labor they supply; the equality consists in the fact that measurement is made with an *equal standard*, labor.' Marx explains that this would not mean complete equality, since one worker would be able to 'supply more labor in the same time, or can labor for a longer time.' Marx assumes that it would be possible to measure each man's contribution to the social wealth by the same standard. In practice, however, it is impossible to say whether a skilled technologist is, or is not, supplying 'more labor in the same time' as a manual laborer; and this enables the Soviet government to maintain that in paying relatively high salaries to factory managers, it is not violating Marxist principles. However, it is obvious that Marx did not envisage the degree of inequality which now exists in the Soviet Union.

6. Some of the arguments used in this section are derived from the well-known theory of Ludwig von Mises. (See his *Socialism*.) Mises declared that in a society where prices were fixed by the government instead of being determined by competition, and where no account was taken of those elements of cost represented by rent and interest, it would be impossible to calculate with sufficient accuracy how the available resources ought to be divided among the different kinds of production in order to ensure the most efficient use of them. Mises believes in *laissez-faire* of the old-fashioned nineteenth-century kind; but the fact that his own beliefs are inacceptable does not invalidate his criticisms of Communism.

Communists have made no serious effort to confute Mises; they merely dismiss him as a bourgeois apologist, and therefore beneath contempt. John Strachey, for example, in his *Theory and Practice of*

Socialism, refers to him once, on which occasion he describes Mises' book as 'a volume, the five hundred pages of which severally and collectively seek to disprove the possibility of the existence of a planned economic system of production for use without once mentioning the existence of such a system in one-sixth of the world.' But Mises did not say that such a system was impossible; he said that it would be inefficient; and there is at present no reason for supposing that he was wrong. Confirmation of the Mises thesis is provided by Boris Brutzkus, in his *Economic Planning in Soviet Russia.* The first section of this book, written in 1920, is a remarkably accurate prophecy of the kind of thing which happened under the first Five-Year Plan.

Socialists, on the other hand, have endeavored to meet Mises' criticisms by suggesting that in a planned society prices might vary, and calculations might be made, precisely as is done under a free-market system. For example, if there were an increased consumer demand for some commodity, its price would be raised; the production of it would then bring greater profits; and the planning board would be able to calculate that it ought to be produced in greater quantities. In other words, the different branches of the productive system would, as it were, play at competition. 'Market Socialism' of this kind might, at least in theory, be reasonably efficient in satisfying the consumer; and the Soviet Union may, in course of time, begin to adopt such methods. However, the fundamental objection remains: that the efficiency of the whole system depends on the efficiency and integrity of the planners, that there can be no adequate democratic control over them, and that they have no sufficient incentive to avoid mistakes and to plan wisely. If it is admitted that free-market methods are necessary for determining prices and guiding production, why not have a genuine free market without any autocratic board of planners?

It should also be pointed out that the economic problems of Soviet planning will become greater as the system grows more productive. No extraordinary wisdom is needed for planning the building of big mass-production factories and power plants, particularly as long as it is possible to take the United States as a model. Almost anything built in the Soviet Union at this stage is likely to have some degree of usefulness. The real difficulties of planning begin when one begins to plan new kinds of consumers' goods.

7. During the first Five-Year Plan the Soviet planners appear to have indulged in a perfect riot of 'gigantomania.' It was assumed that bigness was identical with efficiency; and when it was a matter of erecting large-scale factories and equipping them with machinery bought from the capitalist nations, money was no object. The result was that many of the factories were so large that efficient management was impossible, and that transportation costs became excessive; while some of the state farms were so huge that the laborers spent nearly all their time walking to their work and back.

At that time the colossal size of Soviet factories and machinery was regarded by Communists as a convincing proof of the superiority of Communism over capitalism. R. Palme Dutt begins his *Fascism and Social Revolution* (which is probably the ablest piece of Marxist apologetics ever written in English) by quoting the following sentences from the *Automobile Engineer* of March, 1931: 'American machine-tool makers, having a range of equipment sufficient to meet the needs of the American production plants, have supplied to Russia machine tools outside this range, specially designed to obtain still faster production. An excessive price has been demanded for these special machines on the ground that, while the tools show an improvement in output speed on their standard lines, they have no immediate prospects of finding other customers for them, there being no demand outside Russia for faster production than can be obtained with existing models.' Palme Dutt comments as follows: 'Here, as in a single crystal, is expressed the whole present stage of the general crisis of capitalism, of the exhaustion of the possibilities of productive advance within the fetters of the old private ownership, and the necessity of the socialization of production as the sole condition for further development. In the situation that this picture reveals lies the real root of the issue of Fascism or Communism. In this situation lies the basic cause why precisely at the present stage of social development the issue of Fascism or Communism inescapably confronts existing society.'

Palme Dutt's fundamental assumption, from which the argument of his whole book is developed, is that because the machinery used in the Soviet Union is more elaborate than the machinery used in the capitalist nations, it follows that Communism is superior to capitalism. In reality, the fact which he cites from the *Automobile Engineer* proves nothing of the kind. What it does prove is something which has been known ever since the Pharaohs built the pyramids: namely, that a dictatorial government can afford to spend money more recklessly than can a private businessman. Any piece of machinery must be paid for in human labor. The cost of these particular machines — and as the quotation from the *Automobile Engineer* shows, the Soviet government paid an excessive price for them — was the labor of the Russian peasants who provided the wheat and the timber with which the Soviet officials obtained the necessary foreign exchange. What has to be proved is, first, that the wealth which these machines would produce would be greater than what it cost to purchase them; and secondly, that the Russian people would not have been better off if the Soviet officials had spent their foreign exchange on something else. Neither Palme Dutt nor — at that period — the Soviet government appear to have been aware that such questions could even be asked. In any case, in view of the lack of an adequate costing and pricing system in the Soviet Union, it is probably impossible to answer them.

That the 'bourgeois' economists were fully justified in pointing out that bigger factories and more elaborate machinery were no proof of economic superiority has now been realized by the Communists themselves. Stalin has recently denounced the 'gigantomania' of Soviet engineers and has decreed that factories must be smaller. A writer in *Izvestia* comments as follows (see *The Living Age*, May, 1939): 'As Stalin once put it, "There is a dark side to all successes." That is true of the current situation. First, it takes excessive time to build factories of this giant size. . . . Besides, these industrial giants are complex and unwieldy, they are difficult to manage efficiently. . . . We have been forced to carry the products of a few vast undertakings all over the nation, in the absence of regional production. . . . The country must relinquish the idea that has taken root, particularly in the minds of Soviet engineers, that small undertakings are of necessity backward. . . . In the machine-building industry of the United States, almost all the factories are far smaller than those in the Soviet Union, yet the most efficient machines in the market are made in the United States by factories which we would consider too small for quantity production.'

With reference to the tractors, see L. F. Hubbard, *Soviet Trade and Distribution*, 315. An enormous expenditure on agricultural machinery produced only a very small increase in agricultural productivity. According to Stalin grain production in 1938 was (in spite of a considerable increase in population) only 18.6 per cent above the figure for 1913.

8. For a list of cases where Stakhanovists were murdered (based on reports in *Pravda*), see N. de Basily, *Russia Under Soviet Rule*, 349.

9. Marx studied imperialism, especially British imperialism in India and Ireland; but it did not occur to him that imperialism might become a cause of European wars. The association of imperialism with war was made not by Marx but by Lenin (who of course lived at a time when this association had become obvious). Lenin derived his ideas on this subject largely from the English liberal economist J. A. Hobson.

10. The only wars possible under a liberal free-market system are wars fought to impose free-market rules upon colonial areas. These, it should be pointed out, do not necessarily involve imperialist rivalries. They may (as occurred a number of times in the nineteenth century) be undertaken by several imperialist powers in co-operation, with an Open-Door policy of complete commercial equality.

Of colonial imperialism, it should be pointed out that it is bad not in its essence but only in its methods. It is desirable that all parts of the world should eventually achieve roughly equivalent standards of living; this can be accomplished only by the export of capital equipment from progressive areas to backward ones; and since countries can hardly be expected to make free gifts of their surplus capital, it is necessary to allow them to make profits on such transactions. What is bad about imperialism is the failure to protect the interests and welfare of colonial races. The only satisfactory solution (impossible as — under present conditions — it may be) is control of those races who are not yet capable of responsible self-government by some disinterested international organization.

11. This aspect of the European problem is emphasized by Jerome Frank in *Save America First*.

12. John Strachey, for example, discussing the Nazi dictatorship (in *The American Mercury*, February, 1939), declares that the Nazis could stabilize capitalism if 'the standard of life of the German people could be allowed to rise.' 'But to do this,' he adds, 'would mean directly and deliberately decreasing the share of the German employing class in the national income.... It would amount to their toleration of ever-declining rates of rent, interest, and profit. This, as I agreed above, would make capitalism workable for a long time yet; but no capitalist class has hitherto been willing to contemplate such a course.... To expect a Nazi régime to develop along these lines is to expect it to turn itself inside out. For these reasons we must rule out this alternative as ... fantastic.' These words would seem to imply that capitalism is workable only if the capitalist class makes itself poorer. This, however, is not wholly accurate. Capitalism is workable as long as it does not become clogged with excess savings. A dictatorship must either diminish the total amount of savings, or it must pour them back into circulation through public works and social-welfare schemes. That part of their incomes which the capitalist class actually spend themselves, on their own consumption, on the other hand, need not be diminished; under a business dictatorship it might, on the contrary, become very much larger than at present. Owners of capital might resent losing control over their savings, but they would be more than recompensed by being assured of a very high standard of living. A dictatorship, moreover, can always enforce obedience, even over its own supporters, where a democracy cannot.

13. It is, however, probable that the United States is the only major country where such a choice is still possible. A prolonged period of intensive war preparation leads necessarily to a totali-

tarian economy. The longer the present European crisis lasts, the more closely will the economic systems of Great Britain, Germany, and the Soviet Union come to resemble each other.

Chapter V

1. There is no authoritative full-length exposition of the Marxist view of history. A study of it must be based on scattered passages in the *Correspondence* of Marx and Engels and in the political and economic writings of Marx, Engels, and Lenin (particularly Marx's preface to his *Critique of Political Economy*). The most elaborate exposition by a Marxist is the *Historical Materialism* of Lenin's associate Bukharin. After Bukharin fell into disgrace, however, it was discovered by the Stalinists that his book had been written from a 'mechanistic' rather than a 'dialectical' point of view.

2. For a typical example, see *Marxism and Modern Thought*, by N. I. Bukharin and others.

3. According to Engels: 'Ideology is a process accomplished by the so-called thinker, consciously, indeed, but with a false consciousness. The real motives impelling him remain unknown to him, otherwise it would not be an ideological process at all. Hence he imagines false or apparent motives. Because it is a process of thought he derives both its form and its content from pure thought, either his own or that of his predecessors. He works with mere thought material which he accepts without examination as the product of thought, he does not investigate further for a more remote process independent of thought.' (*Correspondence*, 511.)

4. Quoted in Otto Rühle: *Karl Marx*, 55, 84.

5. *Correspondence*, 484, 475.

6. Engels said in *Anti-Dühring*: 'The ultimate causes of all social changes and political revolutions are to be sought, not in the minds of men... but in changes in the mode of production and exchange.

... The growing realization that existing social conditions are irrational and unjust ... is only a sign that changes have been taking place quietly in the methods of production and forms of exchange, with which the social order, adapted to previous economic conditions, is no longer in accord.' (*A Handbook of Marxism*, 279.)

7. Mr. J. M. Keynes remarks that 'The ideas of economists and political philosophers, both when they are right and when they are wrong, are more powerful than is commonly supposed. Indeed, the world is ruled by little else. Practical men, who believe themselves to be quite exempt from any intellectual influences, are usually the slaves of some defunct economist. Madmen in authority, who hear voices in the air, are distilling their frenzy from some academic scribbler of a few years back. . . . Soon or late, it is ideas, not vested interests, which are dangerous for good or evil.' There is no more striking illustration of this fact than the history of the Soviet Union since 1917.

8. For the Marxist view of science see *Science at the Crossroads*, particularly Hessen's study of Newton.

9. Engels said in his *Ludwig Feuerbach* that 'the demand for final solutions and eternal truths ceases once for all; one is always conscious of the necessary limitation of all acquired knowledge, of the fact that it is conditioned by the circumstances in which it was acquired. . . . That which is recognized now as true has also its latent false side which will later manifest itself, just as that which is now regarded as false has also its true side.' (*A Handbook of Marxism*, 225.)

10. This paragraph should not be taken as implying that the artist ought to remain aloof from politics. The artist is a part of society, and is therefore as much affected by political changes as anybody else; he has, moreover, a peculiar interest in the preservation of those social conditions which will allow him intellectual freedom. Most good artists in most periods of history have fulfilled their duties as citizens; they have not, however, regarded art as merely a

political weapon. In recent years a number of writers have proclaimed, as a new and startling discovery, the fact that the artist is
a part of society; this has been regarded as something which was
known only to the Marxists, and which — in some mysterious way
— proved that all intelligent artists ought to be Communists. But
of course it is quite possible for an artist to be politically active
without being a Communist; good artists have, on the contrary,
sometimes been political reactionaries. The reason why this discovery is regarded as new is that many of the writers who are now
Communists were, before 1929, believers in the ivory-tower view of
art — an attitude very prevalent in the United States of the twenties.
While not new, it therefore appears as new to many recent converts to Communism.

11. Engels said in *Anti-Duhring*: 'We therefore reject every attempt
to impose on us any moral dogma whatsoever as an eternal, ultimate, and forever immutable moral law.... We maintain on the
contrary that all former moral theories are the product, in the last
analysis, of the economic stage which society had reached at that
particular epoch. And as society has hitherto moved in class antagonisms, morality was always a class morality.' (*A Handbook of
Marxism*, 249.)

Engels goes on to explain, however, that the classless society of
the future will develop a new kind of 'really human morality.'
He gives as an example the rule, 'Thou shalt not steal.' In the
classless society such a rule would have no meaning and would
appear ridiculous, because 'at the very most only lunatics would
ever steal.' The utopian character of Engels's ideas about Communism can be gauged from the fact that in the Soviet Union today
the stealing of state property (and almost all property is state property) by anybody above the age of twelve is a capital offence.

12. Moral relativism is not, however, confined to the Marxists
and their Fascist imitators. It is apparent also in recent developments in the study of anthropology and sociology, and in those
philosophical tendencies which are represented by pragmatism and
instrumentalism.

13. The classic statement of dialectical materialism is Engels's *Anti-Duhring*. The most elaborate recent account in English is T. A. Jackson's *Dialectics*. Whatever can be said in favor of it has been said by a recent convert, J. B. S. Haldane, in his *Marxist Philosophy and the Sciences*.

14. The opinion that Marx did not believe in the kind of dialectical materialism now propagated in the Soviet Union is held by Professor Sidney Hook. (See his *Towards the Understanding of Karl Marx*, and *From Hegel to Marx*.) Hook approaches Marxism by way of the instrumentalism of John Dewey, and regards the Marxist philosophy as instrumental to the class needs of the proletariat, not as absolute, objective, or universal truth. Hook abandons, therefore, the belief in the inevitability of Communism. Passages from Marx can be quoted in support of this interpretation (particularly his *Theses on Feuerbach*); but Marx was not a very consistent thinker. Hook is able (a unique achievement) to present Marxism as a rational system, free from mysticisms and contradictions. The objection to his approach, as to all varieties of pragmatism, is that the ultimate interest or value to which thought is instrumental remains very arbitrary. Hook nowhere makes explicit or justifies the basic assumptions which have caused him to regard the viewpoint of the proletariat as superior to that of the bourgeoisie and to consider a proletarian revolution as desirable.

15. Engels, nevertheless, in his *Anti-Duhring*, after explaining that to a certain type of thinker 'it must seem extremely remarkable that consciousness and Nature, thinking and being, the laws of thought and the laws of Nature, should be so closely in correspondence,' declares that 'thought and consciousness... are products of the human brain and that man himself is a product of Nature, which has been developed in and along with its environment; whence it is self-evident that the products of the human brain, being in the last analysis products of Nature, do not contradict the rest of Nature, but are in correspondence with it.' (*A Handbook of Marxism*, 233.)

16. According to Engels in *Anti-Duhring*, 'Motion itself is a con-

tradiction; even simple mechanical change of place can only come about through a body at one and the same moment of time being both in one place and in another place, being in one and same place and also not in it. And the continuous assertion and simultaneous solution of this contradiction is precisely what motion is.... This is even more true of the higher forms of motion of matter, and especially of organic life and its development.... Life consists just precisely in this — that a living thing is at each moment itself and yet something else.' (*A Handbook of Marxism*, 257.) The belief that motion and change involve contradictions which can be solved only by the dialectical method is basic to Marxism. Engels defined dialectics as 'nothing more than the science of the general laws of motion and development of Nature, human society, and thought.' (*A Handbook of Marxism*, 266.)

17. According to Lenin, 'The conflict of mutually exclusive opposites is absolute, just as development and motion are absolute.' Lenin insisted on 'the recognition [discovery] of contradictory, mutually exclusive, and opposite tendencies in *all* manifestations and processes of Nature (*including* spirit and society).' (Quoted in Adoratsky: *Dialectical Materialism*, 57.)

18. J. D. Bernal insists, nevertheless, that 'the essential task of materialist dialectic is the explanation of the appearance of the qualitatively new.' (See *Aspects of Dialectical Materialism*, by various authors, 102.)

Chapter VI

1. Quoted in Otto Rühle: *Karl Marx*, 59, 85, 82.

2. *Das Kapital*, III, 954.

3. For this interpretation of the economic liberalism of Adam Smith, as for a number of other ideas, I am indebted to Eduard Heimann's very valuable *Communism, Fascism, or Democracy*.

Chapter VII

1. For a left-wing Catholic approach to economic problems, see Maritain's *True Humanism*.

2. See John M. Blair: *Seeds of Destruction*, 150, 167, 325–42. The sources from which Blair cites these statistics are various publications of the United States Department of Commerce, and H. G. Moulton: *Income and Economic Progress*.

3. For reasons why prices always rise faster than wages, see Blair, *op. cit.*, 363–68.

4. Professor P. W. Bridgman points out that 'the whole invention of an interest system in combination with a gold standard (or any other material basis) is physically unworkable except for limited intervals of time. A gold dollar placed at compound interest at six per cent annually at the time of Julius Caesar would have swelled by now to occupy a sphere of radius far exceeding the radius of the orbit of Neptune. The interest system is physically impossible except for brief intervals, and with the continual occurrence of catastrophe to start it off again.' (*The Intelligent Individual and Society*, 240.)

5. Gardiner C. Means has shown how, during the depression, the competitive occupations cut prices and maintained production, while the semi-monopolistic industries maintained prices and cut production. (See his *Industrial Prices and their Relative Inflexibility*.) For example:

	Per cent drop in prices	Per cent drop in production
Agricultural implements	6	80
Motor vehicles	16	80
Iron and steel	20	83
Agriculture	63	6
Food products	49	14

From the viewpoint of preserving the free market, big business during the depression adopted in every respect precisely the wrong policies. The free market cannot be preserved unless production and employment are maintained, and prices and earnings are allowed to have a maximum of flexibility. Big business during the depression reduced production in preference to reducing prices, and reduced employment in preference to reducing salaries and wages.

6. This is the basic weakness in the argument of Walter Lippmann's *The Good Society*.

7. The argument of this section is derived mainly from J. M. Keynes: *The General Theory of Employment Interest and Money*.

8. As Mr. Keynes points out, the fundamental weakness of orthodox economics has been its failure to realize that the free-market mechanisms which regulate prices and earnings do not apply to savings. Orthodox economics has always assumed that savings are automatically reinvested, and that the interaction of supply and demand will fix the rate of interest at the appropriate economic level. In consequence, it has never found any satisfactory economic explanation for prolonged periods of depression, and has always ascribed them to violations of the rules of sound economics on the part of some pressure group (most frequently the trade unions). But in reality savings are not automatically reinvested; the rate of interest cannot be forced by competition below a certain minimum (which is apparently — except in the case of borrowings by the government — in the neighborhood of three per cent); and in certain respects the rules which govern saving are the exact opposite of those which govern other economic activities. Orthodox economics has, for example, assumed that just as a fall in the price of some particular commodity will decrease the production of it, so a fall in the rate of interest will discourage the practice of saving. On the contrary, a low interest rate may make it necessary for many people to save more, and not less, than they would have done otherwise (e.g. in the case of people who are saving for their old age).

9. This aspect of the situation is emphasized by Professor Alvin Hansen in his *Full Recovery or Stagnation*.

10. It is, of course, to be assumed that some part of the loans extended by the government would not be repaid, and that the government would thereby, through foreclosure, acquire ownership of certain factories, farms, and houses. But the government would not retain ownership; it would sell such properties as soon as possible, as the H.O.L.C. now does with its foreclosed houses.

11. If stocks, bonds, and other debt claims owned by individuals were cancelled at death, but if such debt claims, when transferred to non-profit-making institutions, continued to be interest-bearing, a probable result would be a large influx of wealth into cultural, educational, scientific, and philanthropic channels. Such a result would seem to be extremely desirable.

12. See A. A. Berle and G. C. Means: *The Modern Corporation and Private Property*. In the two hundred corporations studied by Berle and Means (which control 50 per cent of the corporate wealth, and 22 per cent of the total wealth, of the United States), only 11 per cent by number and 6 per cent by wealth have stockholders who own a majority of the stock. In 44 per cent by number and 58 per cent by wealth stockholding is very widely diffused, there are no large holdings, and control belongs entirely to management, not to ownership. Henry Ford and the Du Pont family are almost the only big industrialists of the old kind, who combine ownership with control.

Blair (*Seeds of Destruction*, 276) quotes figures compiled by the Federal Trade Commission, showing that in 1925, in 4367 representative small corporations, with an average capitalization of less than $2,000,000, the directors and officers owned an average of only 10.7 per cent of their firm's common and 5.8 per cent of its preferred stock.

It should be added that, in spite of the diffusion of stock-ownership, the idea (sometimes expressed during the twenties) that the United States is becoming a nation of capitalists is very far from realization. The total number of stockholders in the country is probably not above four millions — a small minority of the total population — and the holdings of many of these are very small. The amount of stock held by workers in the corporations for which they work is negligible.

13. The principle that, wherever possible, employment should be expanded at the expense of earnings, rather than *vice versa*, is basic to the free market. It can with advantage be extended to a number of non-profit-making activities. An obvious example is teaching in the public-school system.

14. Orthodox economics, the subject-matter of which is relationships of supply and demand, always assumed full investment and full employment. Confronted by the existence of unemployment, the economists blamed the trade unions for not accepting lower wages and thereby making possible fuller employment. They failed, however, to realize that the interest rate was equally important in causing economic maladjustments, and that the working class could not fairly be expected to bear the full burden of such maladjustments. Given full investment and full employment, the classical economics would again become completely valid.

Index

Index

293

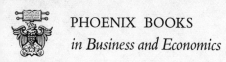

PHOENIX BOOKS
in Business and Economics

CAMBRIDGE ECONOMIC HANDBOOKS
Edited by MILTON FRIEDMAN *and* C. W. GUILLEBAUD

PHOENIX BOOKS
in Political Science and Law

PHOENIX BOOKS
in Philosophy and Religion

PHOENIX BOOKS
in History